St. Olaf College Libraries

Gift of LaVern Rippley

Cleveland and Its Germans

[Cleveland und sein Deutschthum]

Illustrated

Published by the
German-American Biographical Publishing Co.
Cleveland, Ohio
c. 1907

Translated from German
by
Steven Rowan

THE WESTERN RESERVE HISTORICAL SOCIETY
CLEVELAND, OHIO
1998

THE WERNER D. MUELLER REPRINT SERIES

Works Translated From German: Completed
Jacob Mueller. *Memories of a Forty-Eighter*
Cleveland and Its Germans (1897-'98 edition)
Cleveland and Its Germans (1907 editions)

Works Translated From German: In Process
Waechter und Anzeiger Jubilee Edition (1902)

Reprints of Significant Local Titles: Completed
Eric Johannesen. *Cleveland Architecture, 1876-1976* (1979)
John Malvin. *North Into Freedom* (1879, 1988)

Reprints of Significant Local Titles: In Process
Edmund H. Chapman. *Cleveland: Village to Metropolis* (1964, 1981)

First English Edition
Copyright © 1998 by The Western Reserve Historical Society
All rights reserved
Printed in the United States of America
The Western Reserve Historical Society Publication Number 185

Library of Congress Cataloging in Publication

Cleveland und sein Deutschthum. English.
  Cleveland and its Germans / translated by Steven Rowan. -- 1st
English ed.
      p.   cm. -- (The Western Reserve Historical Society
publication. The Werner D. Mueller reprint series)
  Originally published in German: 2nd ed. 1907.
  Includes index.
  ISBN 0-911704-50-7
  1. German Americans--Ohio--Cleveland--History. 2. German
Americans--Ohio--Cleveland--Biography. 3. Cleveland (Ohio) -
-History. I. Rowan, Steven W. II. Western Reserve Historical
Society. III. Title. IV. Series: Western Reserve Historical
Society publication. Werner D. Mueller reprint series.
F499.C69G3313 1998b
977.1'32--dc21   97-51816
                                                               CIP

Table of Contents

Foreword to the English Edition

Throughout its 130 year history, the Western Reserve Historical Society has always pursued a dual, but interrelated mission. It both collects and carefully preserves the evidence of the past in its library and museum, and disseminates information derived from those collections. Its institutional mission, simply stated, is "...providing direct access to the history and heritage of all of the people of Northeastern Ohio." While much of this goal is achieved through exhibits, programs, and public access to the rich resources of its research library, publication has always been a critical component of what we today call creating a more "accessible" past.

The translation and publication of the two editions of _Cleveland and its Germans_ represents a major step in making the past more accessible. For years, scholars and others fluent in German knew that these two volumes contained valuable information concerning the growth and development of Cleveland's German-speaking community, as well as a wealth of biographical information. Yet, many students, genealogists, and other researchers do not read German and the original works have remained effectively closed to them. Today, we are delighted that these books, which chronicle one of northeastern Ohio's major ethnic communities, are available to a much broader audience. As noted by their translator, Professor Steven Rowan, these volumes help "...give Cleveland the best control over its second- and third-magnitude nineteenth-century German citizens of any city in the country..." Their republication in English translation was made possible by the generosity and foresight of Werner D. Mueller; the skills of Professor Rowan; and the Western Reserve Historical Society's interest in seeing that the collections entrusted to its care help us all understand more about our shared historical experiences.

Richard L. Ehrlich
Executive Director

iv

Translator's Preface

What follows is a translation of the entire contents of the second edition of *Cleveland and Its Germans* [*Cleveland und sein Deutschthum*] published by the German-American Historical-Biographical Publishing Co. of Cleveland in 1907. The purpose of the translation is to provide assistance to those using the original copies, which contain images which cannot currently be copied into this format.

This translation was made within the terms of a contract made in 1995 between me and the Western Reserve Historical Society. I wish to thank both John Grabowski and Kermit Pike for their patience and assistance in this project, which appears to crown a sequence of translations made by me for the Society, including Jakob Müller's *Memoirs of a Forty-Eighter*, the fiftieth anniversary edition of the *'Wächter und Anzeiger,'* 1902, and the first edition of <u>*Cleveland and Its Germans*</u>. It has caused me to spend much more time in German Cleveland than I ever expected, and though at times daunting in its scale, it has not been an unpleasant experience.

Steven Rowan
St. Louis, Missouri
Martin Luther King, Jr., Day, 1996

Introduction to the English Edition:
The Swan Song of the Cleveland Germans?

The second edition of *Cleveland and Its Germans* can be scanned for symptoms of the ongoing process of assimilation which would receive a sudden shock of acceleration within a decade with the entry of the United States into World War I. The end of mass immigration from Germany about 1890, the dying out of the old leadership cadre of the Forty-Eighters, and the fading of the spirit of the Civil War meant that the process of assimilation went to work without any significant counter-force. There had always been assimilation, but during the period through about 1890 this was continually challenged by the supply of fresh arrivals and the moral force of the Forty-Eighter tradition. Once the Forty-Eighters were gone, the German community tended to splinter into constituent subgroups: Protestants, Catholics, Jews, workers, craftsmen, entrepreneurs, none of them of sufficient weight to continue to support a distinct linguistic culture in the midst of mass-oriented American society.

The biographies have a dark counterpoint which reflects this process. Time and time again, Germans born in America are praised for their fidelity to German causes "despite" being born here. Those who immigrated as children are also praised, since many did not choose to try to preserve their German identity. Despite the effort of the biographers to paint a positive picture, some German-Americans portrayed there clearly had only marginal links to the German community. They had become Americans who moved most comfortably in the English-speaking milieu, and sustaining two separate linguistic cultures appeared a luxury of little profit. The demise of the German Theater shortly before the second edition is one symptom of many that the time was short for this separate linguistic community.

The book itself is a product typical of the later nineteenth and early twentieth century, the subscription publication. It was created by the German-American Historical-Biographic Company in Cleveland, run by Jacob E. Müller, with the assistance of Hugo Karman. The idea was to write small, flattering biographies and publish them together with photographs, with the subjects expected to subscribe to the publication. "County histories" and "city histories" were created with long, usually indifferently-written historical narratives, followed by the biographies. They then ended up on the coffee-tables of respectable homes and in the back shelves of local and state historical societies.

Despite their mercenary origins, however, such vanity-press products can give us information about people available in no other source. The biographies, though they often glide past anything uncomfortable, provide information such as birth and birthplace, education, training, marriages, names of children, places of business and political affiliation. Read properly, they can be as helpful as obituaries, another complex source.

What makes this collection particularly significant is that it is a "second take," and that it deals with social levels seldom reached by these collections in large cities. In the English-language collective biographies in large cities, the subjects are usually very wealthy and prominent by definition, while a prominent person in the German community was more often a brewmaster, the owner of a grocery or a tavern-keeper. Further, the collection is a second edition, and while a few of the biographies are repeated from 1897-98, with alterations and additions in most cases, conclusions may be drawn about changes in the German community in the course of that decade.

Compared to the 1897-98 edition, the version of 1907 has a much shorter and more stereotyped historical introduction. One learns far less about Cleveland than in the earlier edition, or in the jubilee edition of the *'Wächter und Anzeiger'* of 1902. There are fewer biographies (211 as against 252), and the persons treated seem to be even further down the social chain than had been the case before. Only 43 biographies are repeated, usually with minor changes over time corrected by minor alterations, but some completely rewritten. Some of the newer biographies were of old pioneers who seem to have been missed in the earlier sweep, or who were at last persuaded to subscribe. The almost complete lack of women in the biographies, in the brief, obligatory marriage passage, is a repeat from the earlier edition. There is also a great deal more stridency about German causes, which is an indication of their increasingly precarious position.

What one does learn is the story of individual craftsmen, some among the last generation to pass through the traditional German apprenticeship system. They rarely carried their schooling beyond confirmation at the age of 14, but they would then go into an apprenticeship of between two and four years, followed by a period of "wandering" ("Wanderschaft") through many towns, working in a variety of shops and operations. Then they would return home, do their military service, and emigrate. They tended not to emigrate to avoid military service, unlike many German immigrants in the mid-century, and the number of clearly politically alienated appears small. There is also extensive evidence of "chain migration," with whole extended families coming over serially to one location in the United States. Links between the American and German branches continue to operate as well, with persons passing over only when they are ready to fit into an American situation pioneered by a relative or a friend. Some of the people found here could also be regarded as members of another ethnic group, such as Hungarian or Polish, or who were politically distinct from the German Reich of 1871 (Swiss, Austrians) but these groups often lived easily within the larger German ethnic world, which looked on them in turn as junior members of a general Central European identity.

Religiously, Germans recapitulated the history of Western Christendom by being distributed into various religious traditions, a fact which in some cases accelerated their dissolving into the American mass culture. While some Protestant, Catholic and Jewish communities nurtured German culture by providing schools, hospitals and orphan-homes for German-speakers, in many other cases German worshipers were neglected and encouraged to "Americanize." Departure from overcrowded ethnic neighborhoods often meant that the worshipers moved while the ethnic churches remained behind. Catholic prelates often regarded ethnic parishes as anomalies rather than opportunities, and the existence in Europe of missionary funds for German-speakers raised dark suspicion that Germans wanted a national prelacy of their own in America. In the case of Jewish communities, the wave of new Yiddish-speaking immigration from Polish regions of the Russian Empire and from Austria-Hungary undermined the German identity of German Jews. Zionism would rise in the twentieth century to a major cause, pulling Jews out of their German orientation altogether.

In America, what they found was almost convulsive growth and opportunity for those who could work hard and persistently. Their goal was economic and social independence, which meant the ownership of a shop, grocery or tavern which would free them from dependence on an employer. The qualities admired in these biographies are those of a Teutonic Horatio Alger: pluck, hard work and a rather stolid insistence on the virtue of thoroughness.

But living meant more than just working. Enormous energy was poured into cultural recreation and the serious business of culture. Germans rightly regarded themselves as heirs to a gifted tradition in music, particularly voice, and singing was a major part of their German cultural heritage. Americans who spent years in Germany studying music were "adopted" by the German community as fellow travelers.

The society world of the Germans was built around a series of activities which set them apart from the ordinary run of Americans. Systematic gymnastic exercise, which began as consciousness-raising in a demoralized Prussia after the defeat at the hands of the French at Jena, generated the culture of the Turner Society, which in America was a specific creation of the Forty-Eighters. These societies cultivated not only physical gymnastics but also "spiritual gymnastics," which preserved the ideological content of the American Turner movement. Drinking in the German style was also something which set them apart from the Americans as a whole, who were more given either to serious carousing by the means of whisky or to temperance. German drinking was by its very essence a public activity, part of the affirmation of community, and the demonization of drink by native Americans was another part of the dark undertow to be perceived at the margins of these biographies.

Above all else, those German immigrants who did not wish to assimilate totally wished to cling to their language, which embodied a complex literary tradition requiring schooling, reading, drama and and public use. The use of German in the Cleveland Public Schools, which was clearly on borrowed time in 1907, was the benchmark of whether Germans would be able to sustain a distinct linguistic culture in America. In 1907 the theater was already gone, a victim of the indifference of ordinary German residents. Soon the public teaching of the language would go, and finally the newspapers and other sustinance to a living language. The costs to our general culture of this victory for assimilation were great, and our current debate over the role of English in American life is one which has been played before. The irony is that this victory is more the triumph of the "dictatorship of the majority" so disliked by Tocqueville, an ideology which has allied with mass consumerism to strip minorities of any sort of their legitimacy when they pursue a culture of their own. Viewed from a distance, of course, the survival of a German culture in a town like Cleveland seems to have been doomed from the start, and its survival relied on the fluke of the infusion of a cultural elite leadership in the aftermath of the Revolution of 1848, a fluke sustained by massive German immigration through 1890, when the maturing German economy became capable of absorbing the children it produced, and even began to import labor. At this distance the death of German Cleveland has an inevitable and elegiac quality, but it also warns us of the costs of compulsory conformity in a mass society.

Steven Rowan

Cleveland and Its Germans

Foreword

That simple man must be treated with contempt
Who never considered what he has done.

The following pages describe the process by which the city of Cleveland came into being, from the period of the first settlement in a wilderness barely a century ago, where today our huge buildings jab into the heavens, electric cars cruise through splendid boulevards, and the smoke of innumerable smokestacks rise from the valley and the lakeshore witnessing to the hard work of thousands, working by the sweat of their brow.

The boom which Cleveland has experienced since the publication of our first edition of Cleveland and its Germans, the grandiose development of the situation, the death of so many of our old outstanding Germans and the emergence of those filling their gaps, besides the general development of affairs, moves us to declare a new edition.

We will follow the development of Cleveland to the present day, and in the biographies added, we shall give an example of what German hands and German spirits have accomplished in their new fatherland.

A book of Germans bears the dedication of the Poet far from the homeland:

To the fatherland, hold fast to it,
Hold fast with your whole heart…

The most holy thing which we have brought to the free soil of America is our language. Let us hold fast to it with our entire heart, for our entire strength is rooted in this holy soil so long as a grain of it remains.

Through this new work we have contributed what we could to the unity of Germans and their community, and we issue it with the old adage, "Habent sua fata libelli" ["Books have their own destinies."], convinced that wherever our book goes and whatever times discover it, it will serve like its predecessor as a source of interesting information and a valuable monument to the honor of the Germans of the city of Cleveland.

The Publishers

Table of Contents

Part I

Part II

Part III

Part IV

Index of Biographies

This index is keyed both to full biographical sketches (in the section of the volume following page 80) and to substantive biographical data located in the historical narrative that precedes page 80. An asterisk (*) denotes an individual whose biography was also published in the first (1897-'98) edition of *Cleveland and Its Germans*.

Part I
Chapter 1
Foundation and Development of the City of Cleveland.

America, you have it better
Than our continent, the old,
You have no fallen castles
And no basalt.

The old master Goethe, when he directed the verses above to the United States in his "Delicate Zenias," could add, "And you do not have great cities with their bustling life and striving, with their splendor and misery, with smoking chimneys and unhealthy tenements." Much has changed in the meantime. Today, to be sure, one may still look in vain in America for picturesque castle ruins such as decorate the banks of the Rhine, but it is certainly possible to find decayed, ruined cities whose founders and inhabitants once believed their new settlements would be numbered among the most populous in the land in a few decades. On the other hand, there are little places whose names were barely known by any European, at least in the year Goethe wrote that verse (1827), that have grown to great cities. One of these is Cleveland, the Forest City.

The foundation of Cleveland falls in the year of 1796, but white men had already set foot in the region where Cleveland lies today. The missionary Father La Roche Daillon, who first preached the Gospel of the Christian faith to the Kahquah Indians, also came here, and in 1682 Father Robert Cavelier de la Salle crossed the area on his search for the Mississippi. Traces of an earlier settlement are to be found in the remnants of a fort in Newburg, as well as the remnants, still visible today, of a fortification about six miles east, over the mouth of the Cuyahoga.

After the Peace of Utrecht (1716), the ownership of the states around the Great Lakes, as well as a portion of Canada, went to France, despite all of England's reservations and protests. It was only later political episodes, in which George Washington had a part, that brought these lands to England. The first European settlement in Cuyahoga County dates from 1755. But the famous Indian chief Pontiac attacked the settlement as well as an expedition sent there in 1764, defeating the English. The next year the schooner *Victory* was sent to what is today Rocky River — then called McMahon's Beach on the Rivière des Roches — to retrieve a cannon left on the battle field.

The rebellion of 1776 threw its shadows here as well, and Ohio came to the United States through the Peace of Paris.

On 7 July 1786, some settlers from Moravia came to the vicinity of the Cuyahoga River under the leadership of John Heckenwalder and David Zeisberger. They lived for a while in Independence, but a few months later they had to leave the place due to the lack of food as well as of the tools and supplies for their efforts. In 1789 a settlement nine miles east of the mouth of the river was founded by Joseph Du Chartar.

The ground on which Cleveland stands originally belonged to the state of Connecticut. It received as a result the name "Western Reserve," until Connecticut ceded 500,000 acres of reserve land in 1792 to the federal government to benefit those who had been injured by the war with England. Three years later, Connecticut sold the remaining three million acres to a syndicate of citizens who had organized under the name of the Connecticut Land Company.

The lawyer Moses Cleaveland was the agent of that company. In 1796 the board of the company decided to plot out a central city on the lands, on the plateau at the mouth of the Cuyahoga River, and a surveying expedition was sent for this purpose, at its head General Cleaveland and Seth Pease. When this surveying commission had completed its work, Cleaveland, after whom the city was named and whose statue today stands in Public Square, returned to the East, never to set foot here again. He died in 1806 at the age of 53. It is not known, by the way, why the "a" vanished from the name of the city.

Some white people did remain behind when the surveying expedition departed, consisting of Job Stiles, Joseph Landon and the wife of the first-named man, Tabitha Stiles. Landon soon left, but he was replaced by Edward Paine, later General Paine of Painesville. Paine was a merchant and traded with the Indians. In the next few years several new settlers came to the newly founded community, including James Kingsbury and his family, Lorenzo Carter, Ezekiel Hawley and Daniel Eldridge. The last of these died soon after his arrival, and he was buried in the newly plotted churchyard, which would be located today in the very center of the town if it had not long ago been closed. The first marriage to take place in the new settlement was that of Chole Inches, a girl in the service of Lorenzo Carter, who was able to win the love of a Canadian named Clement. In 1799 Rudolphus Edwards and Nathaniel Doan came here, and the Doan, Carter and Hawley families lived at the start of the century in Cleveland itself, while other settlers gathered in the vicinity in Newburg and Kinsman. In those days the "city" consisted of Water, Superior, Huron, Ontario and Ohio Streets, as well as the thickly wooded Public Square and several side ways and alleys. The first house that was raised was at the corner of Water and Superior Streets.

In 1810 Cuyahoga County was founded and the county seat selected. On 5 April of the same year the first regular sitting of the court was held, in a house standing west of Public Square, replaced by a true court house building two years later. This new court house, a log cabin, stood on the Square. Soon the death penalty was pronounced here, leading to the execution of an Indian who had murdered two settlers in our Sandusky. He was hanged in the Square.

On 28 June 1812, ten days after the declaration of war against England by the United States, a crier announced this fact to the amazed people of Cleveland. On 16 August came news of the humiliating defeat of Hull at Fort Detroit as well as the announcement of the approach of English forces. Anxiety and fear seized the populace, a general flight was planned, and whoever had valuables buried them. Only a small band of brave men armed themselves for active resistance and organized a military column. Joined by men from East Cleveland, Euclid and Newburg, it swelled to 56 armed members. Cleveland was used as a depot for arming and provisioning, and there was a great deal of activity here. In the meantime, however, the committed band found no occasion to put their courage into practice. On 26 August, Brigadier General Simon Perkins arrived with a large force of troops, and later Elisha Dibble appeared with more soldiers. He established his headquarters in Rudolphus Edwards' house at Rocks Corner. Soon there was a skirmish between Perkins' force and English irregulars with the Indians who supported them, which ended rather without result. Over the following winter a small number of soldiers remained in Cleveland, but most of those recruited had been released. Despite that, the town remained the gathering-place for the military.

On 5 August 1813 Oliver Hazard Perry, then a young officer of 26, left Erie with his fleet and anchored with his ships before Cleveland to get provisions. General W. H. Harrison camped in Fort Seneca. On 10 September the English squadron came within sight, and the famous maritime battle of Lake Erie took place. Toward evening of that significant day, Perry had to leave his flagship *Lawrence* after hours of sharp combat and take to the cannon-boat *Niagra*. He put on his dress uniform, took his penant and flag and passed to the *Niagra* in an open boat rowed by four determined sailors under heavy enemy fire, escorted by his brother of 14, Calbraith. He arrived uninjured and broke the enemy line with this ship, which had hardly involved itself in the battle. Eight minutes later the flagship of the British struck its colors. Four other ships had to surrender, and two tried to escape but were pursued by the *Scorpion* and brought back captive. The victory was decisive. The Americans won 6 ships of the line from the English, with 60 cannon and several frigates. The American squadron had only numbered 9 ships with 56 guns.

The State Legislature elevated Cleveland to the status of village in 1814. The first election in the place, which now numbered barely a hundred inhabitants, took place in June, 1815, with the following result: president, Alfred Kelly; recorder, Horace Perry; treasurer, Alonzo Carter; trustees, Samuel Williamson, David Lang and Nathan Perry, Jr.; marshal, John A. Ackley; assessors, George Wallace and John Ridder. In the same year, Leonard Case founded the Commercial Bank of Lake Erie and the first church was raised, at the corner of St. Clair and Seneca Streets.

The village slowly expanded, but one did not hear much about Cleveland until 1832, when the canal to Cincinnati was opened. Trade and exchange received an important stimulus from that. The harbor was improved with an appropriation of $5000 from Congress, and the population grew rapidly. A new church was built, later replaced in 1838 by the "Old Stone Church" still standing on the Square.

On the western side of the river, a settlement with its own township organization had formed under the name of Ohio City. Promoted by the Buffalo Land Company, a speculative undertaking, it developed rapidly. Intense competition for growth between Cleveland and Ohio City arose, which often led to bloody confrontations. Ohio was raised to the status of town by the legislature on 26 March 1836, and it was only five days later, on 3 April 1836, that Cleveland received its charter as a town. To promote business interests, John W. Willey, later the first mayor of Cleveland, and James S. Clark, two land speculators, raised a bridge across the river at Columbus Street, for whose use they charged high tolls. The residents of Pearl Street, however, did not want the farmers of the west side to bring their products to Cleveland and make their purchases there, so they declared the bridge injurious to themselves and destroyed a considerable portion of it. Only a court judgment brought the conflict to an end.

In the meantime, the newly created city of Cleveland held the first municipal elections, with the following results: mayor, John W. Willey; justices of the peace, Richard Hilliard, Nicholas Dockstadter and Joshua Mills; city council members, Morris Hepburn, John R. St. John, William V. Craw, Sherlock T. Andrews, Henry L. Noble, Edward Baldwin, Aaron Strickland, Horace Canfield and Archibald M. F. Smith. The city was divided into three wards, each with a justice of the peace and two members of the city council.

During the years 1838 through 1840, a schoolhouse and two further public buildings were erected. In 1846 the first high school rose, and in rapid succession the gasworks and a telegraphic connection with the outside world. In 1847 the rail connection to Columbus was finished, and soon the amalgamation of Cleveland and Ohio City was begun, which was completed in 1854. Ohio City, which then had a population of about 4000, vanished from the map, and instead "Greater Cleveland" was created. That took place after decisions of the councils of both communities on 3 April 1854.

According to the United States Census, Cleveland had 7 inhabitants in 1800, 57 in 1810; 150 in 1820; 500 in 1825; 1075 in 1830; 5080 in 1835; 6071 in 1840; 9573 in 1845 ; 17,034 in 1850; 25,670 in 1855 and 35,000 in 1857.

In 1856 the waterworks were erected in the west side and the central market house raised. In this year, Salmon P. Chase and Henry B. Payne were candidates for governor, and they carried on an intense campaign. In 1857 the Ohio Canal was continued to the river, and the Cleveland, Columbus and Cincinnati Railway was also extended. Both enterprises brought the city new expansion and prosperity and businesses doubled.

New streets and new business areas arose overnight. Soon the Lake Shore Railway, the Cleveland and Pittsburgh Railway and the lines to Toledo and into the Mahoning Valley were built, and Cleveland's future was assured. All areas of trade received new markets, the wealth of the city expanded, new factories were called to life, and in a word the metropolis of the Western Reserve developed from a rural center to a trading city. Head of the city at this time was Samuel Starkweather, whose capable administration is still held in the greatest regard by old settlers. Starkweather contributed extensively to the blooming of the city.

In October 1860 the East Cleveland Street Railway Company was established, at a time when the city was being called to arms. In the course of the war the city expanded ever more, and what had been a harbor city and a trading city now became a factory city. Shipbuilding was especially pursued, and the introduction of ships of iron and steel made the establishment of ironworks more necessary than ever.

In 1866, after the noise of war had stilled, Union Station was opened at the foot of Water Street. In the same year a health authority was established. In 1867 the Bethel Union and the Northern Ohio Historical Society were established. In 1868 the Jewish orphanage was dedicated and the iron steamer *J. K. White* slid from the ways.

In 1860 Cleveland had 43,835 residents. In 1866, 67,500; in 1870, 92,829; in 1880, 160,146; in 1890, 261,353; 1900: 381,768; the most recently published school census estimates a population of almost 500,000 for Cleveland.

Parallel with the expansion of population, the size occupied by the community also grew. From 1872 to 1873 East Cleveland and a portion of Brooklyn were annexed, in 1875 the construction of a harbor bar was begun, and in 1877 the splendid viaduct of Superior Street was opened to public traffic. Ten years later the Central Viaduct was completed, and now the era of large construction began.

The territory on which the city of Cleveland was located from its foundation extended from the edge of the lake to Huron Street, west to the river and south to what was then Ohio Street and is now Central Avenue. It covered a fourth of a square mile.

In 1852 Willson Avenue was the eastern border of the city. In the following years ever larger suburban complexes were annexed to the city, so that the communities of Newburg, East and West Cleveland and Brooklyn made the present area of the Forest City 32 square miles.

Cleveland has the name of Forest City with justification. Many streets have virtually vanished under trees, so that there are always enough gardens and plots and tree-shaded streets to make the term a proper one. There is hardly any large city in the country in which it is so pleasant to live as it is here on Lake Erie. The means of transportation are modern and adequate, the streets beautiful and broad. Summer is pleasant and even extraordinarily hot days are bearable, as evenings are cool, so that during the night one may recover his strength. The hot rays of the sun are made tolerable by the winds, which have bathed in the blue waves of Lake Erie, so that we do not have to suffer from the heat endured in the cities in the interior of the state. Nor do we suffer from the dirty water of a turbid river.

Due to excellent communications by water and land, Cleveland has become a city of conventions, and its residents have earned a reputation for hospitality to a high degree. We shall have opportunity elsewhere to speak of the other developments in the city; of its stately buildings; its huge markets in wholesale and retail; its exports to all the lands of the world; its factories, which occupy more than 60,000 workers; its bridge system (Cleveland has over 50 bridges); its flourishing educational system; its model fire department and police; its outstanding hospitals; its charitable agencies; its fine cemeteries; a grandiose park system; the many fine homes; its temples of art; and its churches, and so on.

Cleveland is a transfer point for coal. It takes a commanding position on the south shore of Lake Erie, as a harbor for the interior and for export with its own trading fleet, and its port on the Cuyahoga River is one of the best and deepest harbors for interior shipping. Cleveland is also an important point on important rail lines for the trade of the continent, and the finest and most extensive development is promised for the future.

Chapter 2
Cleveland During the War of the Rebellion

As the primary center of the Western Reserve, Cleveland naturally played a large role in the political development of the state and contributed considerably to the election of President Abraham Lincoln. When he left his home in Springfield, Ill., for Washington to take up the presidency, he came from Pittsburgh to make a stop in Cleveland and spent the night. He was received with tremendous jubilation by young and old, great and small at the Euclid Avenue railway station, and he was brought through the festively decorated streets to the hotel, which was located on Superior Street. There J. H. [Irvine U.] Masters, in the place of Mayor Senter who was then in Washington, and Judge Sherlock Andrews greeted him in the name of the city of Cleveland. Despite the fact that the newly elected President was exhausted, he gave a brief address of thanks, in which he referred to the dark clouds on the political horizon of the country and expressed the hope that the freedom of the country would be preserved and that the slaves would also receive their rights. Another great reception was held that evening, in which the surviving warriors of 1812 and the officers of the old Wide Awake regiments, the association created during the electoral campaign of the previous year, presented themselves. The President departed the next day, escorted to the train station by the Cleveland Grays, to proceed on to Washington through Buffalo.

The enthusiasm our city showed the later-martyred president was expressed even more when the North was awakened by the first cannon shot at Fort Sumter to enter the greatest war ever known in world history. From all sides men streamed to the flags, leaving their lives for the sake of the Union and for justice and liberty. The state of Ohio and particularly the city of Cleveland were not in the least left behind. One of the first regiments that reported was the 7th Ohio Volunteers, to which Cleveland contributed three companies, while the rest consisted of citizens from neighboring communities. The regiment assembled at Camp Taylor, near Cleveland. It was mustered in on 30 April, passing then to Columbus to march from there to West Virginia, where it received its baptism of fire in the Kanawha Valley. It then took part in the battles of Winchester and Cedar Mountain, distinguishing itself particularly in the latter affair. Only 300 men came out of that battle unwounded. It was later still active at Fredericksburg, Chancellorsville, Gettysburg, Chattanooga and other, smaller battles.

Special mention should be made of the battle of Lookout Mountain on 24 November 1863, which took place in and above the clouds and which ended with the taking of one of the keys to the entire rebellion. At the battle of Ringgold, Georgia, on 27 November 1863, the regiment lost 50 percent of its men in 30 minutes, including the colonel, lieutenant-colonel, adjutant and 12 company officers. Later in '64 followed the three-day battle of Resaca, Georgia, and New Hope. The German company in this regiment, Company K, had many members of the old Cleveland Turner association, which still recalls these brave men today. These included Major Ernst Krieger, Captain Christ Nesper, Adolph Kohlmann, Wilhelm Voges, E. H. Bohm, E. Schinkel, Henry Rochotte, H. Strahle and Christian Reisse. They even supplied the otherwise-English regiment with three primary officers: Krieger, Resper and Bohm. The Jews belonging to this regiment, distributed among the three Cleveland companies, were all heroes without exception. For example, young Victor Perle died for the Fatherland in the battle of Chancellorsville, Va., on 23 May, 1863, killed as he charged ahead of his regiment, bearing the flag.

A second Cleveland regiment was the 8th Ohio, which fought under General Lander at Romney, then under General Shields in the Shenandoah Valley, at Chancellorsville, and suffered terribly at Gettysburg. After it had distinguished itself again at Cold Harbor and in the battles before St. Petersburg, it returned home crowned with victory in July 1864.

In April 1861 several companies of the 23rd Regiment were also formed at Camp Taylor, to be joined with this regiment in Columbus, Ohio. The first colonel was later the hero of Stone River, General Rosekrans, whose major and successor as colonel was R. B. Hayes, eventually president of the United States. In the ranks as a private stood the present president, William McKinley. The regiment stood and fought through the entire four years of service primarily in West Virginia, distinguishing itself in the battles of South Mountain, Antietam, Winchester, Fishers Hill and Cedar Creek. It was the only regiment in all the wars the United States ever fought that gave the country two presidents.

The unfortunate result of the battle at Bull Run did not discourage the residents of Cleveland, but rather spurred them to new patriotism.

The 37th Ohio Regiment was the third so-called German regiment, forming part of the 300,000 men called up in August 1861 by President Lincoln.

Like the 7th, this regiment received its baptism of fire in the Kanawha Valley, and remained it there for a time as an occupation force. At the start of 1863 it was taken by boat to Arkansas, fighting under General Grant until the taking of Vicksburg. From there it rushed to help raise the siege of Chattanooga, fought at Mission Ridge and then helped drive the Confederates under General Longstreet from eastern Tennessee, where it suffered terribly from a lack of proper clothing and provisions. Then we find the regiment once more at Kennesaw Mountain near Atlanta and finally with General Sherman in the march to the sea. After being stationed for a while in South Carolina, it marched to Louisville, Ky., and was mustered out there and returned to Cleveland. The Germans of Cleveland provided a large contingent to this regiment, and even today they can look back with pride on the deeds of the 37th.

Many members of the Cleveland Singing Society joined this regiment. Among them should particularly be named these well-known Germans, some still alive and some deceased: Major Karl Ankele; the staff surgeons, Konrad and Julius C. Schenk; the quartermaster, Theo. Voges; Captains Louis Quedenfeld, Geo. Böhm, Jacob F. Mary, A. Vallander, C. Sebastian, Louis F. Lambert, Karl Messner, Wilhelm Kraus, and Karl Moritz (later so well known here as "Major"); Lieutenants Heinrich Göcke, Arthur Stoppel, Anton Peterson, Julius Scheidt, Louis Ritter, Henry Votteler and Christ. Pfahl.

A new regiment was formed even later that came under the command of Capt. W. W. Hazen of the regular army. It fought under General Buell near Louisville and took part in the bloody battle at Pittsburg, in which it lost 171 men dead and wounded out of 373 men in half an hour. This is certainly a good sign for the bravery of the regiment. Yet the brave earned their laurels other ways as well, such as in the Battle of Murfreesboro, where they defended a fort with valor, and again in the bloody encounter at Gordon's Mills and Chickamauga, in which they left 100 dead on the field of battle. At the start of 1864 the regiment was so ground down that it returned to Cleveland to recruit more, then went back to join its division in eastern Tennessee. Of the 331 men with which it returned, only 99 were still capable of field service. Fully 150 suffered heroic death on the field of battle, and 80 were sick unto death. Despite this, the remnant marched with General Thomas against the Confederate General Hood, following him to Alabama. In June the regiment went with the remnant of its corps to Texas, where it was mustered out of its four years of service.

Ten companies of the 103rd Ohio came from Cleveland in August, 1862, marching from here in September to Cincinnati to halt the advance of the enemy from Kentucky. From there the regiment was ordered into the eastern part of Kentucky to put an end to the guerilla war of the rebel cavalry. Later, under the leadership of General Burnside, it took part in the march to Nashville, where it endured great hardship in the city when the town was taken by General Longstreet. Then the regiment fought as part of the 23rd Corps in Tennessee and came finally to Raleigh, N. C., from whence it returned to Cleveland to be mustered out.

A further Ohio regiment, the 105th, was also formed in August 1862. With a strength of 1013 men, it soon found itself on the march to Lexington, Kentucky, where it suffered a great deal from the attack of General Kirby Smith. From there the regiment, consisting largely of untrained men, found itself as a reserve losing a large part of its manpower, some through sunstroke but mostly through illness. The 105th distinguished itself in the Battle of Perryville, with heavy losses. Similarly it could boast of service at the Battle of Chickamauga, where it served so bravely that it was praised by General Rosekrans in his order of the day. Later we find the regiment in the encounter at Mission Ridge and finally in Goldsboro, N. C. From there it went to Washington, taking part in the great parade there, and it was finally dissolved on 8 June 1865 in Cleveland. The 105th may feel pride also to have been the first regiment to leave camp after the call for troops on 4 August 1862, and it was the first regiment to be mustered out there after the end of the war.

In the same month as the 103rd and 105th, a second German regiment was formed in Cleveland. After it trained here for a time, it was sent to Cincinnati along with the other Ohio regiments to push back the attack of General Kirby Smith. After that it was was brought to Washington, and took part in the Battle of Chancellorsville, where, despite brave resistance, it was involved in the general collapse of the 11th Army Corps due to the incapacity of the commanding general, O. O. Howard. Its surgeon Dr. Hartmann fell, sword in hand. After this undeserved insult, however, there was splendid compensation in the Battle of Gettysburg. The regiment reached Gettysburg on the morning of 1 July and attacked at once, its chief responsibility being to hold Cemetery Hill. On the second day of this bloody battle, the brave German regiment suffered heavy losses, but it managed to take the flag of the 8th Louisiana Tigers. The total loss of the regiment in the battle of Gettysburg was 400 out of the 550 men with which it had entered the battle. The last service the regiment performed was at the end of the war, on the coast of South Carolina and Florida, from whence it returned home.

Many well-known Cleveland Germans belonged to this regiment, both as officers and in the rank and file. The officer who distinguished himself as the bravest of the brave when he seized an enemy flag in hand-to-hand combat with its bearer, receiving nearly mortal wounds, was our beloved police judge Peter F. Young, then adjutant. Captain Lutz commanded the entire regiment on the second and third days of battle, escaping death only by miracle when he was struck at close range by a musket ball that glanced off the cylinder of the revolver on his left hip, throwing the captain to the ground.

The 124th Regiment was recruited in January 1863 in the northern counties, going first to Kentucky and later to Nashville, Tenn., where it occupied itself with fortification work until the middle of the summer. In September it took part in the battle at Chickamauga, and it suffered terribly from lack of water during this bloody day. It later took part in the Battle of Mission Ridge and helped free Chattanooga from Confederate troops. The last active part the regiment took in a battle was at Nashville. In July, 1865, it was mustered out. The chief act of heroism of the regiment occurred during the Battle of Mission Ridge, where it took an enemy battery with fixed bayonets, then turned their own guns on the fleeing enemy.

Of the other infantry regiments sent into the field by Ohio during the war, eight companies of the 125th Regiment were recruited in Cleveland in October 1862 and sent to Louisville in the January of the following year. It first entered the fire near Nashville, fighting in the battles at Ringgold and at Chickamauga, and earning the name of the Ohio Tiger Regiment from its service in the second day of this hot battle. It was publicly praised by General Rosekrans, under whose eyes it had fought. At Chattanooga and Mission Ridge it once more stood under heavy fire, distinguishing itself by its charge in the Battle of Franklin, and after the taking of Atlanta it learned from the mouth of General Thomas that it had contributed much to the salvation of the army and of Nashville. After seeing further active service in New Orleans and Texas, it was mustered out in Cincinnati in October 1865.

The 128th Ohio Regiment which left Cleveland in August, 1863, went immediately to Kentucky and later helped compel the 3000 men holding the Cumberland Gap to surrender. After a mere six months under arms, it was dissolved in March 1864 in Cleveland.

The city of Cleveland and environs supplied eight companies of the 150th Ohio Regiment. After entering the service of the Union, it did 100 days' service in Washington and the surrounding area. The 169th Regiment also did service there. This regiment had many losses due to illness, but its military appearance made it one of the best regiments Ohio placed in the service of the Union.

The last infantry regiment Ohio sent to war was the 177th. It [p. 26] fought at Murfreesboro, took part in the assault on Fort Fisher, N. C., and was mustered out in July 1865 in Cleveland.

Even if Ohio fielded a respectable number of infantry regiments, still there was no lack of sons of the state who joined cavalry or artillery regiments, happily giving their lives for the cause of the North. So it was that in the autumn of 1861, Senator B. F. Wade and the Honorable John Hutchins were empowered to form a cavalry regiment that went into service as early as October, distinguishing itself in the guerilla war in southwestern Missouri and later fighting in the Indian Territories against the Choctaw Indians, who had allied with the Confederacy. Later it operated in eastern Tennessee with much distinction, in the region of Knoxville. It was there, in the midst of stormy weather, in an exposed outpost, that the unit decided to reorganize as a veterans' regiment. In January, '64, it was sent east to the Army of the Potomac, and it was once recognized by General Sheridan as his most dependable cavalry regiment. Several of its members won the Congressional Medal of Honor.

The 6th Cavalry Regiment belonged most of the time to the Army of the Potomac, but it was seldom gathered as a regiment, as one or another of the three battalions was always being detached to go elsewhere. A well-known Cleveland German, Mr. A. C. Knauff, belonged to the regiment as a captain. His reputation was always the finest.

The 12th Ohio Cavalry Regiment, organized in October 1863, fought in North Carolina, and it was involved in the capture of Jefferson Davis.

The 14th Ohio Light Artillery, also called into being by Senator Wade and Mr. Hutchins, took part in the battle of Pittsburg Landing, then went with General John A. Logan to Jackson, Tenn., marching back via Corinth and remained there until it was mustered out in Cleveland.

Two more batteries were made up particularly of the children of Cleveland. The 19th was entirely employees of the railways joining here, winning high praise for their valor under the command of their bosses Joe Shields and Frank Wilson. It was usually attached to the 23rd Army Corps, and with this unit it later fought its way to Atlanta and beyond, participating in the march to the sea and through the Carolinas and Virginia to Washington.

The 20th battery, organized by Capt. Louis Smithnight, was first known as the Sigel Battery as it was recruited for Sigel's Corps, but at the time Kirby Smith invaded Kentucky it was ordered there and remained in the West. Due to the resignation of its captain after a serious wound, the battery remained for some time in less than the best condition until it took on new blood in the ranks, after which it won back its old confidence. One of the best of its officers was Wm. A. Neracher from here. It also had Capt. W. Backus and Lieutenant Henry Höhn.

The 1st Regiment, Light Artillery of Ohio also included a large number of Cleveland's sons. Its colonel was the beloved old General James Barnett, who is still living. Batteries A, B, H, J and K were all Clevelanders, and among their officers good names were made by Capt. C. Heckmann, Lieutenant Krebel and particularly Capt. Hugo Dilger of J. The batteries were scattered among all the various armies, but they were all distinguished in their conduct. A certain number of these old artillerists joined the Cleveland police after the war, and many reached high posts: for example, Henry Höhn of the 20th Battery became Chief of Police, and others became lieutenants and captains.

A small example of the valor of the sons of Cleveland, and particularly the Germans, is shown by a short true episode from the life of Sergeant E. H. Bohm of Company K, 7th Ohio Infantry Regiment.

It was 1861. Company K had been ordered to guard Carnifex Ferry on the Gauley River, four miles south of Cross Lane, when on 20 August the order came from headquarters to take a scouting patrol across the river into enemy positions there. Capt. Bohm, at the time still a sergeant, was one of the first to volunteer to take part in the dangerous mission, and he was given command of the force of 20 men. Shortly before departure, Capt. Schutte of Company K joined the expedition, armed only with a revolver and in civilian clothes. The ferry boat reached the opposite shore of the river, and after a march of an hour the troop reached a crossroads via side-paths through hilly country choked with thick woods. A corporal and five men were sent to scout one road, while Sergeant Bohm with the remnant of the men and Capt. Schutte marched down the other road.

After the little band had gone three miles through thickly forested terrain along a road going zig-zag, up and down, they spied in the distance six riders from the 1st Virginia Confederate Cavalry Regiment, which was also on a scouting mission. As soon as these caught sight of the bluecoats, they took flight, followed on the double by Sergeant Bohm and his people. In no time they emerged from the thicket into a rather large clearing lying in a depression, in whose center lay a solid log farmhouse, surrounded by cornfields. The inhabitants of the farmhouse fled at the approach of the Yankees and took refuge in the wooded hills surrounding the clearing. Here Sergeant Bohm had his men line up and advance slowly toward the heights where the cavalry had vanished, after he had assured himself that the farmhouse was empty and no enemy attack was to be expected from there. A shot coming from a distance of 50 yards from the heights, however, convinced Bohm and his people that the enemy being sought was closer than desired or expected.

This shot was only a signal, and in an instant came a volley of more than 200 muskets, pouring a veritable rain of bullets on the little force. Completely surprised and under attack from an invisible enemy with secure cover, they sent several rounds already loaded in the direction from which the shots had come, and they made their way back to the farmhouse as best they could. Barricading themselves with the furniture, mattresses and such, they were in the position, with their better weapons (Enfield repeating rifles) to hold off the Confederates for a while. During the withdrawal, Captain Schütte, who had been at Bohm's side, was mortally wounded, and a private on his other side received a shot through the knee. Although struck by several bullets that either glanced off his equipment or tore his cap from his head, Sergeant Bohm managed to get his dying captain out of the way of enemy bullets and into the farmhouse. Despite the dying man's request for Bohm to leave him to his fate and seek his own salvation in flight with most of the lightly wounded, who made their way protected by the cornfield, Bohm remained with his dying superior, to be made a prisoner of war with a few of his comrades. As repayment for his valor, he had to enjoy the hospitality of the enemy jails at Libby Prison, Va., Parish Prison, New Orleans, and Salisbury Prison, N. C. When Colonel Croghan, commander of the First Virginia Confederate Cavalry Regiment, who found death about three months later from a bullet of the 7th Ohio Infantry Regiment, heard of Sergeant Bohm's magnanimous action, he did all in his power to lighten Bohm's lot as a prisoner of war until he was taken to Libby Prison.

Even as the men of Ohio and particularly of the city of Cleveland were ready to flock to the colors and answer Lincoln's call, so also the women and girls were ready to do all in their powers to show their patriotism. As soon as the first cannon shot fell and the fury of war had shown its torch, women's associations began forming in Cleveland to support the troops rushing to the colors, whether it was a matter of provisions or clothing, or to assist those left behind with advice or deed. After the first battles, the wounded were brought to various places, and bandages and lint were sent to heal the wounds as well as possible. In this matter the Soldiers Aid Society of Ohio was particularly active.

One of the most important institutions the women of Cleveland brought into being in this difficult time was the Soldiers Home, which was under the control of the aforementioned society. In it, troops passing through were fed and cared for if necessary.

On Washington's birthday, 22 February, under the name of the Northern Ohio Sanitary Fair, a great bazaar was held in a great temporary building of 64,000 square feet on Public Square, at which General James M. Garfield delivered the opening address. The success of this was great, benefiting the sick and wounded soldiers of the Fatherland.

On the whole, Cuyahoga County sent over 9000 men to the army, of whom more than a quarter were Germans, which can easily be determined from the lists of names.

The Germans of Cleveland may thus be rightly proud of their role in the bloody conflicts of the War of the Rebellion, whether they went to the colors or worked more quietly.

A thankful citizenry has not forgotten what the sons of Cleveland and the county have done for the Fatherland, and in their memory was erected on the southeastern corner of Public Square the Soldiers and Sailors Monument. The first stimulus to the erecting such a monument came in 1879 from the Camp Barnett Soldiers and Sailors Society, which presented plans in October of the previous year, at a reunion of soldiers and sailors, where it received enthusiastic applause.

After the State Legislature passed a law empowering the county commission to raise a small tax to erect the monument, the matter took on solid form in May, 1887, when Capt. Scofield, as chairman of the monument committee, reported to the county commissioners that they had chosen the southeast portion of Public Square for the monument. Then there was a major battle between the Park Commission, which owned Public Square, and the members of the Monument Committee. The struggle wavered back and forth among the courts, until finally the monument committee emerged as victors. The monument consists of a memorial hall in which the names of almost 9000 warriors, as well as those of members of the Womens Aid Society, are immortalized, with a column crowning it, on its pinnacle a statue of Freedom. On the sides there are various military groups.

On 4 July 1894, the monument was dedicated with great pomp, to the cheers of thousands of citizens and residents gathered there. Governor William McKinley and former governor Foraker held the addresses, while a chorus of 3000 voices took over the musical part of the program. In the evening the entire city, particularly Public Square, was illuminated, and the festively-clothed crowds streamed through the streets. The warrior's monunent is a decoration to the city and is worthy of Cleveland and of Cuyahoga County.

Chapter 3
Cleveland's Further Growth. City matters. Viaducts

Even though the Mexican War of 1846 already had a great influence on Cleveland's development, it was even more the war of 1861-65 which caused the city to shoot up suddenly. It is not just that the population of the city doubled during those dreadful years, but also that the great coal seams and iron digs of Lake Superior came ever more together, and a great iron industry arose for which Cleveland today is still known throughout the entire United States. Through the war, Cleveland, which had been known as a trading city, also became a city of factories. In 1865 no less than 56,000 tons of coal were brought to Cleveland, nearly double what it had been in 1860. The importation of iron also grew significantly, and in 1865 iron fabrication amounted to nearly $6 million, certainly a fine sum for such a relatively young city. Trade in wood and in oil rose continually, and the city boasted of no fewer than 30 oil refineries. In 1865 the first baseball game also took place, in which Oberlin played Cleveland, and Oberlin won. As insignificant as this might seem to a layman, it does show that Cleveland already felt itself to be a city, opening the way for the national sport of the Americans.

Naturally such a rapidly developing city demanded an improved municipal administration, and improvements were in fact begun at once. The first was the raising of a better water supply, for as early as 1866 it was established that the water used by the populace up to that time, drawn from the Cuyahoga River and the drains of the city, was injurious to health. After various improvements had been made, in 1870 a new water station was established about a mile-and-a-half from the lake shore. This was 36 feet under the surface, held down by 5 anchors and weighted with 1000 tons of stones.

The establishment of the fire department came in 1829, when the first pumper was obtained. In the autumn of 1862, after long and bitter battles, purchase of the first steam pumper was approved. Until that time the crews consisted entirely of volunteers. Then a municipal fire department was established, and the fire telegraph system was introduced in 1864. In 1873 the five-member fire commission was created, and through this the effectiveness of the department considerably increased.

As a result of various conditions the commission was somewhat altered in 1876, in such a way that it consisted of the chairman of the committee of City Council for fire and water matters, along with four citizens elected for four years by the people. Through this restructured commission, significant improvements were introduced, and order was brought to this crucial department. After the great fire on the "flats" in 1884, there was clear realization of the need to build a fire boat, and after considerable discussion one was voted with an appropriation of $28,000. This first boat received the name *Weatherly*, though it was rebuilt a few years later and renamed the *J. H. Farley*. In 1893 it was moved to obtain a second fire boat, named *Clevelander*, which cost the city the considerable sum of $40,000.

Through 1866 the police stood under the sole control of the mayor and the city marshal, while the money of the department was administered by the city council. In the year mentioned the matter changed when the State legislature created a new commission, consisting of four members named by the governor and the mayor ex officio. This commission had the entire administration of the department in its hands and was empowered to name a superintendent. The commissioners themselves received no compensation, and policemen were only hired for as long as their abilities and conduct permitted. After only two years, however, in 1868, there was another change, in which the commissioners were no longer named by the governor but through a vote of the people.

It was a remarkable time for Cleveland when the government building was built on Public Square, and the proposal was then made to move the entire municipal administration there to be housed in buildings. At the same time, the county commissioners received permission from the secretary of the city council to tear down the old courthouse on the southwest portion of the Square. As a result it came to considerable friction which reached such a scale that in March 1857 Public Square was fenced off in order to make any court orders moot. The struggle was between the city and the owners of lots on Superior and other streets opening on the Square. No side was willing to give in until finally, in 1867, the matter was referred to the courts. The courts decided that Superior Street was originally meant as a through street from Water Street to Erie Street, and for that reason the city had no right to close off Public Square without compensating the bordering landowners. In response to this decision the municipal administration appealed, then relented, and in August 1867 the Square was finally opened once more to traffic.

The space reserved for the various branches of the municipal administration looked quite shabby until the start of 1875. The city hall was a plain building on the south side of Public Square, where the mayor and the various other city officials had their offices, and the other departments were scattered here and there about the city. This could not continue, and in February of the year mentioned the municipal administration rented the Case Block for 25 years at $36,000 per year. In time this also proved not to be adequate for a growing city, so that in 1894 the State Legislature approved the use of Public Square, on which a city hall adequate to the need of a metropolis could be built. The landowners bordering on the Square opposed the erection of a city hall with all possible energy, and they were successful, so that the municipal authorities were forced to seek another place to build.

In 1871, in response to general demand for public places of recreation, the mayor named the first park commission. Since then the city can boast of owning parks that rank with the most beautiful of any city in the country, obtained partly through purchase, partly through gifts, and as soon as the improvements already begun are completed, the entire city will be covered with a net of splendid riding and walking paths as well as parks. Wade and Gordon Parks, named after the gentlemen who gave both of these fine parks to the city, are today bound by elegant boulevards.

In 1878, Public Square was first lighted by electricity, and in 1881 four high masts were erected from which the city could be provided with light. But these soon proved impractical, so that today only one of the four survives, standing in the middle of Public Square, shortened now by a hundred feet. Nearly all the principal arteries of traffic in the city have electric lighting, while side streets are illuminated by gaslight or gasoline.

With the growth of the population, the number of administrative offices grew more with every year, so that in 1885 there were 23 of them. The members of these boards had little responsibility, so it was inevitable that irregularities arose and came to the light of day which made alteration of the system inevitable. The Ohio Legislature then passed laws introducing the so-called Federal Plan to put this trouble to rest. This plan was replaced by the present Cox code in 1904. In 1896 the municipality was empowered by the Legislature to issue bonds for almost $5 million for municipal improvements. Objections against the issuing of this great sum were laid to rest by the Ohio Supreme Court the same year.

Something of great importance for the Cleveland of the future is the noted Group Plan, which is destined to make Euclid Avenue, already a place with a reputation of unequaled beauty, into a place of which Pindar might sing the rebirth of the most splendid of the Greek cities, at least so far as the city center is concerned.

The new postal building, the first of the plan, is already in the course of completion. It will be followed by a new courthouse, the new city hall, the library and the grandiose rail station, and when the Group Plan is complete, the area of the lake front northeast of the Square will become a miracle of public palaces, columned halls and parks which will be the pride of Clevelanders and the astonishment of visitors, so that no city in the United States will equal Cleveland.

With all the growth, the means of transportation, particularly between the east side and west side, proved totally inadequate, and as early as 1836 the raising of a bridge was recommended as pressingly necessary. The project was seen as impossible until 1871, when Mayor Buhrer once more moved the construction of a high bridge.

After much battling back and forth by various businessmen of the east and west, as well as attacks on the constitutionality of the permission of the state legislature to issue $1,100,000 in bonds for building a bridge, the entire matter was submitted to a public vote, in which the great majority favored building the bridge. The opponents, who thought their interests injured by the construction of the new artery, made all efforts to subvert construction, but they were not successful. In December 1878 the great structure was given over to public traffic with corresponding ceremony. Cost of construction was $2,150,000. The bridge is more than half a mile long, 46 feet wide, and 64 feet high.

As was to be expected, the advantages of the new artery of traffic soon became palpable, and the south side now began earnestly to promote being joined to the east side and the west side. In 1883 the citizens of Cleveland in a vote declared themselves in favor of constructing an iron piered bridge from Jennings Avenue over the river and from Scranton Avenue to Ontario Street.

On 11 April the referendum was made into law, and despite all objections by the usual opponents, it was not altered. Ten years after the opening of the Superior Street Viaduct in December 1888, the Central Viaduct was opened to traffic. This structure, entirely of iron, is a mile long, has a width of 56 feet, and rises 101 feet above the level of Scranton Avenue. In the very next year, the City Council passed a resolution to build a similar iron bridge over the Walworth Run, joining Jennings Avenue with Abbey Street. The officials who approved this project began construction, despite the usual protests.

The enormous traffic passing at almost every time of day over the three viaducts demonstrates that they were absolute necessities. Unfortunately, there was a terrible accident on the Central Viaduct on 16 November 1895. An electric car loaded with passengers fell over the edge of the raised draw bridge in the dark. All of the interior passengers, as well as conductor located inside the car, found their deaths in the filthy waters of the river. The motorman managed to save himself by leaping shortly before the catastrophe, as did a few of the passengers on the exterior of the car. At the investigative hearing held immediately after the accident, nothing precise could be established. The motorman insisted that he had stopped before the safety barrier before the bridge and that he received the signal from the conductor to proceed, so that he put the car in motion. He said he had not seen the red signal lights, which bridge personnel were supposed to place as a warning. The end result of the hearings was that the conductor who drowned with the passengers in the river was made responsible for the accident. News of this dreadful episode spread like lightning through the land. As a result better security measures were taken, not just in Cleveland, to prevent a similar catastrophe, which not only meant the loss of life but also high liability compensation.

Chapter 4
Municipal and County Administration

Around the end of the eighties a general dissatisfaction arose among the Cleveland citizenry over the operation of the various commissions or boards that regulated municipal affairs. During the winter of 1886-87, Judge E. J. Blandin gave public expression to his plan for a better public administration, supporting the election of a supreme executive who would name the officials to regulate municipal matters, similar to the manner of the national government. Mr. Blandin's motion found great support, as was always the case, although it was stubbornly opposed by certain sides. So it was only after difficult struggles that the state legislature unanimously approved the measure in early 1891, which still is known as the Federal Plan and remained in force until 1903.

According to this plan, the mayor was the actual leader of business as responsible head. He possessed the necessary powers, and in the course of time the new municipal law functioned well. But as will be enumerated later, U. S. Senator M. A. Hanna had the "federal plan" revoked by his state legislature, replacing it with the one currently on the books. The purpose of this act was to reduce the mayor's power and to replace it with a new board system. Under the law code, the mayor, the three directors of public works, law, and the police judge are all elected by the people. The Police and Fire Department are under the service authority, which is named by the mayor and must consist of a Democrat and a Republican.

The city council consists of 32 members, 26 representatives of the city wards and six members at large. Their offices, and those of all municipal offices, is two years.

In the absence or incapacity of the mayor, his functions are carried out by the vice-mayor, who is also president of the city council.

Over the last few years a great deal has happened due to the continual growth, with greater demands on sewers as well as street improvement, laying out of new parks, etc.

Following is a list of the various mayors of Cleveland since organization in 1836:

John W. Willey, 1836-37
Joshua Mills, 1838-39
Nik. [Nicholaas] Dockstader, 1840
John W. Allen, 1841
Joshua Mills, 1842
Nelson Hayward, 1843
Sam. Starkweather, 1844-45
George Hoadley, 1846
Joshua M. Harris, 1847
Lorenzo A. Kelsey, 1848
Flavel W. Bingham, 1849
William Case, 1850-51
Abner C. Brownell, 1852-54
William B. Castle, 1855-56
Sam. Starkweather, 1857-58
George B. Senter, 1859-60
Edward S. Flint, 1861-62
J. R. [Irvine U.] Masters, 1863-64

Herman Chapin, 1864-66
Stephan Buhrer, 1867-70
F. W. Pelton, 1871-72
Charles A. Otis, 1873-74
N. P. Payne, 1875-76
W. G. Rose, 1877-78
R. R. Herrick, 1879-82
John H. Farley, 1883-84
George W. Gardner, 1885-86
B. D. Babcock, 1887-88
George W. Gardner, 1889-90
William G. Rose, 1891-94
Robert Blee, 1893-95
Robert E. McKisson 1895-98
John R. Farley 1899-1901
Tom L. Johnson 1901 to the present.

The foundation of Cuyahoga County falls into the end of the last century. Since this time the borders have been frequently altered, and it consists of 20 townships as follows: Bedford, Brecksville, Brooklyn, Chagrin Falls, Cleveland, Dover, East Cleveland, Euclid, Independence, Mayfield, Middleburg, Newburg, Olmstead, Orange, Parma, Rockport, Royalton, Solon, Strongsville and Warrensville.

The administration is essentially the same as in all 87 other counties of the state of Ohio, and a body of county commissioners elected for three-year terms is responsible for representing the interests of all in the county to make changes and improvements such as building bridges, maintaining roads, etc. In the number of its inhabitants it is barely exceeded by Hamilton County, hence taking the second place among the 88 counties, with an area of 500 square miles. The total worth of property in the entire county, including Cleveland, is more than $200 million.

The history of modern metropolitan Cleveland only dates from the last ten years. It had its start with the youthful mayor, Robert E. McKisson, and reached its highest development under its present head, Tom L. Johnson. Between the two administrations lies that of Mayor John Farley, a man of personal qualities but also of reactionary conservatism. Many of the great public works such as the new sewer system, the new water works, and large-scale street paving, were planned and partly begun under Mayor McKisson. This exciting young mayor lost a political struggle at the end of his second term when he turned against the head of his party, Marcus A. Hanna, which was a headstrong act, since his defeat was inevitable. He was followed by John Farley, a Democrat of the old school, who practiced thrift, and could do little for the development of a metropolis. Innovations and improvements cost money, and they cannot be done on reduced taxes. McKisson owed his defeat to his split with Mark Hanna, and Mayor Farley went down because of his devotion to Hanna. He did not even seek the renomination of his party, he had so injured his cause with the people by trying to carry out a promise made to Hanna. It was a matter of the renewal of a streetcar charter. The days were gone, however, the good old days, when corporations could get privileges from a willing city council for a pittance. A new time had arrived when aroused citizens would troop to the homes of the city fathers with a rope for having traded the city's millions for a piece of cake. Under these conditions, even a powerful man such as Farley had to fall.

The streetcar question is intimately involved with the most recent history of our city. It makes and unmakes mayors and city councilmen, and since it is not resolved to the present day, as is also the case with other monopolies, it will continue to play a role in the future.

A man who was municipal auditor under Farley and understood the spirit of the times was the noted politician Charles P. Salen. When he saw that Farley's political career was running downhill, he thought of the former streetcar man and congressman Tom L. Johnson, whose campaign he had led, but who was living in New York at the time if not yet a resident. Salen called on Johnson to return to his old home of Cleveland and run for mayor. Tom L. Johnson came, saw and conquered. Despite the opposition of the powerful Republican Hanna machine, the citizens of Cleveland elected Tom L. Johnson their head on 1 April 1901, and then reelected him. It is altogether likely that he will run again in autumn, 1907.

Opponents have portrayed him as a man with many hobby-horses, pursuing impossibilities and chimeras. On the contrary, he has shown himself to be a man with both feet solidly planted on the ground of reality, as one might assume with a man who made himself a millionaire many times over by working for twenty years since his youth in the streetcar business. What led many to judge him falsely was his tendency to be ahead of his time. Once in office, he seized the opportunities before him. He quickly saw that the growth of the city demanded larger resources. It was necessary to gain a larger income, and for this purpose he created a new city taxation board and the taxing school which soon grew famous. On 30 July of the same year the taxation authorities increased the value of semi-public corporations by $20 million, assuring the city $600,000 in increased income.

Then Hanna arose, setting in motion the entire Republican state machinery and causing the state taxing authority to declare this increased evaluation as invalid. The mayor turned in vain to the courts. Yet the people reelected him mayor on 1 April. The courts quickly abolished the taxation school, and the Republican legislature abolished the taxation authority. Despite these defeats, the struggle of the mayor was not without success. Since then the corporations have raised the value of their taxable property voluntarily.

The railroads whose lines run through the city and the county had always been evaluated too low by the county auditor, in the view of the mayor. He turned to the assessors with figures. When he was rejected there as well, he turned to the state supreme court. It referred him to the legislature, and in April, 1902, he appeared before that body. Once more he was preaching to the deaf. These efforts were not entirely in vain, however, since the Republican governor Harris has recently named a commission with the purpose of reforming the entire taxation system in the sense of the mayor of Cleveland.

His activity in the area of taxation led Mayor Johnson into state politics, and in order to be more effective in this he ran for governor in 1903, although his most elevated friends advised him against it. Hanna was beaten five times in the city and county, but he remained victor in the state as a whole. Mayor Johnson endured a painful defeat, but the next mayoral election poured balsam on the wound when he was elected for the third time as mayor. Senator Hanna had more confidence in his strength than his body permitted, and when he began working for his reelection as senator at the start of the following year his overtired body was overcome by a nervous fever.

The mayor's political struggles, his efforts to win tax revenues, his successful effort to introduce a fare of 2¢ per mile on the railroads, the abolition of fees in county offices, the completion of the new water works and the new water tunnel, the beginning of the group plan, his attacks on the Republican boss system in the state, the cleaning of streets, their general paving, and all the other battles were as nothing compared with his fights with his stubborn campaigns against the streetcar companies. Hanna had had the entire municipal law upset by the legislature in order to clip Mayor Johnson's wings.

Even this coup failed in its effect. Johnson remained mayor and is fighting to assert himself even today for a fare of 3¢ to be introduced, an amount which is not too low. To show he is right, he has invited the Forest City Railway Company to build a 3¢ streetcar line. The city council laid out the line, but on 11 May 1902 the Cleveland Electric Railway Company obtained a court order against the construction of the line. Under a new ordinance, considerably improved and strengthened, a second attempt was made to construct the line. The monopoly turned to the courts again and finally obtained an order against the city council and administration from the state supreme court so that nothing could be done until the next election. All important municipal business lay fallow. When the mayor was reelected under the new code, new routes were laid out, new charters issued for the 3¢ line, and rails began being laid in Denison Avenue. Now orders of suspension and trails of all sorts rained on the branches of the Cleveland Electric Railroad Company. Ordinances in favor were moved in the city council, but these could no longer be passed as in earlier years. The mayor proposed to the monopoly that it should lease its lines to the city. The monopoly demanded an excessive price which was quickly rejected. The construction of the 3¢ line made progress in the meantime, and trials multiplied. The monopoly turned to the U. S. Supreme Court. The lines of the 3¢ line now reached from Denison Avenue to Detroit Street, and in fall, 1906, the enterprise was opened to the jubilation of the public. There was not much left for the monopoly to do than meet the lower fare, but a breach had been made in its walls. The struggle has been carried on with such intensity by both sides that it can only end in a defeat.

The mayor, a man in his early fifties, marked with few wrinkles, is surprisingly lively, natural and democratic in his bearing. He has extraordinary intellectual gifts, a solid character and great persistence at keeping a plan. His favorite pastimes are mathematics and mechanics. He is also inventive, and he is a master at calculation, so that he sees through very difficult problems with ease. His insight into human beings is not always infallible, so that when he makes errors it is in this direction. He likes to surround himself with young people whose energy and liveliness match his own nature. He exercises a great influence on his surroundings, and his personal magnetism extends to others.

Even though he is less popular with the great businessmen of which he is one due to his financial position, this is because he does not associate with them and uses methods which seem rather like Barnum to them. Hence it is said that he is not a true man of the people. But whoever gets to know him sees that he is in earnest and genuinely wishes to serve the people. It is part of his nature to do things differently.

His use of tents in his campaigns is a striking proof of this. For his opponents this was a circus, but two years later they saw the advantages of a tent, and in the end Mark Hanna himself spoke to a tent meeting.

The administration of a city of Cleveland's size demands a big business man, and even severe critics must admit that Tom L. Johnson is the man in the right place, despite all his errors put to his account and which are seen in him by those with little direct knowledge or by those whose vision is clouded by political prejudice.

Chapter 5
Cleveland's Schools and Other Educational Institutions. Churches, etc.

Cleveland can look back on its successes in education, reaching back not yet fifty years, with pride. In 1836 the lack of public schools had become so palpable that the city decided to establish one and hired a schoolmaster for this purpose. The schools, which had hitherto been privately taught, had shown themselves not capable of satisfying the needs of the continuously growing population. During the first quarter 229 children were instructed, and the payment for this purpose amounted to $131.12. From these small beginnings, Cleveland has raised education to a level agreed upon by all sides as the heights. In October 1836 the city council of the time named a school board, made up of three members who administered the schools in this manner until 1859. After an ordinance was passed in 1837, a tax of 1.5 mills was passed for school purposes. In 1840 the first school buildings were erected on Rockwell Street and Prospect Street, of which the Rockwell building is still in the possession of the school board. The building on Prospect was sold in 1895 as no longer being suited to modern demands. In 1852 the city council, under which the control of schools stood, created the office of school superintendent, naming Mr. And. Freese to this position. In 1846 the Central High School was founded, and in 1854 West High School.

From 1859 to 1892 the public schools were contolled by a school board elected by the people, and until 1862 the school board depended on the city council for all its acts, and was otherwise without power.

In 1868 a law was passed by the Ohio Legislature granting the school board the right to raise money without involvement by the city council.

In March 1892, after the coming into force of the Federal Plan, the Ohio state legislature approved the complete reorganization of the educational authority. The administration of all school matters was vested in a board consisting of seven members elected by the people, with a chief executive called a school director, to be elected by the people.

A new school law was adopted in 1905 which was so composed as to be extended to the entire city. The number of board members remained the same, but now the school director was elected by the board, as was the superintendent.

This director had the right to name all subordinate officers, including the superintendent of instruction. The latter, however, had the right to name the teaching personnel in keeping with his own judgment. The complete course takes 12 years to complete, four years for the elementary subjects, four for grammar subjects and four years for instruction in the high schools.

Today there are a hundred schoolhouses in the city with almost 1800 male and female teachers, a half-dozen high schools and two craft schools.

Intellectual sustenance comes from the local public library, with over 250,000 volumes and five branches with many small book stations in all parts of the city and handsomely decorated reading rooms where the best-known newspapers are also made available. These stand at the free disposal of every citizen, in addition to a series of well-endowed private libraries.

Adalbert [Adelbert] College was originally founded as an institute for training readers and theologians in Hudson in 1826, but in March, 1880, on the motion of Mr. Amasa Stone, a trustee, it was moved to Cleveland and its name was altered to Adabert College of Western Reserve University. Mr. Stone bequeathed the institution half a million dollars under the condition that the institute henceforth bear the name of Adalbert College in memory of his son, who had studied at Yale and had drowned while swimming. Two buildings were raised, one with room for 60 students, the other with a lecture hall, a library, a museum and a chapel. In 1888 an athletic facility was erected and a laboratory for physics and supplied with proper equipment by Mr. S. Mather, was presented for use in 1894. The Hatch Library, a gift from Mr. H. R. Hatch, came into the possession of the institute the next year.

The Case School for [of] Applied Sciences owes its development to the liberality of the famous philanthropist Leonard Case. The school was opened in the Case Block on Rockwell Street with five teachers and 16 students on 3 October 1881. In 1882 a well-located lot was purchased on Euclid Avenue opposite Wade Park, and the construction of the school was begun in 1886. The necessary money was contributed by generous citizens.

Opening was possible as early as 1885, and three departments were established for physics, chemistry and civil engineering. A total of $25,000 was given for the instruments and equipment of the laboratories. Unfortunately both building and contents were destroyed by fire on 27 October 1886. The building only had a little insurance, and there was none on the instruments, so that the loss was a painful one. Despite that, reconstruction was begun at once, and today several splendid buildings decorate the spot, containing laboratories and shops for mechanics, mining and electricity.

Alongside its public schools, Cleveland also possesses a large number of ecclesiastical schools of various denominations, which enjoy considerable attendance.

Brooklyn has been called the city of churches, and Cleveland follows Brooklyn with the next-largest number of churches. Cleveland has 23 different denominations with more than 250 churches, with the day schools and Sunday schools associated with them. Most of the buildings are true show pieces, making a special witness to the prosperity of the congregational membership.

We are allowed to choose a few from the great number of these imposing structures. The first of these is the Catholic Cathedral with the residence of the bishop and the school building joined to it, at the corner of Superior and Erie Street; then the First Methodist Episcopal Church and Trinity Cathedral on Euclid Avenue; the Plymouth Congregational Church, at the corner of Prospect and Perry Streets; and the two Jewish Temples on Willson Avenue. Each of the various denominations seeks to outbid the other with the erection of every new building, whether in interior decoration or outer construction, building splendid structures on the primary streets and making a most imposing impression on the visitor.

Beyond this great number of imposing churches, Cleveland also has more than 50 large and small structures for missionary use, temperance and similar purposes. Among the various denominations, the Catholics have more than 40 churches, followed by the Methodist Episcopal Church with as many, the Congregationalists with 30; the Baptists with 30; the Protestant-Episcopal Church with 24; the Presbyterians with 21; the Evangelical Lutherans with 20; the Jews with 12; the Evangelical Reformed with 11; the Reformed Church of the Disciples of Christ with 10; the Evangelical United Brethren with 9; the United Brethren in Christ with 1; the Evangelical Community with 11; the Quakers with 3; the Netherlands Reformed, the Free Baptists and the Dutch Reformed with 2 churches each; the Reformed Protestant Episcopal, the Free Methodists, the Universalists, the Unitarians and the Swedenborgians with one church each. As may be seen from the statistics above, there is adequate provision for the religious well-being of the population of Cleveland.

Cleveland hence enjoys the reputation of being one of the most pious cities in the country. One organization which has come into being largely through church support which has grown greatly in the last few years which dedicates itself to the moral elevation and education of young men is the Y.M.C.A. (Young Men's Christian Association). Founded in May, 1867, after several moves it became possible for the society to obtain an elegant home at the corner of Prospect and Erie in the course of the years 1888-1889. The cost of erecting this imposing building with its elegant façade ran to a quarter-million dollars. The society has three branches, one at the corner of Hamilton and Alabama Street, the other in Collinwood and the third on Broadway. A further building is in the course of construction for the Young Women's Christian Association on Prospect Avenue.

Chapter 6
Charitable Institutions. Hospitals and Medical Colleges

Cleveland does not simply take a prominent position among the cities of the country for its educational and religious institutions but has also accomplished something outstanding in the area of the care of the poor and the sick, as is universally acknowledged. In 1849 the officials of the city saw themselves compelled to mollify the unemployment and the misery resulting in the aftermath of a dearth of business by establishing a permanent poorhouse, and construction on it was begun on the south side, between Scranton Avenue and Valentine Street, in 1850. The construction lasted five years, and it still proved not to be adequate to the demand, so that in 1885 two additions were made, one as a hospital, the other to care for the mentally ill. Soon it was necessary to expand the institution, already demanding considerable space, and in 1889 the municipal hospital was built on the north side of the poorhouse. The institution can care for more than 400 persons. The hospital for the mentally ill has room for 375 persons. In 1858 an attempt was made to use a portion of the building as a correctional facility, but the plan soon proved impractical and was let fall.

In addition to these institutions there is another enterprise which exceeds all the other efforts in the area of charity and which is supposed to be an aspect of the grandiose Group Plan described elsewhere. It is the farm colony in Warrensville, ten miles outside the city, for which the city has purchased almost 2000 acres. Located on charming hills, the terrain has a view of the distant lake. Under the direction of the municipal director of welfare, Dr. H. R. Cooley, the project has already started to unite all the municipal welfare and reform institutions to create a true republic of recipients of care. Every class of recipients will have its own building and a plot of land with which to compete in cultivation and beautification, while the whole will operate under central control.

The plan is comprehensive, containing a home for convalescents, a sanatorium for tuberculars, a children's hospital, a penal hospital, a hospital for communicable diseases, an infirmary and a work house, as well as a summer camp for relatives of persons in the various hospitals, so that they may visit, as well as a number of farms and gardens. Many temporary quarters have already been erected there, and the permanent structures shall be erected one after another, the large infirmary first. In connection with that will come the steam laundry, the bathhouse, the bakery, the cookhouse and the power plant. The individual countryside buildings for the various types of admittees will lie scattered around. The entire complex of the infirmary will be located on the top of a hill overlooking a forested valley. The landscape spreading about it, including gardens for fruits and vegetables, will give the inmates something to do and pass their time, and they will not only make their stay more profitable, but also more pleasant than for many others held in a public welfare facility, and the entire farm colony will place its stamp on the whole region, encompassing about 2000 acres.

Rails have been laid from Warrensville Road in order to reach the farm colony more easily, so that there will be easier communication with the city. It is also planned to have a special car for transporting ill persons built, so that patients may be quickly and safely transported in times of epidemic.

For the care of orphans and such small ones entrusted to public care for whatever reason, Cleveland has more than a dozen permanent institutions. Among them special mention is deserved by the Protestant Orphanage on St. Clair Street, created due to the efforts of the philanthropists L. Case, J. H. Wade, Joseph Perkins and Dr. Alleynne Maynard, who contributed $10,000 for the erection of a hospital in conjunction with the institution. The institution is an imposing building, offering room to shelter 300 children.

The Jewish Orphanage on Woodland Avenue enjoys the reputation as one of the best institutions of its sort in the entire country. This project, called into existence by a Jewish philanthropic society The Sons of the Covenant in 1863, found considerable support, and in 1868 this Jewish orphans' asylum was given over to its purpose.

Since that time perennial expansions have been needed, and today the Jewish Orphanage is without a doubt an imposing building and a credit to its street, with its surrounding garden like a park. It offers support to 500 children, and it enjoys the reputation throughout the country as one of the best-run institions of its type. It is no surprise, as a result, that the applications for acceptance into the institutions are considerable.

The Catholic Boys' Orphanage, run by sisters at Monroe and Willett Streets, was founded by Bishop Rappe in 1852. From small beginnings in a little wooden house with support for only 12 boys, there arose in the course of years a fine building in which today several hundred parentless children find a replacement for home, and preparations are being made to expand the institution. Special mention should be made of the childs' care institution on Detroit Street, The Cleveland City Industrial School, in which children, whichever faith their parents belonged to, are received. Philanthropic citizens contribute to the upkeep of the asylum. Through the munificence of the late Amasa Stone, who gave $37,000, and a lot of 60 acres on Detroit Street provided as a gift by Mr. Leonard Case and other gentlemen of the Childrens' Support Society, it was possible to move the institution from Champlain Street, where the Central Police Station is located, to its present location. It would exceed our powers to enumerate all the larger and smaller philanthropic institutions dedicated to the physical and spiritual well-being of fellow beings not blessed with good fortune.

So far as large hospitals, of which Cleveland has a considerable number, the first has to be the Cleveland State Hospital, created as a result of an act by the state legislature in 1852 and opened in 1855. At the beginning it was only designed for 120 patients, and this soon proved to be too small. In 1872 a tremendous fire destroyed the building, and then designs were made for the main building and construction begun. In 1887 the insane asylum was once more attacked by fire. The burned part was quickly rebuilt, and at the same time the chapel, the recreation hall, the laundry, the boilers and other necessary structures were built. In 1893 two large annexes were built onto the structure, already grown enormous, and now further expansions and improvements are planned. Instead of the small number of 120 patients, the asylum today harbors thousands of unfortunate within its walls, and it is now overfilled. The costs for building alone amounts to a $1.5 million. The oldest hospital, if not the most important, is the one built at the behest of the states of Illinois, Indiana, Ohio and Kentucky by the national government, the U. S. Marine Hospital, on the shore of the lake. The structure, begun in 1844, was only completed in 1850, costing nearly $120,000, including the lot. During the Civil War, it served as a soldiers' hospital.

In 1874 the Cleveland Hospital Association leased the Marine Hospital for 20 years and made major improvements. After the expiration of the lease, the institution returned to the hands of the United States, which manages it at this time.

Lakeside Hospital has the efforts of Dr. Woodruff of the First Presbyterian Church to thank for its existence. It is one of the loveliest and best-equipped hospitals in this city. It lies on the shore of the lake, near the Marine Hospital, with room for 225 patients, and it has spent more than a half million dollars on its building and equipment.

The fourth important hospital established here, St. Vincent's Charity Hospital, was established in 1865 on a lot bounded by Central Avenue and Perry and Marion Streets, under the care of the Sisters of St. Augustine. Thirty rooms are available for private patients, 2 wards each for 20 men or women are available, and there us an operating theater with a seating capacity for 200 persons.

The next is the Cleveland Homeopathic Hospital, better known as the Huron Street Hospital, which arose in 1868 out of an original association of allopaths and homeopaths. The homeopaths separated from the association, acquiring the building known under the name of the Old Hudson Institute, and used it for training and as a hospital until 1872, when they constructed a lovely building on the place where it is still located. In 1878 further roomy structures were added, and in autumn of the same year it was dedicated to its purpose, while the operation rooms, lecture halls, etc., were moved to the other structure.

One of the newer hospitals whose reputation has spread widely beyond the borders of our city and county is St. Alexis Hospital, belonging to the Sisters of St. Francis under the control of the able Sister Leonarda. A long-felt need was met by this establishment. The area surrounding the hospital has a large population made up of workers, who often lack the means to get help when sick or injured.

In 1884 the order purchased a private home and equipped it for the care of the sick. In the course of the first year 24 patients were taken in and 2 sisters took care of the work. Today, after the passing of 14 years, more than 1500 patients are supplied with the best medical care, most of them for free. The large stone building on Broadway, which was considerably expanded last year through an addition, is not only a decoration for the street, but for the entire neighborhood.

The municipal hospital, under the control of the municipal director for poor relief, as already mentioned, is an addition to the vast poorhouse on Scranton Avenue, consisting of a main building and an annex of 16 rooms. Other than what has been mentioned, Cleveland possesses a great number of similar institutions, such as St. John's Hospital on Detroit Street, St. Clair Hospital on St. Clair and Belden Streets, the German Hospital on Franklin Avenue, the Cleveland General Hospital on Woodland Avenue and the Evangelical Lutheran Hospital on Hanover Street and Franklin Circle, not to mention the places for healing female and child diseases.

The needs of those seeking seeking professional training in medicine are satisfied by four medical schools and a school of pharmacy.

The institution founded in 1834, The Medical College of the Western Reserve, was the first of its sort to be called into being and had its quarters on the corner of Ontario and Prospect Streets, until a structure built for the purpose could be raised at the corner of Erie and St. Clair Streets.

The Cleveland University for Medicine and Surgery was opened in the autumn of 1850, two years after the first teaching institution of this sort was opened in Philadelphia. Support and contributions for this new enterprise came from all quarters, and the most important authorities in the homeopathic area joined the faculty. After several abortive efforts moved it back and forth, the institution, now known as The Western College of Homeopathic Medicine was able to find a home of its own on Huron Street in 1892. In 1894 the name Cleveland University of Medicine and Surgery was adopted, and the institution owns three buildings on Huron Street, including the hospital, the college and the lying-in clinic.

The Cleveland College of Physicians and Surgeons was founded in 1865 by the noted German physician Dr. G. C. E. Weber. In 1871 it joined with Wooster University, and in 1878 it joined the Western Reserve College. In March, 1896, the institution dissolved its ties with Wooster, the present name was adopted and soon followed the association with Ohio Wesleyan University, one of the best institutions of higher education in the country. The list of the physicians working there as teachers shows a large number of Germans. The fourth and last of the local medical schools received its charter of incorporation on 28 July 1890, under the name of Cleveland Medical College. Its faculty consisted of its incorporators.

Enthused by the success of the first year of 1890-91, it was decided to construct a building for the purpose with the latest medical equipment, and this was built on Bolivar Street, where it enjoys considerable support from the disciples of Aesculapius [Asclepius].

The Cleveland Pharmaceutical Association has existed here for almost 20 years. When it was founded in 1879, German-American pharmacists did not take a small part. For ten years the Association pursued the goal of bringing pharmacists closer together, as well as raising social life among themselves.

Then, on 6 October 1882, on the motion of Mr. E. A. Schellenträger, it was decided to create a pharmacy school, so that young people could be trained for the profession of pharmacy. At the very next session, the services of Mr. N. Rosenwasser were won to present lectures on chemistry and medical matters during the 20-week course on one afternoon a week. During the first year, Mr. Rosenwasser held 20 lectures on medicine. The next year the same number of presentations were made, but they were done in two divisions, one for medicine and the other for chemistry, and instruction was transferred to Mr. H. W. Stecher and Dr. C. W. Kolbe.

During the following year, continuous changes were made with improvements in mind, of which the most significant was the division into a junior and senior course. Further, the addition of several subjects of study and the expansion of the hours of instruction also took place. In the course of the year this institution, under recognized and capable leadership, rose so high that it could be compared with any pharmaceutical college in the country.

The examinations held by the Association at the end of every school term demonstrated that much had been accomplished. The administration was empowered by state authorities to grant the diploma of pharmaceutical chemist after the completion of a three-year course of seven months each, followed by a successful examination by an authority named by the school.

Chapter 7
Cleveland's Railways and Streetcar Lines

Railways are justifiably called the trailblazers of civilization. Cleveland owes its commercial successes to its geographic location, suitable to railway transportation. Cleveland has made great progress in the last few years not only as a crossroads of the most important railways in the country, but also as a harbor city. The first attempt made in 1835 by Mr. Allen of Willoughby to bind Cleveland with the outside world by rail was a decided failure. The business depression of 1837 gave the enterprise its death blow. The next attempt was crowned with success, when the Cleveland, Columbus & Cincinnati Line (now part of the Big Four railway) received permission to construct the line, but the depression of 1837 had such an impact that the project could not be launched for several years. It was only in 1845, after business had improved somewhat, that the line was promoted again, and after the charter issued by the state was amended and renewed, the first efforts at construction began. After overcoming tremendous difficulties, of which the lack of money as well as the opposition operating in all public enterprises were the chief, the line between Cleveland and Columbus was finally ready.

On 22 February 1851 the first train left Columbus, bringing legislators, officials and other influential people to Cleveland. At the very beginning, the railroad proved itself to be a successful undertaking. At the end of the 1850s, the division from Galion to Indianapolis was opened, and the name Cleveland, Columbus, Cincinnati & Indianapolis Railway was taken. In June 1889 the line was joined with the Cleveland, Cincinnati & St. Louis system, being called The Big Four Railroad.

In 1890 certain sidelines were joined to the system and the capital stock of the Cincinnati, Wabash & Michigan line bought out, but it wasn't until July 1892 that the E. W. M. R. R. was joined to the Big Four. The company has its seat in Cincinnati, and it embraces a length of 2250 miles, not including the leased side lines.

On 14 March 1836 the Cleveland, Warren & Pittsburgh Railroad Co. received permission to build a line to Pennsylvania through eastern Ohio. As a result of the bad times prevailing then, the enterprise slumbered for a time, only to be revived in 1845. The path originally planned was altered, and a more direct and cheaper way to the Ohio River was chosen. In 1849 construction was begun, and in 1850 the line was incorporated under the name of the Cleveland & Pittsburgh Railroad. In 1852 the stretch between Cleveland and Rochester, Pa., was ready. Through a lease contract signed on 1 December 1871, the line passed for the period of 999 years to the Pennsylvania Railroad. The length of the Cleveland-Pittsburgh line is 224 miles.

The Lake Shore & Michigan Southern Railroad arose in 1869 out of eight various companies, which combined into one. The railway administration made the best proof of the progress in railroading over the last decade in 1895. On 24 October 1895 a train drawn by Locomotive 564 left Chicago and traveled the distance between Chicago and Buffalo in 481 minutes, 7 seconds. The Lake Shore & Michigan Southern is today one of the most important and best-equipped railroads in the country. On the whole, her rail network, consists of the Lake Shore Railroad combined with the Cleveland, Plainesville & Ashtabula and the Cleveland & Toledo Railroads, and later in 1869 with the Buffalo & Erie Railroad, an extent of 1440 miles of which 540 are main line and the rest side lines. Rates for passengers as well as freight are the cheapest imaginable.

In 1851 the legislature amended the charter establishing the Cleveland, Akron & Columbus Railroad, originally a branch of the Cleveland-Pittsburgh line, establishing a special company to make a connecting line at any opportune point. The following March the line to Millersburg in Holmes County was built and received in 1853 the name Cleveland, Zanesville & Cincinnati Railroad. The comany soon fell on difficult times, was publicly auctioned, and was purchased by G. W. Cass and John J. Marvin and joined in 1865 to the Pittsburgh, Fort Wayne &Chicago Railroad. With the takeover of the entire property of the P. F. W. & C. R. R. in 1869 by the Pennsylvania Railroad, this line also passed into their possession. In November, 1869, the Penn. R. R. sold all its rights in the C. Z. & C. R. R. to the newly created Pittsburgh, Mt. Vernon, Columbus & London Railroad. After various exchanges not very advantageous to the stockholders, the line went into the hands of the Cleveland, Akron & Columbus Railroad, and since June 1882 it is in their possession. The total length of the rails is almost 200 miles.

A considerable number of railroads touch our city on their progress through the country, such as the New York, Pennsylvania & Ohio line or the Cleveland & Wheeling line. The Cleveland Terminal & Valley line, better known as the Valley Line, handling traffic between here and Valley Junction, 17 miles from Canton, failed in 1895, and was reorganized in the same year, and is now one of the branches of the Baltimore & Ohio system.

The New York, Chicago & St. Louis line, better known under the name of the Nickel Plate Road, whose length to Chicago over Cleveland is 523 miles, was created in the brief time of less than 2 years. The erection of this was a marvel of modern railroad technology, and it was opened for traffic in October 1882. In the following months the line was taken over by the Vanderbilts. In March 1885 the line failed, the president W. H. Vanderbilt died, and vice president D. W. Caldwell was named receiver. In May 1887 the company was reorganized under its old name, and it is today regarded as a dividend-paying enterprise.

In January 1859 the city council was petitioned to permit a street railway, and after permission was granted in March, installation began. The beginning capital amounted to $15,000, and the line was to reach from Doans Corners to Public Square, the fare from dawn to 9 PM was 5 ¢, and for the night hours 10 ¢.

As always with novelties, no matter how advantageous they might be for the individual or the community, a certain opposition had to be fought down, and in September an ordinance favored by the entrepreneurs was passed. This empowered A. S. Sterins, Ellery Williams and others to lay a single line from the eastern end of Kinsman Street to Erie Street, from Erie to Superior Street and the Square, and from there to Bank, then to Wall and Bath Street. The length of the line was 4.5 miles, and this was put into service early the next year, with an equipment of 8 cars and 40 horses. The prejudice prevailing up to that time against the construction and operation of horse lines gradually vanished, and in 1868 the Garden Street Line, now the Central Avenue Line, was built. In 1872 the Broadway and Newburg Horse Line was incorporated, and it was granted certain privileges by the city council, such as the use of the rails of the East Cleveland and Kinsman Street Comany in the heart of the city.

In 1869 the Brooklyn Street Railway was built, with its end point at the West Side Market House. The way to the East Side then had to be reached by omnibus, and through the expansion of this line through Pearl Street across the viaduct to the Woodland Cemetery, the public was saved much money and trouble. In February 1872 the Southside Street Railway was incorporated, and for a while it used the so-called Bobtail Cars, which moved at a snail's pace through the steeply rising and falling streets, until the construction of the Central Viaduct made the route shorter and more direct.

In 1889 the present line from Superior through Seneca and Scranton Avenue to Clark Avenue was erected. The Superior Street line was opened to traffic in 1874, and in 1885 a horse line on Payne Avenue was created, which had to make way in 1889 for the cable car line. The St. Clair Street Railway was built in 1871 and ran from Water Street through St. Clair to Case Avenue.

The West Side Street Railway had to confront great difficulties of terrain presented by crossing the river and negotiating the steep Champlain Street on the east side, as well as the even steeper Detroit Street hill. Through the construction of the viaducts, these hindrances were overcome. With the expansion of the city, even greater challenges were taken on by public transportation, and the street rail system was expanded, so that in 1891 23 various lines were in operation, which led to an amalgamation into two. Seventeen lines form the system of the Cleveland Electric Rail Co., or the Big Consolidated, while six belong to the Cleveland City Rail Co., or the Little Consolidated.

All cars are propelled by electricity, with the exception of the Superior and Payne Avenue lines, which were constructed for cable. The fares of the two lines is five cents, and transfers are issued which are only valid for the company issuing.

In 1902 all the lines were united under the Cleveland Electric Railway Company, and since the two surviving cable lines were also changed into electrical lines, and the Steam Car called the "dummy," operating in Newburg and on Broadway has disappeared, the total streetcar operation of Cleveland has become electric and placed in the hands of a single company. Although considerable savings were realized, there was no reduction of the fare, which remains at 5¢ or 11 tickets for 50¢.

Soon after his inauguration Mayor Johnson began agitating for a fare of 3¢, and Mayor Johnson did manage to find a man who was willing to build a new line. The ordinance which permitted the first route, through Denison Avenue, was approved by the city council on 9 December 1901, and this was the beginning of the streetcar war which is still raging in all its intensity. Two days later the State Attorney General Sheets launched a successful proceeding against the municipal administration. The citizens responded by reelecting Mayor Johnson and all other Democratic candidates at the next election. On 11 May 1902 the district court issued a cessation order against the construction of a 3¢ line, and on 30 June of the same year this order was rendered permanent. The city council was prevented by the state supreme court from doing anything, and Senator Hanna arranged for a new municipal governance law to be passed through the legislature. Under this law, Mayor Johnson was reelected once more in early 1903. The senator once more sought to have the legislature extend the charters for the streetcars. Mayor Johnson now ran for governor to prevent that. He lost this campaign, but the senator died early the next year, his strength exhausted from the struggle. The streetcar battle went on. The next step in the war was the foundation or revival of the Forest City Railway Company, which made its first bid to construct a 3¢ line on 31 October 1903. The Cleveland Electric Railway Company then made a proposal with a fare of 2¢ and deposited a sum of $20,000, which still is in the hands of the city, as is the case with many other guarantees which have been placed under the same conditions. Work began on the 3¢ line in Denison Avenue, and in November of the same year there were two miles of tracks. Then came the court order, made by Albert J. Day, halting further work. The order was only reversed on 6 December 1905 by the Ohio Supreme Court, and from this time on the Forest City Rail Company has been able to make more progress.

In the meantime the city council adopted an ordinance which called for a fare of 3¢ on all lines. The Cleveland Electric forced a trial which it won before Federal Judge Wing, who issued a court order preventing the introduction of the ordinance. In a subsequent trial the line managed to have the Federal Superior Court establish that the charter for the Woodland Avenue line only ran out in February 1908, as was the case with the other lines on the West Side. A second trial on the operation on Central Avenue and Quincy Line, was lost by the railway in the same court, which declared at the start of this year that the charters in these streets ran out in March, 1905. When the 3¢ line tried to lay track in the streets, a certain W. W. Raynold sought a court order, which he received in superior court. This should have decided the matter whether a new company needed consent to lay track when there were already tracks in the same street.

The history of the streetcars over the last few years is a story of court orders and trials which cannot be reviewed in detail. It suffices to say that the 3¢ line ran its first cars last November (1906) in Denison Avenue and Fulton Road through to Detroit Avenue. From there passengers were taken by bus to the corner of Detroit and Pearl Street, where they were brought over the Superior Viaduct to Water Street via streetcars.

Cleveland Electric hindered access to Public Square through a further court order, so that the "ash-can line" which was already laid in Superior Street had to be taken up before it was finished. Then there was a temporary general cessation order on the grounds that Mayor Johnson was financially involved in the 3¢ line. In the meantime the Forest City Railway Company had leased its property to the Municipal Traction Company, and when it was hit by the cessation order, the Low Fare Company was founded and the property moved there. This is the company which is currently seeking to build the 3¢ line.

A proposal earlier made by Mayor Johnson that Cleveland Electric lease its property to the 3¢ line under the protection of the city found so much response by the end of February that Cleveland Electric did an inventory of its holdings. Mr. A. B. Du Pont did the assessment for the 3¢ line. Efforts continued for more than two months, and there was an armistice during this period. The findings differed dramatically, however, with Cleveland Electric estimating the value of its property at $33 million, while Mr. Du Pont estimated it at $22 million. A committee of the city council proposed that Cleveland Electric be paid $60 a share. The proposal was rejected, as was one for $85 a share made the year before. President Andrews further declared that his line was not for lease. It only desired a charter for 20 years at 7 tickets for 25¢ or 5¢ cash per trip. The line introduced the fare during the truce, but raised it as soon as war was declared again on the 3¢ line.

Cleveland can thank its rapid growth to its propitious situation as a harbor city on the chain of five Great Lakes. The eight states that border these lakes have a population of more than 30 million persons, and in the proper season the traffic on these water highways will not be exceeded by any other artery of transportation in the world. The exploitation of these waterways has made it possible for transport costs to be a ninth of what they once were when the transit of persons and goods was exclusively in the hands of the railroads. Goods, for example, can be transported by water a distance of 1000 miles to the west for less than sending these by railroad a quarter of the distance, south or north.

In 1816 the first steamboat, *Walk on the Water*, made its maiden voyage between here and Buffalo, taking 44 hours to do so, but the steamer's life was a short one. In 1827 the first steamboat built by Levy Johnson, *The Enterprise*, came down the ways. From this time on, maritime construction has risen to such heights that Cleveland wins first rank after the shipbuilders of the Clyde in Scotland.

The first steamship built in the United States with a capacity over 1000 tons, at the time the largest in the world, left the ways in 1844 in Cleveland, receiving the name of *Empire*, making the trip to Buffalo in 12.5 hours. This was soon followed by the construction of the most modern boats. The wooden ships had to make way for elegant and fast boats, and today steamers such as the *North West* and *North Land* and others ply the route from Duluth to Buffalo. They can be measured by the same standards of luxury applied to ocean steamers. If the means of passage permitted, Cleveland could compete directly in the production of ocean-going military, freight and passenger ships. The two largest establishments, the Globe Iron Works and the Cleveland Shipbuilding Co., are the firms that manufacture passenger and freight steamers.

Part II
Chapter 1
The Significance of Germans for the Flourishing of Cleveland

Even if one would not be fully justified in saying that Germans have given contemporary Cleveland its essential form, still an important proportion of its population is German or of German descent. According to the most recent governmental census, the number of Germans in our town amounts to about 40 percent. And whoever observes the factories, whoever passes down commercial streets and seeks after the names of the owners of businesses, he will discover uncommonly many German names, which would be a proof that Germans have been most deeply involved in the building of the city and that German energy and entrepreneurial spirit has done the most to make Cleveland what it is today.

Yet, on the other hand, whenever philistinism and pettiness emerges, and sniping or envy spreads abroad, it is also the Germans who have a part in it. We Germans, with our many good qualities, also have our hereditary vices, which can sometimes be historically traced and which have not vanished even with the erection of the new massive structure of the German Empire. The most outstanding failing is envious localistic pettiness, which is to be noted in the smallest detail. This "internal struggle" has greatly injured Germans from the beginning, even if it is not always of the most serious nature.

Yet the Germans of our fair city have shown themselves on great occasions to be capable of great deeds. They were among the first to send their sons into battle to save the Union, and at that time they were united and led with true enthusiasm. And they were also united when it was a question of opposing efforts of a nativist and anti-liberty direction. They are still united in not permitting themselves to be robbed of their language, their customs and usages, and they are united in wanting to be good Americans while keeping their German way of life. The fact that Germans have divided themselves, here as everywhere else, into a thousand associations and little clubs damages nothing, and it is fortunate that they do not all belong to one and the same party. The fact that the whip of party does not hold them in rank and file, that they can preserve their independence in the best sense of the word, has been demonstrated in the political struggles of the last several years. Today, as 65 or 50 years ago, their influence remains crucial in influencing conditions in our city.

The German element that immigrated to the United States is made of entirely different materials from other nationalities. This as well has its historical cause. German emigration began in the generation after the Thirty Years War, which ruined the position of Germany in the world, destroying the German middle class and with it the power and energy of the nation. What had once been an adventurous and powerful German citizenry was numbed and ruined, and what had been free men became anxious Philistines subject to the whims of fate. The alienation of the nation from its own nature achieved its highest peak. The oppressed townsman and peasants recovered only gradually and with difficulty from the hardest blows, and it was only toward the end of that century that they began to raise themselves from moral and physical depression and raise their gaze to greater ideas. It was not that they could have dared to defy their oppressors at home and put a bloody end to the spiritless comedy with a violent blow. They were too weak and exhausted to do that, and the despotism of the princes was all the stronger, nourished by France.

No, the oppressed subject escaped misery at home only through flight. Hesitantly, barely trusting their own strength, they responded to enticement from abroad, marvelling at everything foreign as something to be praised, and when it could be done, they departed the Fatherland without regret or pain. As a result emigration took on continually greater scale, turning to the north and to the south and particularly to America. In time it grew to a scale that even the strongest governmental ban availed little against the "evil," which grew day by day. Germany, which was poor enough as it was, continued to pass a great deal of its productive force, its human and monetary capital, overseas, receiving in return only French customs and vices, alien luxuries and adventurers. The reason for emigration varied from one area to another, and often several motivations operated at once. Either there was political and religious oppression, such as war for the sake of the faith, or there were social abuses, such as hunger, dearth, disease, relative overpopulation and unemployment. But there was also an imprecise pressure for bettering one's own situation or the enticing example of the prosperity of earlier emigrants. Our writers even speak of a supposed Teutonic tendency to wander as the real reason for emigration, but such arbitrary assumptions beg the question of whether anyone who is happy at home will easily take up the wanderer's staff. Even the few exceptions confirm the rule. The first German immigrants who landed in Pennsylvania were driven from their homes by confessional intolerance, and their next followers, who settled in New York, fled from hunger and French oppression.

Our area saw little or nothing from these emigrations. It was only in the 1830s that the first columns of the great German immigration brought Cleveland the blessing that so affected the prosperity of America in general and of Cleveland in particular. One might say that the destiny of our city was decided in 1833.

The first 35 years in the existence of the newly founded city passed without real disturbance, but also without any remarkable progress. The little place Moses Cleaveland chose for his "City of the Future" — for every new settlement had the same hope in those days — was spared elemental catastrophes and dreadful visitations, and no insurmountable obstacles had been placed in its way. Despite that, there was also no real progress, and in 1830, when Cleveland was 34 years old, it had hardly outgrown its childrens' shoes and numbered only 1075 inhabitants. Residents waited and hoped for some sort of push, and their hearts must often have harbored doubts about the future of their community.

That was changed with one blow in 1833. New hordes of immigrants from Germany appeared as if dropped from heaven, seeking a new home, a new Fatherland. This was the first column of the great armies of immigrants who sought new places to work in the aftermath of the French July Revolution of 1830.

These immigrants were mostly people of intelligence and substance, the best element America had recruited up until then and in some senses the best among those who came from across the ocean to the present day. The bureaucratic and police-state atmosphere of their oppressed fatherland had simply become intolerable to these people. America has the French July Revolution of 1830, which was followed by a liberal uprising in Southern Germany, to thank for this fine addition to its population. Following the suppression of this uprising under the power of Metternich, a hunt for demagogues and liberals such as Germany had seldom or never seen unfolded with the approval of the princes and their favorites, which was a blemish on German history. Every free movement, every free idea, was persecuted and suppressed with arbitrary gruesomeness, and the reaction against the rights and liberties of the people raged so badly that even some of the conservative citizens were no longer able to watch passively and were compelled to turn their backs on their fatherland and seek a new, free homeland in America. This gave a push to German emigration, which grew in strength from year to year until the even stronger push of 1848 and 1849, which had a decisive significance for the destiny of Germans in America, as well as on the political and social life in the New World as a whole.

Cleveland was among the areas receiving a great number from this immigration of 1833, reinforced from week to week by new recruits. They arrived and settled with family and possessions, with their strong hands and healthy limbs, with their money and goods, hope and courage, and with them the passivity of the little population vanished, altering the physiognomy of the town and its bordering townships. Such immigrants, bringing with them gold and silver, were welcome guests. Soon the forests were cleared from the land; garden plots, flowered meadows and vineyards appeared; streets were cleared and began to come alive; trade and commerce awoke from their winter's slumber; hands were active in the shops; and passivity made way for courage. The city began to rise to fulfill its later mission.

Handicrafts, which in those days were still a goldmine, lay almost exclusively in the hands of Germans, who were hard-working, modest and thrifty, satisfied with what they could make. They were happy to own a home of their own, to eat and sleep under their own roof and to be their own masters in a free country. The reach of these Germans spread continually. The activity of trade and business, not yet lamed by monopolies or trusts, could still pay off, and the fortunate owners of restaurants and inns, whose noble calling it was to serve the thirsty and the hungry, still had good times for their philanthropic activities. For a long time the art with which the Germans slaked their thirst in happy sociability was not challenged, just as even today the *Gemütlichkeit* of the German element remains peculiar to themselves, a proud inheritance.

Thus a comfortable prosperity spread everywhere, and satisfaction reigned even among the workers. Certainly the wages were low, and three-quarters of those were paid in the form of vouchers to shopkeepers, but the wages were steady and, despite the shortage of cash, there was little concern about getting enough to eat, there was no hunger that could not be fulfilled and there was no worrying about the daily bread. Food was cheap and the needs of people modest and measured.

Under these conditions, Cleveland prospered; its shops expanded, homes and gardens became more beautiful, and the limits of the town grew. In the course of the decade, until 1840, the population grew seven-fold, and the next decade brought the population to 18,000. Thanks to the immigration of 1849 and the further develoment of 1850-60, the population reached the total of 44,000.

The Germans of Cleveland did not belong to the class of speculators, those "go-ahead" erntrepreneurs who risk more than they have to lose in their passionate quest for quick profits and their own economic advance. They were more positively involved in politics than is the case today. As a result the Germans became one of the factors which contributed positively to the rise and prosperity of the city, and it would only be a bad German or a prejudiced American who would not admit this freely.

With the arrival of the great decade from 1850 to 1860, the image of American life altered basically, and a new cultural era was inaugurated. Pro-slavery propaganda was at its zenith and was bolder than ever. Yet at the same time the public conscience, which for so long been indifferent to the institution of slavery, began to stir and to exhort the people about its holy duty. The anti-slavery movement grew rapidly, patriotic men of clever decisiveness placed themselves at its head and enthusiastic fighters joined up. A fresh, agitating spirit had descended on the progressive press, and within both of the old political parties, which had once stood under the sway of slaveholders, one could perceive the start of collapse. It was precisely at this opportune moment that the Forty-Eighter fighters for liberty crossed the ocean. Barely acclimatized, they did not hesitate an instant to place themselves in the service of liberty in their new fatherland, enlisting under the banner of the anti-slavery forces. Ten years and more the struggle proceeded with intellectual weapons and varying success, until victory over slavery was won on the blood-soaked field. The great cultural services the immigrant Forty-Eighters performed for their adopted fatherland are recognized by history and cannot be more closely reviewed here. In any case, it can be asserted with certainty that without the German element, slavery would have survived years, perhaps decades longer, as a constitutional institution.

Just as the French July Revolution of 1830 indirectly stimulated the strong emigration to America, so also the French February Revolution of 1848 and the repression of the German uprising conjured up by it led to the German migration to America, which bestowed the greatest benefits on our country, to the loss of our old fatherland. Thousands, hundreds of thousands of educated, liberty-loving and energetic men were driven into exile. There were new settlements in every state of the Union, and this event and this emigration also redounded to Cleveland's benefit. Many hundreds of the new immigrants settled within the limits of the Forest City, people who had completely broken with the past and now had no idea what new path to begin here. Their idealistic and free views had saved them for America.

From this time on the German language and the advantages of German intellect and character were preserved and supported, after a few earlier attempts. Efforts were made to provide a place for the lively arts. Singing societies and Turner associations were founded for their stated purposes, but also to agitate against slavery, to struggle against nativist tendencies, to oppose party servility and political corruption, as well as to take a stand against intolerance and zealotry of any sort.

Despite concerns for winning our daily bread and despite the lack of money, work began at once on founding and building a Turner Hall. Even though it was of modest dimensions, still liberal Germans found it to be a suitable home for their German ideas. A German school was also raised. The Germans of Cleveland quickly won important influence and complete equality in politics, due to their restless efforts. But Germans also fell to fighting among themselves almost at once. The battle of brothers between the older Germans and the younger Germans, between the "Grays" and the "Greens," soon flamed up, with the result that even in the slavery question there were divisions between these two parties that were ever more intense.

At the close of the decade, Cleveland had taken another decisive step forward toward further development, despite all struggles and storms. Germans, who included 15,000 souls and amounted to about an eighth of the population in 1860, had grown dramatically in their economic position, and had achieved an enviable prosperity. In business and industry they had risen considerably, and there were some who had hardly known where to hang their hats a decade before who were now established masters and owners of prosperous businesses.

Then came the war, which demanded so many bloody sacrifices. The pages of history record the enthusiasm with which our German brothers gathered under the Star-Spangled Banner to defend their new fatherland. They sealed their peacetime cultural achievements on bloody fields of battle with their heroic deeds.

The great events of the years of 1870 and 1871 brought new waves of immigrants. Since then, the number of German immigrants has declined from year to year, but Germans do not need to be ashamed of the role they have played and still play when the history of Cleveland's development is written.

What corner of the town could be found where there is not some sort of witness to German industriousness? What house or palace does not have some German sweat stuck to it? Where is there a workshop or factory where German talent is not represented, or any institution of arts or learning that does not give evidence of German energy? Isn't it the German who unconsciously drives to fulfill the needs of his heart and soul, which brings some light, warmth and joy into meaningless effort and striving? Hasn't the introduction of musical festivals, banquets and worthy popular entertainments been a considerable piece of cultural work?

The German who understands that true German identity is not at odds with true Americanism will be mindful of the obligation that the heritage of the past imposes on him, a holy bequest from his forbearers. The entry of this expanding city into the second century of its existence must result in the community of Cleveland becoming a place of intellectual freedom, in the noble fulfillment of the welfare of citizens, and our city shall be expanded in this direction. If the present generation takes the same role in this cultural work it has taken in the past, then Germans need have no concerns for the future.

Chapter 2
The German Press of the City of Cleveland

As has already been emphasized elsewhere, the Germans here have always been intimately connected with the growth and development of the city of Cleveland. Yet it was only in 1847 that the time arrived for the founding of a German newspaper. The former judges Eduard Hessenmüller and Wangelin founded a little German paper, which survived only with difficulty. It was the *Germania*, whose editor was a Mr. Rothnagel from Canton. The paper was quickly sold to the central committee of the Whig Party, although this party was not in sympathy with the needs of the new German migration. Then, in 1852, the *Wächter am Erie* appeared, edited by August Thieme, a man of the 1848 Revolution. The first number of the newspaper appeared on 9 August 1852. In 1856 another German paper appeared under the name of the *Cleveland Courir*, but it did not enjoy a long existence and did not prosper. From time to time over the next 20 years, newspapers appeared alongside the *Wächter am Erie*, of which none except the *Anzeiger* was able to survive. In the 1870s the *Columbia* and the *Germania* rose and vanished, and at the start of the eighties *Die Biene* flourished for a time. Despite this, a new paper was founded in 1888 by the Republican Party, since the *Wächter* was too liberal for them. In December of that year the *Germania* was called into existence with significant resources, but poor management exhausted these resources within a year, and the editorial offices were closed by the sheriff on the day after Christmas 1889. A few months earlier, however, a fourth German newspaper was founded, called the *Deutsche Presse*, the first German penny-paper, and it spread rapidly. Two years later this newspaper was bought out by the *Anzeiger*, so that the field was clear for the two principal newspapers once more. It should be remarked that there have always been a few German weekly newspapers in Cleveland, but few of them have been able to achieve much influence. The last great move in the German newspaper world took place in 1893, when the *Anzeiger und Deutsche Presse* merged with the *Wächter am Erie*. This brings us to the present situation, where the *Wächter und Anzeiger* holds a position which would be the envy of the largest English papers.

The first number of the *Wächter am Erie* appeared on 9 August 1852. At that time Cleveland had no more than 20,000 residents, of whom a quarter were Germans. The year of 1848 had driven rather a lot of Germans to America to seek a home. The German press experienced a considerable growth as a result, and it served in turn as the herald of societies and clubs, such as the Turner societies, singing societies, the German stage and other German institutions of education.

In Cleveland there was a brave little band of "Greens," already mentioned, which went to work like bees to promote everything then associated with the concept of liberalism. Karl Heinzen had long been welcome here, and he was happy to come. The demand for a newspaper that would promote and support these ideas became steadily more palpable. The *Germania* which was here was far too slow and circumspect, so that after long preparation and discussion the *Wächter am Erie* was finally called to life. As a result of efforts by Jacob Müller and Louis Ritter, a joint-stock company was established, and in the summer of 1852, August Thieme was called from Buffalo, where he then was living.

August Thieme made a long speech before a gathering in Weidenkopf's Hall to present his ideas about establishing a German newspaper that would represent the principles of democracy, and shares worth $400 were sold. They went to work with these modest resources. Heinrich F. Rochotte, an experienced and capable typesetter, agreed to establish a printing shop. A large room in the top floor of the *Plain Dealer* Building was rented, at the corner of Superior and South Water Street (where the Bratenahl Block is presently located), and they went to work.

It was decided to publish the paper for the time being twice a week. The first number was printed on the press of the *Plain Dealer*. Naturally there was little time to waste, and there was joyful effort on behalf of high principles.

From the very beginning the *Wächter* entered the lists for the abolition of slavery. This horrified many of the old-line Democrats, the "trimmers." They regarded the right of property in black human beings to be as holy as any other form of property, and anyone unwilling to recognize this was a communist and a subversive. They heaped the new paper with bitter scorn, and when they were told that the paper was from the outset an independent German popular newspaper, they still believed that its Democratic sympathies entailed support for the pro-slavery platform passed in Baltimore. The *Wächter*, on the contrary, supported the principles that the Democratic Party embodied in Jefferson's time. As a result, the trimmers became enemies of the *Wächter*, and most of them have remained enemies through the decades since then. After a year of operation it was seen to be best to have the paper in solid hands, so it was sold to August Thieme and a typesetter. Under the new leadership the paper appeared three times a week, but this novelty did not last long, so that soon it was changed to a weekly, only to appear twice a week later. In the meantime the struggle between the "Grays" and the "Greens" grew steadily more passionate. There existed a genuine danger that the split of the Germans would become unbridgeable when a movement arose that caused internal unity to be restored, as if by magic. This was the period of the Know-Nothings, who celebrated their triumphs everywhere with remarkable successes in Cleveland, in Cuyahoga County and in the state of Ohio. The *Wächter* immediately took the field against the movement with all decisiveness, which as it contained no lasting principle, no issue to sustain a national party, had transitory success. Germans opposed this marvelous chimera with closed ranks, and the majority joined the Republican Party, which had energetically opposed the monstrosity. The *Wächter* acted with energy, and as early as 1855, even before the Frémont campaign, it supported that significant battler for freedom, Salmon P. Chase, as candidate for governor. During the Frémont campaign of 1856, the *Wächter* appeared as a daily, but could not maintain this over the long run and reduced frequency for a while after the elections. The paper was only made a daily again on 27 September 1866, and there has been no interruption since then. By then the *Wächter* had moved to Michigan Street, and business boomed. In 1871, in order to expand the business, Thieme established the Wächter am Erie Printing Co., which was incorporated with a number of representatives of the German community here with a capital of $50,000, while editorial control remained in experienced hands. In 1872, during the Greeley campaign, the *Wächter* left the Republican Party, which had already begun to give in to the spirit of intolerance and become the party of monopoly and corruption. The *Wächter* also supported the Tilden campaign in the elections of 1876. From that point on the paper remained Democratic, battling the intolerant moralism that flourished among Republicans with all its might. After Thieme's death in 1879 the Wächter am Erie Printing Co. continued under the chairmanship of former Lieutenant Governor Jacob Müller. The editorship was taken over by Julius Kurzer, who had assisted Thieme during his lifetime. The company went through many changes, but the liberal element always remained on top.

After Jacob Müller was named by President Cleveland as consul general at Frankfurt am Main, so that he was compelled to leave Cleveland for an extended period of time, Dr. Wolfenstein became interim leader of the paper, later followed by C. L. Hotze, who reorganized the <u>Wächter am Erie</u> Co. and brought the control of the shares into his own hands. In the meantime Mr. Kurzer had died, and he was succeeded as editor in chief of the *Wächter* by Dr. Christian Horix, who soon died in the full bloom of age.

Carl Claussen, who had been managing editor from 1883, took over after Dr. Horix, leading the paper until 1888, passing his office to Ernst Kluffmann and L. F. Korth after him. Under the management of Mr. Hotze the *Wächter* had a hard struggle, as competing papers spouted out of the ground like mushrooms, and it was only when Charles W. Mädje took the wheel with a strong hand that the newspaper rose once more to respect and influence.

The "Wächter" has been edited by August Thieme; Gustav Balzer; Julius Kurzer; Carl Claussen, who twice was chief writer; Dr. Christian Horix; Ernst Kluffmann; and L. F. Korth.

The *Cleveland Anzeiger*, which existed and prospered here for nearly 25 years, was called to life in 1871 by Heinrich Gentz and originally appeared three times a week. The next year the paper passed into the hand of a joint stock company, which obtained it primarily for the Grant presidential campaign and passed it to the firm of Bohm, Kraus & Co. in the same year. From then on, the *Anzeiger* appeared as a daily. In 1874 the company transferred the newspaper to Major C. W. Kraus, who kept control of the management in his hand for three years, passing it to Mr. Kaufmann in 1877. The *Anzeiger* became a morning newspaper in 1886 and remained one until 7 April 1890, but otherwise passed its entire existence as an afternoon paper.

The rise of the paper came when Mr. Wm. Kaufmann came here and purchased it. Until 1881 he managed the business together with Emil Pätow, when he founded the <u>Anzeiger</u> Publishing Co. Kaufmann was more than just an able journalist with rich experience, but also a capable businessman, so he managed to make the *Anzeiger* one of the best German newspapers in the country, as well as a business success. During the years when the *Anzeiger* was a morning paper, it was bettered by only a few German newspapers in the United States. It was Kaufmann's special pride to make a paper for the family table, offering material that was many-sided and interesting. The *Anzeiger* was created as a Republican newspaper, and it followed this political faith until 1890 without becoming guilty of toadyism. Gradually, however, it came ever closer to Kaufmann's ideal of political independence, and in its last years before merger the *Anzeiger* was a completeley independent newspaper that would support the best candidate, regardless of party.

At the time of merger, the *Anzeiger* was in excellent shape, as was the case with the *Wächter*, and neither paper was compelled to take the step. In 1891 Mr. Kaufmann purchased the majority of the shares of the *Deutsche Presse*, which had already obtained the circulation of the *Germania* through purchase. Further, at the time of the merger he had risen to one of the best businesses in the country through the stereotype and insert delivery business he had established. The *Anzeiger* was edited by Gustav Balzer, Dr. Bernhardt Miller, Wm. Kaufmann and Carl Arnold.

To make the unification of the two German dailies possible, a German Consolidated News Co. was created, which purchased the shares of both enterprises in the course of 1893 and brought the new organization into being. At the same time the German Press and Plate Company was created to unite the stereotype and insert delivery systems of both papers. The consolidation of the two German dailies, which took place in October 1893, was not a commandment of necessity but a result of a considered decision of the leaders of both enterprises, who had become convinced over the course of time that a German daily that cost a penny could not survive if it had to fight competition. In addition, both Mr. Kaufmann and Mr. Mädje and others had become convinced to concentrate forces in order to increase the influence of Germans and of the reform movement in general through a greater circulation. And what these gentlemen sought to obtain through merger actually did take place.

Since then the *Wächter und Anzeiger* has improved in all departments. It has one of the best printing plants not only in the state but also in the entire country, and it is in the position of promptly printing and distributing its very large edition, which is far above 30,000. Nearly 90 men are occupied in the various departments, not including the 40 carriers who fetch the edition from the printing plant every day. Further, the newspaper is handled by 75 newspaper agencies, which occupy more than 1200 newsboys to spread it to all parts of the town, and there is a large circle of subscribers in neighboring towns and villages.

So far as the political position of the *Wächter und Anzeiger* goes, it has sought for years to take a neutral position on all questions of pressing local and national importance. It has used its independence in the public interest, and even though it does not please the strict party man by doing so, it has earned the applause of all intelligent German citizens. It relies on progress in the intellectual and moral development of national character and on the demands made by economic conditions. The *Wächter und Anzeiger* is published by the German Consolidated Newspaper Co., whose board consists of the following persons: Chas. W. Maedje, Wm. Kaufmann, Jul. F. Grothe, Herm. Schmidt and Wm. H. Beavis, with the following officers: Chas. W. Maedje, president; Herm. Schmidt, vice president; and J. F. Grothe, secretary. The publication house is at 1566-70 West 3rd Street.

The present editorial staff of the paper consists of the editor in chief, Mr. Simon Hickler, as well as the following: Rich. Brenne, local editor; Carl Lorenz, Sunday editor; Wm. Hense, music and theatrical critic; J. H. Gerlich, reporter on courts and societies; Carl Neugart, reporter; Emil Karpowsky, telegraph editor; as well as the following coworkers: A. von Ehrenberg, serial and special reporter; Robert Lenz, humor; H. F. Urban, New York; Alex. von Huhn, Berlin; E. Max Hasselbach, Washington; Wm. Kaufmann, Dresden; Eugen Schmidt, Paris; Hugo Heyn, Coburg; E. Schierenberg, Wiesbaden; Anton Turajski, correspondent; H. Holm, correspondent; Mrs. Caroline Tuerk, editor for the women's page.

The *Deutsche Presse*, the first German penny-paper in Cleveland and in Ohio, was founded by Jacob E. Müller in June 1889. Until that time the three dailies had a very restricted edition. Müller, who had been involved in local journalism since 1869, knew this well. He blamed this on the management, specifically on the high prices, as Germans here were usually able to speak English and could take the cheaper English newspapers. The enormous success that he had in a short time with the *Deutsche Presse* shows he was not mistaken. It is possible to assert that a true German readership here was only created by the appearance of the *Deutsche Presse*. The other papers were so shaken that they also began to appear as penny-papers. After two years of existence, the majority of shares of the Deutsche Presse Publishing Co. was purchased by Wm. Kaufmann, and the *Deutsche Presse* merged with the *Anzeiger*.

Since 1 May 1906, after years in which there was only one German daily despite the size of its German population, a second German daily appeared in the form of the *Cleveland Herold*, which had appeared as a weekly for more than five years. Just as is the case with the English afternoon papers, the daily *Herold* appears every day, except Sunday, and it has taken it upon itself to represent the interests of the Germans without respect to party. It is published at 1280 Ontario Street and is published by a joint-stock company. The leadership lies in the hands of messrs. John Reich, Charles W. Haake and Albert Urban.

At the start of the eighties, as a movement arose to improve the lot of laborers and as socialist ideas spread from Europe found reception here, German socialist workers called to life the *Clevelander Volksfreund* in April 1886. It undertook to promote the interests of workers as much as possible and to win support for modern socialism. The management of the paper lay in the hands of a society created by workers, which elected seven men every year in January to handle business. Their first editor, August Keitel, who died in January 1893, had to deal with many problems in the first years. He was a good speaker who knew how to make propaganda for his cause. His successor, K. Ibsen, succeeded in continuing the ideas begun by Mr. Keitel, and he managed to win a large number of subscribers, particularly among workers.

Besides the daily and Sunday editions of the *Wächter und Anzeiger*, the *Cleveland Herold* and the weekly *Volksfreund*, the *Deutsch-Amerikanische Kriegerzeitung* is published here under the able leadership of Mr. Rudolph von Ahlefeld.

Yet to do right by the German population, much has happened over the last 50 years not only in the area of politics and society, but also in religion. The publication house of the Evangelische Gemeinschaft was founded in 1816 in New Berlin, Pennsylvania, and it was moved to Cleveland in 1853. Through the continual increase of the Gemeinschaft, it became possible to erect a large, five-story building whose construction and equipping cost more than half a million dollars.

The first newspaper published in German by the Gemeinschaft, *Der Christliche Botschafter*, was established in 1835, and it is currently the oldest and largest German weekly in the United States, with a readership of more than 20,000 subscribers. Another literary product of the same publishing house is the monthly, *Das Evangelische Magazin*, which first appeared in 1865 and today has a circulation of 15,000 copies.

The publishing house also has a Sunday-school literature running to editions of 170,000 copies.

The total number of printed works read by members of the Gemeinschaft amounts to 216,000. The profits obtained by this enterprise are used largely for charity.

Other than the institution just described, the Baptists have a large bulding for publishing on Payne Avenue, where the *Sendbote* is published, and the German Reformed Church of the United States also has an extensive publishing house on Pearl Street. This institution produces the *Kirchenzeitung* and other religious periodicals for Sunday schools. The *Stimme der Wahrheit* represents the interests of Catholics in Cleveland and environs, appearing at 701 Lorain Street.

Chapter 3
Cleveland's Musical History

It is the great service of the Germans to the New World that they brought with them the cultivation of music. What would life be like in America without the ennobling influence which the activities of the singing societies and musical performances excercise, without the notes which musical and song-filled Germans provide?

Feelings of pride and elevation must overcome the German when he looks back on the past and contemplates how his people broke new ground here and fulfilled their mission.

When we contemplate the musical life of Cleveland today, we find confirmed the statement of an insightful American critic that the musical measure of an American city varied according to the amount of its German population, seeing that Cleveland is one of the most outstanding places promoting the musical arts in the Union thanks to its high percentage of Germans in the population.

When we go back to the beginnings of the city, the prelude to its foundation, when the white inhabitants were still dealing with the Indians, the first person to spread civilized music in contrast to the wild notes of the Indians was a man with a German name, Haas, who traded with the redskins and came perhaps four times a year to the banks of the Cuyahoga, playing his fiddle on these occasions, playing his popular dances and songs.

Somewhat later another German, whose name does not reach posterity, came to Cleveland, which had grown to be a large village, and he brought a sort of harmonium, spreading musical enjoyment.

In the 1820s and 1830s a large number of German immigrants settled. A demonstration that the cultivation of music was one of their primary concerns and that it had begun to take root here is shown by the fact that when German farmers from the county came to Cleveland, performance of vocal and instrumental music was always part of festival programs, and these very much impressed the Americans in those days.

In the 1840s we find the first piano in Cleveland. In the 1850s there came a swarm of intelligent, educated German immigrants brought by the revolutionary movement, bringing with them a corresponding life to Cleveland, and the indications of German music and its influence grow ever clearer and more precise. It was then when the first singing society, the "Frohsinn," was established, and with its emergence the systematic cultivation of song began.

This first singing society was established in 1848. A well-known political refugee, Heber, took over its leadership, and it soon grew into a society with many members. When the director was seized by gold fever and left for California, leadership passed to Gottlieb Votteler the organ builder, and he retained this position until the society dissolved in 1850 because it did not match the expectations of the members. Singing went on despite this, and after Heber's return from California a mixed chorus was organized which rehearsed in Seifert's casino which understood how to counter the problems of the world with good cheer.

The majority of the singers joined the Free Men's League, forming a singing section. This league was made up of the most outstanding representatives of the Germans, interested in preserving German language and ways and establishing German schools. The directors of this section were F. Georg and Carl Adam. The latter, an outstanding musician who did great things with the people available, was a Forty-Eighter from Prague, but he did not find the necessary sympathy among the singers, and since Cleveland had been designated the site of the festival of the North American Singing League, the singing section withdrew from the Free

Men's League in October, 1858, and founded the "Cleveland Singing Society," electing Mr. Fritz Adel as director.

In what was then Ohio City, the present West Side, the Liederkranz and the Liedertafel had been called into existence, led by the schoolteacher Carl Räder and the bookkeeper Chas. Sältzer. They amalgamated in 1858 with the West Side Men's Chorus, and these were absorbed at the start of the 1870s into the Orpheus, for many years the best society in the city and still in existence today.

In 1863 the Harmonie was founded, and in 1872 the Heights Men's Chorus. Both societies still hold a prominent position in the song life of Cleveland. The first director of the Harmonie was Chas. Köbler, in those days an esteemed pianist. Among the singing societies called into being in the most recent times the Turner Men's Chorus must be mentioned as one of the most accomplished, under the leadership of Dr. M. Francisci.

The Vocal Society, founded by Americans in 1858, should be mentioned here as the first imitation of the German style of singing. Americans soon began to develop a taste for choral singing, and they sought to do what the Germans did. The Vocal Society proved to be a lively group and had a great rise when Alfred Arthur took over the society in 1873. The four-part chorus often numbered more than 100 singers. The Vocal Society lost its preeminent position a few years ago when Prof. Arthur established his musical school and dedicated himself primarily to teaching, and its place was taken by the Singers' Club, whose leader was C. B. Ellinwood, a fine bass and singing teacher who had once worked at Arthur's singing school. Later Chas. E. Clemens was the club's director, and the concerts given in the Chamber of Commerce building every winter with the assistance of leading soloists were an event in the musical season of Cleveland.

Also to be mentioned in this context is the Bach Society, which the aforementioned musician Alfred Arthur called to life in 1878 as an imposing church choir with 200 voices at the Woodland Presbyterian Church. Its later director was Carl F. Radde, the son of the noted German jeweler on Woodland Avenue.

In keeping with this model, the Rubinstein Club was established as a ladies' chorus of 80 voices under the direction of Dr. M. Freye.

The principal cultivators of song remain the German singing societies, however, which have been taken as the model for the English clubs mentioned as well as many smaller ones.

Chapter 4
The German Churches and Societies

The most important bearers of German culture in America, alongside the German press, are the German churches and German societies. As was the case in the last century, so also today the religious congregations are extremely active in preserving German language and customs, and they should be esteemed for this by all Germans. Cleveland has more than 70 German congregations, divided by confession into eleven Lutheran, nine Reformed, nine Evangelical Community, seven Catholic, twelve Evangelical Protestant, five Methodist, four United Brethren, four Baptist, six Jewish, one Episcopalian, one Community of Christ, one Mission and one Christian Allied congregation. Each of these congregations has its own church, and a conservative estimate holds that a total of 15,000 adults belong. The Catholics and the Lutherans have their own schools.

Germans are also active in charity, especially in founding the German Old Peoples' Home on Detroit Street, which is a credit to the city, giving many German ladies of the better class the opportunity to express their humane, social sense.

Social life is promoted by German societies, in which Germans join together due to inclination, goals, etc., in a laudable manner.

The founding of the first societies goes back to pioneering days, and it was in particular singing societies which formed. This is thoroughly given in the chapter on the musical history of Cleveland. Besides the singing societies, which currently number over 30, there are Turner societies, including the Germania, Social, Star and Forwards Turner Societies, all of which have their own singing sections as well as their own gymnastic halls, distinguishing themselves through their liveliness. Further there is over a hundred support societies and lodges, 24 homeland societies, four veterans' societies and a dozen other associations such as the German School Society, the German Medical Association, two German pioneer societies and a German gun club.

Rare are the Germans who have abstained from joining one or several societies.

German societies are particularly concerned to make festivities involving Germans into something worth while.

Singing festivals are the first of these festivals to be mentioned, besides Turner festivals, although there has not yet been a national Turner festival in Cleveland, then the Humboldt celebration in 1869 and the German memorial day in 1890, where the Germans of Cleveland unrolled their entire significance and placed all of the rest of Cleveland in the shadows.

In the most recent time, June, 1907, the erection of the Schiller-Goethe monument in Wade Park moved all Germans to an imposing celebration.

Part III
Chapter 1
Financial Institutions

The fact that Cleveland has achieved greatness in finances is best proved by its banks and monetary institutions. It is said that Cleveland capitalists do not easily pass up an opportunity to invest their money at a profit, and the grandiose banking system of Cleveland is the best proof that this reputation is earned. In no other city of the West has the banking system had nearly as positive results, and the astonishing progress of the last years have only gone to fulfill the prophesy that Cleveland will become one of the most significant financial centers in the country, but that progress also guarantees that it will remain on its previous course and is approaching an even more glittering future.

How much German hard work, German persistence and goal-oriented German enterprising spirit has contributed and is yet contributing will be clear to the reader beyond any doubt when he recalls the many German names whose bearers have shown themselves worthy of great trust as directors or officers of local financial institutions. And the fact that German-Americans are so strongly represented in the local financial world, that so many German-American capitalists hold leading positions in local financial institutions, has advanced even less-endowed German-Americans. They are increasingly willing to entrust their savings to banks, and they have not had any reason to regret that. The percentage of German savings deposits is much larger in Cleveland than that of the savings deposits of other nationalities.

One may get an idea of the expansion of banking in Cleveland if one considers that Cincinnati, which is recognized as one of the great financial cities, has half as much money invested in its banks than in those of the Forest City. The total capital of the 36 banks, savings banks and trust companies of Cleveland amounts to $21,569,912.50. The surplus of undistributed profits amounts to $17,979,750. The seven national banks possess assets and liabilities amounting to $75,000,000. The First National Bank is among the few banks in the country with more than $20,000,000 in deposits. The deposits of two other financial institutions, the Bank of Commerce National Association, and the Union National Bank amount to more than $10,000,000; according to the account of February 1907 the assets of the first bank is $24,053,930, that of the latter $11,068,442 and $11,440,307 respectively.

The large banks have shown themselves to be very enterprising. Many branches have been established in the suburbs, and in the center of the city itself many have increased and rebuilt their central buildings. Following the direction of the time, many banks have consolidated, reducing expenses. This tendency can only help to improve the situation and make further development possible.

In 1883 there were five national banks in Cleveland, three savings banks and four private banks. In 1907 there are nine national banks, 15 savings banks and 14 trust companies. The first banks had to deal with great difficulties, since the legislature continually issued new laws which made the flourishing of the business impossible. Later growth was limited by the ultraconservative conduct of bankers, but this laid the cornerstone for the stability which in the end won general confidence. In these early days Cleveland banks were involved in the construction of railroads, which contributed to making Cleveland a major shipping center, and they have more recently been involved in industrial establishments.

It is certainly of interest to note that the first bank established in Cleveland, the Commercial Bank of Lake Erie, was called to life by the Bank Law of 1816. Alfred Kelly was president and Leonard Case was cashier. The village was small then, and in 1820 the bank failed. In 1832 the bank was reorganized with Leonard Case as president and Truman P. Handy as cashier. After the expiration of its charter in 1842 the business was closed, since state officials denied a renewal. In 1844 it was organized under a new charter with a capital of $500,000. Mr. Handy was elected president and remained in this position until 1877.

One of the earliest banks was City Bank, which was originally called the Fireman's Insurance Co., but according to its charter it was able to do some banking business. In 1845 it obtained a full charter as a bank, electing Reuben Sheldon as president and T. C. Severance as cashier. In 1865 the name was changed to National City Bank; in 1885 the charter was renewed, and the bank continues today.

Cleveland has one bank which has a unique position among all the banks of the country. It is the Society for Savings, Ohio's largest bank. It has no capital, but rather according to the terms of a special charter it is to act in the interests of the depositors, to whom profits are paid and to whose benefit they are accumulated. The charter was passed by the legislature on 22 March 1846, and the society was organized on 18 June of the same year with the following officers: John W. Allen, president; Reuben Hitchcock, Dudley Baldwin and F. W. Wingham, vice presidents; S. H. Mather, secretary; J. S. Tatnor, treasurer. In 1850 depsits amounted to a bit more than $17,000. Since organization transactions have amounted to $350,000,000.

The rise of trust companies constitutes an important chapter of financial history. These companies have been particularly successful in Cleveland, and they have extended their activities into the most variious fields.

The Citizens Savings & Trust Co.

The Citizens Savings & Trust Co. was established in 1868. It is the oldest and largest trust company in Ohio. With capital and surplus to the amount of $6 million, it offers undoubted security for their savings deposits. It pays four percent on savings deposits and two percent on checking accounts. Foreign exchange and letters of credit are issued. The bank has also opened a postal banking department which makes it possible to receive deposits from all parts of the civilized world. External depositors receive the same security and interest for their deposits as with locals.

Since the bank has so many female customers, it has established a "women's department" headed by a woman who is always ready to give female customers all possible information and to assist them in the transaction of business. This department also has a prettily furnished room in which there is a serving woman to provide every comfort for female visitors.

The safe of the bank is to be found in the main hallway, so that it is not necessary for the personnel to climb stairs. The safe is absolutely fireproof and secure from theft. Private rooms are available in which one may inspect certificates, cut coupons or hold consultations.

The Citizens' Savings & Trust Co. carries out wills and holds them, functions as executor of the will, as administrator of estates as well as guardian. It collects rents and dividends, pays taxes, renews insurance and distributes incomes. It adminsters money for educational and charitable institutions. It functions as trustee for bonds for railroad companies or other corporations. It also transfers and registers the stock of corporations.

The company mentioned is the oldest and strongest trustee company in Ohio. It has been regarded for years as a rock in the sea of finances. Its total assets amount to more than $42,000,000, of which more than $30,000,000 are deposits. The following list of officers and directors of the Citizens Savings and Trust Co. offers a good guarantee that confidence placed in this banking institution is well-earned.

Officers: chairman of the board, J. H. Wade; president, H. R. Newcomb; first vice president, D. Z. Norton; second vice president, Wm. G. Mather; third vice president, D. Leuty; fourth vice president, Horace B. Corner; secretary, J. R. Nutt; treasurer, E. B. Hale; assistant secretaries, O. C. Nelson and H. S. Newberry; assistant treasurer, Geo. Lemnitz, W. M. Baldwin and W. H. Fowler.

Cleveland Trust Co.

The Cleveland Trust Co. marks 1894 as its year of foundation. It is hence still a relatively young business phenomenon. The beginning of its banking activity was on 10 September 1995. The founders and organizers, people of standing in the local business world, understood and disposed of adequate means to start work in the right manner, moving into large quarters, equipping them in the grandest manner to make the greatest impression, then to draw an adequate number of the best officers and employees to be had, and to get the operation underway so as to make it a model, like placing a palace car on the rails.

The truly palatial quarters at the corner of Euclid Avenue and Erie Street are approaching completion, and these will provide the future location for the Cleveland Trust Company. Until now it has retained its elegant offices in the Garfield Building, known to passers-by as well as clients.

To give those who have not visited it an idea of the scale and significance of the treasure of the Cleveland Trust Company, it should be reported that it began eight years ago with a fund of barely $900,000, which last year had grown to $24.5 million in deposits. It speaks for itself and is easy to grasp that there is no monetary transaction which is not performed here, and that the management of deposits makes up only a part of the great work of the bank. In handling its entire business the main bank is assisted by ten branch banks, which have arisen in rapid succession in all parts of the city.

The president of the Cleveland Trust Company is Calvary Morris. When the building at the corner of Euclid Avenue and Erie Street, at the beginning of our great retail area and at the entrance to the most beautiful of our avenues, is finished and occupied, it will stand as one of the premier banks of Cleveland, since no other bank has built such a building for its own use alone.

The Reserve Trust Co.

The Reserve Trust Co. of Cleveland, whose office is located in the Hollenden Hotel building at the corner of Superior Avenue and Sixth Street, N. E., was opened for business in 1903. It has displayed its financial success and indubitable flourishing with excusable pride. The administration of the Reserve Trust Co. lies in the hands of progressive, conscientious officers, led in turn by a conservative board. The result is that the progress of the institution has been rapid as well as brilliant, but one which is consonant with healthy principles for the management of a bank.

The bank is open to all customers. The bank management is convinced that all customers benefit the bank, just as the bank is beneficial to all customers. The officers are always ready to speak with any customers or persons who wish to become customers, giving them advice. All business with the bank is done with total confidentiality. Money may be deposited in this bank by mail, and any other transaction carried out that way as well. The motto of the bank is, "First security, then liberality." It pays 4% on savings deposits, 2% on checking accounts.

The following are the officers of the bank: president, Adam Graham; vice president and executive officer, T. J. Moffett; vice presidents, Henry Steinbrenner and Ernst Müller; secretary and treasurer, Wm. N. Perrin; assistant secretaries and treasurers, H. A. Stahl, J. E. Graham, L. E. Holmden; manager of the Genessee branch, H. A. Wangereien; manager of the Superior branch, Jos. Bade; directors, Joseph Carabelli, H. B. Chapmen, L. D. Coman, C. E. Ferrell, W. E. Futsch, Thos. H. Geer, Adam Graham, Paul Howland, H. E. McMillen, T. J. Moffett, Ernst Müller, F. H. Peters, Wm. N. Perrin, E. W. Reaugh, Paul C. Searles, J. C. Sparrow, Dr. A. O.

Spence, Henry Steinbrenner, H. A. Stahl, Leslie H. Webb. The following buildings are the property of the Reserve Trust Co.: corner of Woodland and 55th Street; 7921 Woodland Avenue, corner of 80th Street E., and 8117 Wade Park Avenue, near 82nd Street, N. E.

The Guardian Savings and Trust Co.

This banking company opened for business on 10 December 1894 in the Wade Building, 108 Superior Street. In May, 1902, it opened a branch at 63 Euclid Avenue, and two years later the property was purchased on which the present twelve-story building of the Guardian Savings and Trust Co. is located. The branch at 63 Euclid was given up. The new building is uniquely attractive both for its design and for its construction and equipment. All possible comforts for banking are present.

In the Wade Building, then 108 Superior Street (now 805 Superior Avenue N. W.), the original home of Superior Savings and Trust Company, the bank has a branch for the convenience of its customers. This branch is located in the middle of the district for the coal, steel and shipping businesses, and it has facilities for quick handling of all business.

The Guardian Savings and Trust Company does both commercial banking and savings business. It pays two percent on checking accounts and up to four percent on savings accounts up to $10,000, and three percent on savings accounts over $10,000. It extends loans on real property as well as on other good collateral, and interest is set by the market. It also issues letters of credit, buys and sells foreign exchange.

The trust department of the bank is under the control of experienced and reliable persons. It involves itself in transactions of all sorts permitted under the laws of the state of Ohio. The real estate division stands under particularly experienced persons. It deals with purchases, sales and leases of all sorts, and it is in the position to provide reliable information when it is otherwise hard to obtain. The entire floor below the bank is given to the vaults. These vaults are absolutely secure against fire, breakins or acts of rebellion.

The Guardian Savings and Trust Co., disposing of assets of more than $14,000,000, was originally capitalized with $500,000, achieved a surplus in less than ten years, after which its capital was increased to $1,000,000. The capital and surplus now amount to $2,000,000, and the deposits over $12,000,000.

The directors of the business are active businessmen who also provide security deposits in various undertakings. They are all people with the greatest experience and worthy of the greatest trust.

The Euclid Avenue Trust Co.

The Euclid Avenue Trust Company was founded with a capital of $500,000, and it began its operations on 15 December 1904. Their chief office lies in the heart of the retail district on Euclid Avenue, opposite the Arcade Building and next to the opera house, the most advantageous location possible. The bank owns its own building, in which it occupies more than 6000 square feet. The decoration is in Italian marble, mahogany and glass. The building is rightly regarded as one of the best bank buildings in the state.

The renovation and refurnishing of the main office, completed six months ago, made it possible for the management of the bank to provide the best service in all departments.

The bank has a paid-up capital of $200,000, a surplus of $50,000 and deposits of more than $100,000. Last year the increase in deposits amounted to more than $400,000. One year after organization, the bank deposited $100,000 with the state of Ohio to guarantee the administration of trusts. It is entirely qualified to act as trustee, guardian, executor, administrator and transfer agent. It handles the administration of real estate as well as movable goods, and it issues both foreign exchange and letters of credit.

The trust which the public has in this financial institute is shown by the fact that it already has more than 10,000 satisfied depositors, although it has existed little more than three years. Its progressive spirit and its effort to give as many customers as possible the opportunity for comfortable banking, is shown by the fact that the Euclid Avenue Trust Company was the first bank in Cleveland to open its main office every evening (except Sunday) from 6 to 11.

The management of the bank finds that opening in the evening pleases businessmen in the inner city, particularly the customers of our savings department who are unable to visit during the day.

The officers of the bank greet everyone who wishes to open an account. Only a dollar is needed to open a savings account paying 4%. Depositors always receive interest for their money, and they may draw the money and interest at any time.

It outstanding board of directors is a guarantee of its conservative, successful and capable management. The officers of the bank are: Wm. H. Crafts, president; H. D. Marble, first vice president; J. S. Malone, second vice president; R. S. Thomas, secretary and treasurer; W. J. Gawen, Jr., assistant secretary and treasurer.

E. H. Klaustermeyer, one of the directors, is an outstanding German citizen of Cleveland.

Clark Avenue Savings Bank Co.

The history of the Clark Avenue Savings Bank Co. is one of great success since Thomas J. Holmden became its secretary and treasurer in 1905. Mr. Holmden has been in the banking business for 20 years. He started out as a representative in the Union National Bank, and he has obtained basic experience in all the departments of banking. In 1905 he gave up his position in the First National Bank to take the position of secretary and treasurer of the Clark Avenue Savings Bank. At that time deposits at this bank on Clark Avenue, near the Big Four Railroad, amounted to only about $75,000. As soon as Holmden took over business, it was demonstrated how necessary a bank in that area was. In the very first year deposits rose by $125,000, to a total of about $200,000. Soon work was begun on the railway interchange, and it became necessary for the bank to seek a new location. It found this at the corner of Clark Avenue and Isabella Street (now West 50th Street S. W.), where it began to build a permanent home of which not only its investors but the entire public in that neighborhood could be proud. The bank moved into its new home on 6 October 1906. A reception was held by its friends. Although the weather was dreadful on the day and evening of this reception, with heavy rain, the number of guests inspired by the new quarters was great, and on the evening of the reception 110 new savings accounts were opened. The increase in business has never let up. This year as well the bank has gained hundreds of new customers, so that the amount of deposits has risen above $300,000. The bank is in a flourishing condition, and its officers are always ready to assist the depositors with word and deed.

The following list of officers and directors is the best guarantee for the conservative leadership of the business:

Officers: Alex J. McCrea, president; John Theurer, J. G. Robinson and Geo. J. Sommer, vice presidents; Thomas J. Holmden, secretary and treasurer.

Directors: Theodor Kundtz, Theodor Kundtz Sewing Machine Cabinet Works; J. B. Chapek, president of the Cuyahoga Abstract Co.; M. Cermak, shoes and boots, 5211 Clark Avenue; B. Sprosty, rentier, 4811 Clark Avenue; Alex J. McCrea, president of the Ohio Provision Company; John Theurer, president of the Theurer-Norton Provision Com; Henry Terwood, building contractor, 280 Courtland Street; Otto Zickes, pharmacist, 4521 Clark Avenue; W. J. Krewson, Krewson Bros., corner of Gordon and Bridge Street; H. P. Ranney, superintendent with American Ship Co.; C. L. Nickel, Cuyahoga Abstract Co.; P. J. Haas, cut goods, 6529 Lorain

Avenue; T. S. Robinson, president of the R. B. Biscuit Co.; Geo. J. Sommer, manager of the Gehring Brewing Co.; J. A. Smith, Smith, Taft & Arter, architects.

The Depositors' Savings & Trust Co.

The Depositors' Savings & Trust Company was organized in the autumn of 1906, and it began its operations on 15 December of that year. It was the conviction of the founder of this bank that there was still room in Cleveland for a savings bank and trust company which could be used to greater advantage by the common people than was the case with the available strongly capitalized savings banks.

The capital was originally set at $500,000, but it was decided to pay $300,000 at the outset and the remaining $200,000 the following year, so that the total capitalization amounts to a half million, and the paid-in surplus $175,000.

The new bank arranged temporary quarters in 312 Superior Avenue N. E., where it will be located during 1907 until about 1 May 1908. Then it will move into splendid banking quarters presently occupied by the First National Bank on Euclid Avenue.

The following are the officers and directos of the Depositors' Savings and Trust Company: Tom L. Johnson, president; Leopold Einstein, vice president; E. W. Doty, secretary; John P. Kraus, treasurer; Paul D. Jones, assistant treasurer; Newton D. Baker, C. J. Brokenshire, James Caldwell, J. Jay Collver, William Dall, William Diehl, M. A. Fanning, G. E. Harbaugh, Otto Leisy, Walter H. Lucas, George R. McKay, C. H. Miller, F. C. Osborn, Lyman A. Reed and Thomas P. Schmidt.

Chapter 2
Private Institutions. Trade, Art and Science

In many respects Cleveland may compare itself with any large city in the world in its present state. In no respect is this more the case than with the large private institutes, of which the most outstanding follow.

The Spencerian Commercial School

The Spencerian Commercial School on Euclid Avenue was founded in 1848 and was the first of the famous Bryant & Stratton Business Colleges.

P. R. Spencer, E. R. Felton and H. T. Loomis were the principals of the school from 1881 to 1895, at the time of its incorporation. Among the incorporators there were many outstanding local businessmen. In 1895 H. T. Loomis became leader of the school, which he remained until July, 1902, when leadership passed into the hands of E. E. Merville and Miss C. T. Arnold.

The teaching staff of the institute is currently sixteen. Subjects of instruction are bookkeeping, calligraphy, mercantile arithmetic, commercial correspondence, commercial law, calculation, customs and trade, banking, office procedure and auditing, in short all the aspects of mercantile activity. The course in stenography includes stenography and typing, the maintenance of typewriters, typing transcription, dictation to stenographic notation, tabulation, copying and filing, and commercial correspondence.

Courses are divided into day and evening courses. The first last from 8:30 to 11:30 AM and 12:30 to 3:30 PM, with 14 day breaks each in the winter and summer. The tuition for a course of a full year is $110, and a half-year in commerce or stenography $65. The evening courses run from 1 September to 1 March, from 7 to 9 PM on Monday, Wednesday and Friday. The tuition for the 39 weeks is $45. There is also a civil service course of eight weeks, teaching spelling and grammar, arithmetic, letter-writing, penmanship, geography and transcription, and the tuition is $8.

Diplomas are granted in June of each year on the basis of tests in the specialties of the courses in question, assuming not only adequate performance but also complete payment.

The Spencerian Commercial School is not only the most important in Cleveland, but it is also regarded as the finest commercial school in all of America. In terms of business, other matters aside, America can be regarded as a model in institutions and methods, and it is generally regarded as such. American office equipment, including both furniture and aids, such as typewriters, files, chairs, etc., have been copied and adopted everywhere. Even American bookkeeping is regarded as the most efficient, and it is taught and applied as such overseas.

Thus it is that the equipment of the Spencerian School is regarded as a model both in its externals and in its teaching method.

The building, in the classic style, in the form of a large Latin H, so that light may come in from three sides into the teaching rooms and model offices, built with all American elegance and practicality.

The very location of the college may be regarded as ideal, for it lies both near the center of business as well as at the start of the residential district, on the most beautiful street in Cleveland, also called the most beautiful in the entire world.

The Spencerian Business College, or as it is now called, the Spencerian Commercial School, is also an institution of which Cleveland may be proud, preparing both local youth and those from outside Cleveland for the struggle for existence in the mercantile career.

No fewer than 37,000 sons of Mercury have graduated from the Spencerian Business College, including people who have gone far, to the highest positions in the business world, and the reputation of the school is so high that graduation suffices to win positions in the best business houses. But persons other than the sons of Mercury, strictly defined, who are interested in later positions in offices, have also received a useful training in the institute.

Central Institute

An institute which enjoys the highest reputation far beyond Cleveland is the "Central Institute," whose fine building, equipped with everything required for its purpose, stands at the corner of Willson and Scoville Avenue. So far as is known, the Central Institute is the only teaching institution in the country in which young people are actually trained in two years of day school or three years of night school to enter a college. It was founded in 1889 and has since grown continuously and earned a steadily higher reputation.

The drive to earn money quickly is known to cause an enormous number of young people to give up school before they themselves realize how necessary a good scholarly education is for life. In the Central Institute they are able to make up for this oversight and recover what they have missed with a relatively small expenditure of time and money. Young people who have already accomplished something can keep their gains and cover the costs of instruction with a small part of their own earnings. The Institute has day and night classes in which there is instruction 50 weeks out of the year.

The leadership of the Institute is outstanding in every way, and the leaders are assisted by an outstanding staff of male and female teachers who are trained in their specialties. It is no wonder that there are constantly colleges, technical schools, law schools, dentistry and medical schools which accept students but recommend that they make up deficits in instruction at this institution. The Institute is attended by many young people who have graduated high school in rural areas but are still not adequately prepared for certain institutions of higher learning. An additional year in the Central Institute and their shortfall is repaired.

The Institute has three primary departments: a department for basic training in all areas of commercial science, a department for engineering in all branches, and a department for the special preparation of students destined for the highest specialized institutions. Its engineering department, for example, has provided Cleveland employers with more capable employees than any other institution.

The officers of the Central Institute are: James G. Hobbie, president; F. M. Sanderson, vice president, and A. E. Manbeck, secretary and treasurer.

The Metropolitan Business College

The demand for capable mercantile employees, managers, bookkeepers, correspondents, stenographers, etc., of both sexes, has gone hand in hand with the general boom which trade and crafts have experienced in the United States, so that anyone with the necessary training and ability is assured of employment in this specialty.

As a central point with growing industry, Cleveland has developed into one of the premier cities in the United States, and it is natural that there are those who have recognized this need and sought to supply it. Among these needs is one for schools to train young people for commercial functions, and Cleveland has a number of the best of its kind.

Among these, the Metropolitan Business College has an outstanding position. An ensemble of the most outstanding teachers works at this school, training ambitious young people day and night, year in and out, systematically initiating them for their later profession.

Many of these pupils have managed to achieve independence, thanks to the education received here, and they have risen to the highest and most responsible posts, which would never have been possible if they had not made the small sacrifices which are demanded for a fundamental education.

The Metropolitan Business College at the corner of Pearl and Lorain Street educates its pupils in all specialties in the profession, so that it is the fault of the student if they do not gain the knowledge to achieve later success.

This institution is regarded as one of the most outstanding in Cleveland and in Ohio. Its location on the West Side makes it easy for residents of this part of town not to have to send their sons and daughters over the viaduct to supply them with training for a commercial career.

The Metropolitan school is allied with the Ohio Business College at the corner of Erie and Huron Streets in that the pupils enrolled in one may attend classes in the other, so that the entire area is covered and opportunities are also given to those living in the center of the city and on the East Side.

The principal of the Metropolitan Business College is Mr. E. E. Admire, a person well known in the industrial world, and the institution has his leadership to thank for the outstanding teachers it has and the success his pupils have won, as well as the reputation the school enjoys.

The Edmiston Business College

The Edmiston Business College is an institution which helps boys and girls to a successful future. Before he opened the Edmiston Business College, H. T. Edmiston served eight years with the S. T. Williams Co., one of the most important concerns for bookkeeping experts. During these eight years he dedicated himself to designing bookkeeping systems for companies and corporations. This work not only taught him the science of bookkeeping, but also gave him a clear understanding of what is asked of the young men and women who seek office positions. The Edmiston Business College, 3028 W. 25th (Pearl) Street, corner of Walton Street, was opened 12 years ago by Mr. Edmiston, and he has led it since its opening. The Edmiston Business College is today the Cleveland school which has been the longest under the same management. It is today recognized as the most important school of its sort in the state of Ohio. Its growth was not spasmodic but rather a matter of continuous growth from the beginning to the present day. Its course of instruction has obviously pleased the public, which may be shown by the fact that two, three, in many cases even four students have come from the same family. Equipping the school so well in all its various departments has cost money, time and effort, and it has required careful, decisive management.

Further there are other reasons which have made the school so popular. They are simple but powerful. When Mr. Edmiston began his business college project, he was obviously determined to commit himself and to earn the trust and support of the citizens of Cleveland. He knew that his reputation had to rest on accomplishments and not on superficial appearances. He insisted that each of his students be fundamentally trained before going into business life, and he will never recommend a student for a position if he is not convinced that he is well prepared to satisfy the businessman in question. This method has had the result that not only the students but also the businessmen trust him.

For several years the demand for graduates of the school has exceeded the number he is able to deliver. Teachers stand at the head of each department who are experts in their field. Men of broad experience stand at the head of his departments of business procedure and bookkeeping. A court reporter heads the department for stenography. A specialist in handwriting heads the department of penmanship, and the same is the case for all six departments of the college. Graduates of Edmiston understand how to handle how to get started on problems, and they handle the material correctly.

One may write or telephone for the elegant 50 page catalogue of the college; this will give precise information concerning the school as well as the means by which it may help you.

The Day Stenography School

One of the best-known educational institutions in Cleveland and the sole one in its field is the Day Stenography School in the American Trust Building, Public Square. The roominess and comfortable appointment of the school rooms provide the most comfortable experience imaginable, and the participants in the courses find everything they might need used and at hand.

The school is the foundation of Alfred Day, one of the most popular and outstanding teachers and writers in the country. Day looks back on 37 years in his area of teaching, in the course of which he has obtained an enviable reputation. Partly in person, partly by correspondence, he has instructed more than 14,000 pupils, from the Atlantic to the Pacific and from Quebec to the Gulf of Mexico. No one who wishes to be a stenographer, whether as a reporter or anything else, can receive a better education than in Day's school, where every pupil is guaranteed success.

The following textbooks were written by Professor Day: *Aid to Graham, Complete Shorthand Manual, Shorthand Copy Book, Student's Assistant, Shorthand Dictionary, Day's Dictation Book, Day's Standard Shorthand*. His *Complete Shorthand Manual* has been adopted as the standard textbook in the Cleveland Public Schools. His final work, *Day's Standard Shorthand*, was a true revolution in the area of stenography, since it incorporated a system which was easy to learn, easy to write, easy to read, of the greatest speed combined with readability, the ideal of stenography, and learnable in half the time the old systems demanded, and at much less cost. The entire world can demonstrate the truth of his claims through its successes.

Professor Day is an old veteran from the Civil War. He graduated the university in Lawrence, N. Y. Over his many years as a teacher of stenography, he had the greatest number of students of any teacher. His school is the sole one in northern Ohio teaching stenography and typing alone.

Cleveland School of Music

Mr. Alfred Arthur, director of the Cleveland School of Music, came here in 1871. Soon after his arrival he became director of the Germania Orchestra, which was then well known. He became known as a soloist on the cornet; he was highly qualified in orchestral music, and under his direction the Germania Orchestra gave a series of symphony concerts in 1872. The capable musician and director soon won a reputation as a teacher of song and as a choral leader.

As a result the Cleveland Vocal Society was organized under his leadership in 1872, and he retained leadership until 1902. In that year the society ended its performances since it could not find a suitable location.

It was also Mr. Arthur who organized the Bach Choir of the Woodland Avenue Presbyterian Church, as well as the Sacred Music Society of the Pilgrim Church.

In 1884 Mr. Arthur came up with the idea of founding a music school, and the success which he had with it shows what a need there was for such an institution. Soon the space set aside for the school did not suffice, so that it was moved to the Kendall Building. But there as well the location was not adequate over the long run, and Mr. Arthur leased the entire northwest wing of the seventh floor of the Arcade Building. In 1903 Mr. Arthur, always ready to do anything for his school, gave up these quarters as well, since the noise of traffic was disturbing him and his students, and he bought a building of his own, now 3101 Prospect Avenue, which provided his school with an undisturbed and adequate home after all necessary construction was completed.

Alongside the director, Mr. Arthur, Mrs. Iselle Tomlins-Ramsey serves as singing teacher, as do Mr. Marinus Solomons, Mr. J. N. Rogers, Miss Isabella Beaton, Mrs. Flora

Brinsmade, Mr. A. F. Arthur as piano teacher, Mr. F. H. Rogers and Mr. A. F. Arthur as teachers of organ, Mr. Joseph Kos and Miss Mabel Wrighton as teachers of violin, Mrs. Harriet L. Role as teacher of elocution, all of them capable and outstanding musical talents.

It should also be mentioned that Mr. Arthur has authored a series of textbooks on song, and further he has composed several songs and three operas, "Adeline," "Caraliers," and "The Water Carriers." The last of these was successfully performed in 1886 in the opera house here.

Cleveland thus possesses not only a music teacher and director with great accomplishments in Mr. Arthur, but also a productive musical genius.

The Windsor Institute for Speech Defects and Retarded Children

Among Cleveland's institutions dedicated to teaching, the Windsor Institute, 4405 Windsor Avenue, holds a special place, since it is the sole one of its type, not only in the city but also in the entire state. Its founder and leader is W. L. Rosenberg, a man whose education and natural ability is suited to fufill the mission which his institute has taken on: the healing of all speaking problems and the treatment of those physically and mentally retarded children unable to speak, or cannot read or write.

The institute was founded in 1900, and since its foundation it has grown steadily, so that today it disposes of its own building and employs several teachers. Dr. Rosenberg's literary talents have produced one of the best monographs in the area of stuttering, if not the very best work ever written on this area of speech. His institution is a beneficial home for these unfortunates, and its manager, Miss Maria Bessie Rosenberg, is the best and most motherly lady one could imagine for the position. Mrs. Rosenberg is of Canadian-Scots origin, while Dr. W. L. Rosenberg is a born Westphalian of Lutheran background, sharing a poetic vein with his countryman Ferdinand Freiligrath, since he is known in German-American circles as a poet as well as a dramatist with a very sharp pen. His fundamental involvement with the psychology and physiology of writing has made him one of the best graphological analysts in the country, and due to his deep study he ranks as one of the most broadly educated German-Americans. He was born on 10 January 1850, and he is the father of two equally talented children.

The Electrical Massage Institute

The founder of this institution, Dr. James Stotter, is one of the most popular physicians in Cleveland, whose name is particularly well known in German circles. During the fifteen years he has been here, Dr. Stotter has won a great circle of friends and patients through his fundamental scientific training and practical experience as well as through his personal amiability. He dedicates himself completely to his patients.

Dr. Stotter was born in Hungary. He studied at the University of Vienna, and after completing his medical test as a medic he joined the Vienna Garrison Hospital no. 1, where he had many opportunities to participate in surgical operations and to learn how to do them.

In 1890 he followed siblings and parents who had already emigrated to America, and he settled in Cleveland. He immediately expanded his activities and soon had earned the trust of his countrymen and won an extensive practice.

In 1894 he married an old love from his student days, a charming young Viennese. In 1896 he took a study trip to Europe and completed his medical knowledge in the clinics of Vienna and other great cities. After an absence of nine months he returned to Cleveland, greeted by friends and clients with lively satisfaction. The palpable and interesting result of this study trip was the creation of the Electric Massage Institute in the Lennox Building, at the corner of Euclid and Ninth Street, the only one of its sort in the United States. The practical arrangement of the seven halls of this institute and their equipping with the latest instruments of healing is worth seeing. Among other things, it contains a machine for X-rays to investigate internal illnesses in human bodies, as well as devices to investigate the blood and excretions, so that the physician may immediately discover the variety of illness and its source. Among the electric instruments there is also a device from London to help heal cancer without operations and advanced skin ailments. The newest treatment of rheumatic illnesses is achieved through dry hot air, so that the patient receives heat up to 500 without sensing the least discomfort. The electric bath is found in another hall, while in another water is used as a means of healing, and in another massage, and then come the laboratories for treating illnesses of the ear, eye, nose and throat.

The treatment of these last illnesses is Dr. Stotter's specialty, and he has achieved great success in this area, for which he has flattering letters of thanks.

Home Painless Dentists
America stands at the forefront in dentistry. "American Dentists" are found in all countries, and they are known as the best dental practitioners.

In a well-known Cleveland building on the northwest corner of Public Square, the noted Marshall pharmacy is located. On its lowest floor are the workshops of the Home Painless Dentists. Signs with large letters show the name on the side of the Square as well as in the Superior Street side, and at night an electrical device plays at the corner of the building, serving as a guiding star.

It is well known that a total sense of well-being depends heavily on dental health, so that the greatest care should be given to the care of the teeth. A dentist should not be sought only when a tooth demands extraction through piercing pain. Rather the teeth should be periodically cleaned, capped or filled.

If it does come to the loss of teeth, which are both an ornament and a necessity for chewing, they must be replaced.

This insitution is one of the most outstanding in Cleveland and contains all the means created by science to make operations painless, so that the patient does not have to hesitate to submit to the artistry of the dentist to assist his failings and replace them.

Despite the English title, German is spoken in the workshop. Some of the physicians are Germans. Here, as wherever good work is being done, Germans are represented strongly.

Chapter 3
The Piano Industry

The love of music is inborn in people and it must be said to the credit of America that nowhere is it so intensely cultivated, nor are more liberal sacrifices made for it than here.

The piano is the proper instrument to bring music into the family, and given the strongly marked character of American family life, it has found entry into almost every American family which can afford it. As a result, the piano industry is not only one of the most flourishing industries, but it has resulted in the creation of instruments which are without equal, and why should it not be that some of the best are produced here, where the stream of immigration have long brought us the best from every art and craft?

It is certainly interesting to look at the piano industry. Among the most important piano factories in America, with a major installation in Cleveland, is doubtless the Starr Piano Company, whose factory is in Richmond, Indiana, and which sends pianos all over the world.

The founder of the house of Starr was Benjamin Starr, the youngest son of Charles West Starr, who was born in Philadelphia in 1795, and who was one of the pioneers of what was then "the West." He was one of the builders of the town of Richmond. After the Starr Piano Factory had existed for many years, it took on new life when the Starr Piano Company was incorporated under the leadership of John Lumsdon of St. Louis in 1893, and today there are no fewer than 65,000 Starr pianos in the best and most respected families.

One may receive an impression of this enormous establishment by contemplating the fact that the factory area has a floor area of eight acres, the wood storage one of 33 acres. It is known that the quality of a piano rests upon the use of the proper wood and its right treatment. The wood storage of this factory continually holds several million board feet of the most varied woods needed to build a piano, stored in select qualities, which passes through various phases of treatment. After it has been stored in the ordinary air, it is brought through air drying, for which the factory has several of the newest and most perfected systems.

It should be said here that the factory uses only the most reliable domestic and foreign sources for wood as with all other materials. It is because of this, as well as the painstaking care taken at all the other stages of production of the instrument, that pianos emerge which enjoy a worldwide reputation. The standards used are demonstrated by the fact that about 4000 pianos are under production at any particular moment, under the most careful supervision, so that none is passed too quickly or with the slightest defect to the next department. One of them is produced every twenty minutes.

The extent to which the leader of this factory is concerned to exploit all factors which can contribute to the production of the best instruments is shown by the fact that every care is taken to provide the workers with a hygenic setting, and a look at the factory leaves one with an impression of cleanliness and healthfulness, so that the productivity of the workers is the best imaginable. All the tools, from the 85-horse power Corliss machine to the smallest technical aid, are used with the greatest care and the richest profusion in all departments, occupying 725 workers in all.

When one considers the whole, seeing the care and foresight applied in obtaining the materials and applying labor, how the construction of the pianos is controlled by scientifically trained experts on making pianos and under hands which have been practiced for decades, it can be seen how a splendid piano emerges from this concentrated and well-planned work, one every twenty minutes, perfect within and without, passing on to the shops, and then to provide a marvelous harmony in the family circle.

A piano, after all, is not just a means to music, it is also a decoration for a house, and the various branches of crafts and arts work together to complete the work represented by a piano.

In all of these branches, from the beginning to each detail, down last dab, only the best may be chosen and only the best done. Only the factory which is in the position to do that, building its efforts on this basis, can achieve the success the Starr Company has won and claim the place in the piano market which its pianos have achieved.

The pianos of the house of Starr have not only achieved a world reputation, marked with distinction at all exhibits, but the operations of the factory from which they come is a true picture of American industry, demonstrating what it can achieve in this area, nothing less than the best and most splendid and in the largest volume.

B. Dreher's Sons

B. Dreher's Sons piano business was founded 53 years ago by Baptist Dreher, one of the old settlers on the soil of Cleveland. The solid construction and the outstanding qualities of the instruments which come from this factory, as well as solid business principles are what brought the enormous success which he and his sons achieved.

Today the firm of Dreher's Sons is in the first ranks of piano companies in America with an annual production of more than 1500 instruments.

When the Arcade Building was completed, the company also moved into the best locations on the first floor of Euclid Avenue as well as at the Superior Street entrance. As splendid as the shops were, they still did not prove adequate over the long run. The increasing demand for pianos in general and the invention of ever new instruments made expansion necessary. Quarters were rented above the shops on the second floor and joined by an elevator. which continued up to the third floor, which the company eventually intends to occupy as well, and for which an expansion is already planned.

Among the popular new instrument is the pianola, for which the Dreher shop has a "library" of 25,000 rolls, soon to be expanded by 10,000 more.

The Dreher business draws a great deal of its custom from its music hall, which has a concert organ costing thousands of dollars. Every day, many visiting lovers of music from the city and beyond stream into the shop to meet in this milieu and worship music.

Mr. Henry Dreher, the leader of the sales department, is himself a fine musician who has received a thorough musical education both here and abroad. Mr. Dreher is a member of the foremost clubs in Cleveland, and he also belongs to the Freemasons, and he also is in close contact with all the more important musical associations, whose sphere embraces the entire Union, so that he is always up to date with the advances of the musical world.

The F. L. Raymond Co.

Among the finest pianos, produced with the greatest care out of the most carefully selected materials are those of the F. L. Raymond Co., and it is enough for a connoisseur to view to construction of the instrument, to try the play and tone in order to bring forth not just recognition but marvel.

The Raymond instrument truly deserves a place of honor among the most noble and artistic constructions of its genre. The technically capable and patient treatment of the wood and its careful selection, the use of the best string materials, painstaking care in production and assembly of the parts to the smallest detail, the rational observance of all mechanical rules based on years of experience, as described in detail in the brochures produced by the company, all have the effect of creating a work of art corresponding to the highest demands in every way, and for which the company supplies a ten year guarantee.

It should be mentioned here that the carvings and decorations are all made by hand, just as everything machine-like and quick has been excluded in the entire construction of a

Raymond piano, a principle which has been held by the company for half a century, since its origins, and which it is not about to abandon.

A Raymond piano is an unequalled jewel for the family which owns it, and the evaluations of piano dealers and those who know music is adequate recommendation, since they declare it to be the most perfect achievement in the area of musical construction up to now.

Chapter 4
The Cleveland Electric Railway Co.

From the stage of the primitive horse-rail car and the no-less primitive transportation service in those days when Cleveland was still emerging from its days as a community in the backwoods with a local market, the great problem of transportation was posed how to deal with the thousands as they came and filled up the empty places. That problem was resolved as the city which grew to half a million in half a century, and it was solved in such a way that Cleveland may serve as a model for any city of its size.

The earliest of the streetcar lines, created to aid the transportation of our beginning city and its residents scattered east, west and south have all been stripped of their horses and electrified, and they have been transformed from something inadequate to an operation growing into giant proportions and intensity. Today it is essentially one company which masters the wide-spread and fully-developed streetcar traffic, the Cleveland Electric Railway.

From the furthest end of the city the whispering cars bring the worker, the businessman, the shopping wife, to the center of the city or wherever else along the 235 miles of track, for five cents, and the company promises to reduce prices so that seven tickets can be had for 25 cents. Then, for example, a trip from South Brooklyn to Brighton Village via Jennings Avenue, across the viaduct and then to the Square, then up Euclid Avenue to East Cleveland Village, 13 miles in all, will cost 3.5 cents. A cheap enjoyment.

The streetcar system is not only the most significant factor in the industrial and social life of Cleveland, it is also as much a factor in social and hygenic relations.

It takes the worker and officers out of the noise and dust of the business district to healthy and quiet homes on working days, and on Sundays and holidays it sets him and his family in the elegant cars and let them go wherever their hearts desire. No city is as rich in parks as Cleveland. The oldest park in the Forest City is Public Square, where almost all the streetcar lines go, since it is the center of business. Even today the Square is a place of refreshment at all times. Many benches are provided there, both in the waiting rooms of the streetcar lines and elsewhere, around the fountains and along the mounting places. On evenings, when the lights gleam, many sit there and refresh themselves in an entertaining and pleasant manner.

Four miles east of the Square is the beautiful and grand Wade Park, the chief park of Cleveland, far from the hustle and bustle of street traffic, in the pure air, with its high, shady trees, its zoological collection, the lake with its boats, the walking paths going far and wide, the benches and meadows, racecourses and the picnic places which enliven it. Wade Park can be reached by streetcar in 20 minutes from the Square.

Opposite Wade Park is the lovely campus of Adelbert College and the Case Institute. Not far from there is the Lake View Cemetery and the monument of the murdered President Garfield.

On the West Side is found the lovely Brookside Park, reachable via the Pearl Street, the Scranton and Rhodes Avenue lines, then Edgewater Park, reached by the Detroit Street Line.

North of the fine property of the North Ohio Insane Asylum lies Garfield Park, reachable by the St. Clair and Broadway lines.

On the east side of the Lakeshore is the great Gordon Park, to be reached by the same lines.

Alongside these public parks there are private parks, such as Forest City Park on the Willson Avenue Line, the Manhattan Beach Park on the Adams Avenue line in Collinwood, and Euclid Beach Park on the Lakeshore, also in Collinwood, nearly 13 miles from the Square, and each reached by a streetcar line.

Further, there are the suburban lines reaching in all directions to the east, west and south into the cities of north Ohio and to the picnic places and summer freshness. Some of them start at the Square, some at the end stations of the Cleveland Electric Railway Co.

Considering the role streetcar traffic plays in business and recreational life of Cleveland today, the progress made by the growth of public transportation is astounding. The Cleveland Electric Railway Co. is headed by the sons of the same pioneers who first saw the necessity of streetcars in the Forest City and laid the groundwork for it with heavy sacrifices and struggle with endless problems.

Horace E. Andrews is the president of the Cleveland Electric Railway Co. He as well as John J. Stanley, vice president and general manager, are successors to pioneers of Cleveland public transportation. They have grown up through and in it, and they have brought it to its present perfect state.

Chapter 5
Cleveland's Brewing Industry

The history of the Cleveland brewing industry is involved inextricably with the history of Germans and with the story of the city's industrial progress.

Since the foundation of the first brewery in Cleveland barely half a century has passed. Before this time the American public did not even know the name of "beer." The national drink in those days was ale. It took years before the general public learned to like beer, and this gradually lifted the industry until it is today one of the most important in the Forest City.

Germans have every right to be proud that it was they who introduced and developed this mighty industry. Despite hostilities and attacks by nativists and puritans against healthful beer, which people did not want to take the place of either water or liquor, German persistence and entrepreneurial spirit (which has free play here) combined to establish the industry which today has over 5000 workers with an annual market of $8,000,000.

In 1850 there was still no beer brewery in the proper sense of the word in Cleveland. What did exist here were ale and flat-beer breweries, of which the largest, Ive's, stood where the factory of the White Sewing Machine Co. is now located. Further, in those days J. M. Hughes was on West River Street, the Eagle Brewery on Michigan Street, and the Keyes brewery on St. Clair Street, which continues to the present day.

The brewery established in 1855-56 by the Stumpf brothers at the corner of Davenport and Lake Street, where the Gund Brewery now stands, was the first true beer brewery. The second one was that of Matthias Mack on Vermont Street, near the present water works. Then came John Dangeleisen, who established a brewery on Forest Street, near Broadway, followed by a brewer named Müller, from which developed the later Leisy Brewery. In 1857 Leonhard Schlather came, and a year later C. C. Gehring.

At the beginning, all of these breweries were then equipped in the most primitive manner possible. All of them were combined with taverns, and they produced no more than was needed for their guests and the neighborhood. Later this or that brewer would declare himself ready to brew for other taverns as well. Moved by the steadily growing demand, they finally closed their own taverns and set about brewing beer in earnest. It is interesting to hear how primitive brewing was in those days. Everything was "hand made." The malt was ground in a little mill. A horse was often used to turn it. The kettles had a capacity of about four barrels. There was no brewing in the summer, since there were no facilities to store ice. In the winter the brewer brewed as much beer as they could keep in their own cellars, and they sold as long as there was a supply. Some brewers went to Buffalo and other cities in the summer and got beer there.

During the Civil War all business was down, even the breweries. After the conclusion of peace, with the rise of immigration, the brewing industry really crossed the barrier to becoming a really big industry. The first ice cellar was built in 1870, and one may see that as the beginning of development, which now took giant steps.

Seventeen breweries comprise the brewing industry of Cleveland today.

The following dates may be given concerning their development:

The Isaac Leisy Brewery is the largest brewery not just in Cleveland, but in the whole of northern Ohio.

As mentioned at the outset, the foundation for it was laid by the brewer Müller. Later the premises passed into the possession of Fritz Haltnorth. In 1873 Isaac Leisy came to Cleveland on the occasion of a brewers' convention, and since he decided to stay here, he began negotiating with Haltnorth, which led to his taking the brewery over. At first he operated it together with his brother August, but in 1882 August withdrew from the business, and from then on Isaac Leisy was the sole owner of the brewery.

No brewer ever had greater energy than Isaac Leisy, and only that made it possible for the brewery, which he took over in 1873 producing 12,000 barrels to grow in 20 years to fourteen times the production. The Leisy brewery was expanded time and again. Leisy was concerned about the exterior at the same time, and the brewery is not only a decoration of Vega Street and of all Cleveland, but it is the most beautiful in Ohio.

It is known what a promoter of Germans and their efforts was lost when Isaac Leisy left this world in 1892.

Since 1892 Leisy, his father's son in every respect, is leader of the brewery. He has attended domestic and overseas technical schools, and he is also adept at theory. After the death of his father he has steered the firm with a capable hand, and he has rejected the offers of the trust to buy the brewery for $3 million.

In 1893 Otto Leisy married Miss Elizabeth Geber from Mannheim, and he is the father of two children. As is well known, his father was from Friedelsheim near Dürkheim on the Haardt in the Rhenish Palatinate, and he himself was born in Keokuk, Iowa, in 1863, where his father ran a brewery with his brother John after a sojourn in St. Louis and before he came to Cleveland.

The Leisy brewery produces 500,000 barrels a year. The building which does the actual production is 400 feet long and 200 feet wide, and it is regarded as a model of its type by technical persons. The ice and cooling machines are of the newest construction. No expenditure has been spared on the lovely construction of the stables.

Leisy has over 250 employees here and elsewhere, and the weekly wages amount to $5500.

Otto Leisy has a country estate of 30 acres in Fairmount Heights. On the heighest point of the Heights rises the modern Swiss-style villa, and the road hence snakes through a park planted with large trees. The idyllic grounds are the exclusive work of Mr. Otto Leisy, who designed the plans for the parks and terrace himself with great artistic understanding. The park may be seen as one of the most beautiful properties in Cleveland.

During the last year Mr. Otto Leisy had a splendid house built in Colonial style on this property, which he properly calls "Hochwald."

It should be stressed again that Mr. Leisy inherited his ingenious sense of business, his specifically German realism, from his father, combined with an American spirit of entrepreneurship. It should be particularly stressed that he has remained at heart a good German, and he retains the same sympathy for German interests, German institutions and German charitable undertakings which marked his father and have assured him an unforgetting memorial for all times.

In so far as business is concerned, the principle is followed that only entirely pure, unfalsified wares, beer from malt and hops, without any damaging chemicals, are brought to market, and this is done as religiously now as at the beginning. This condition is the reason for its phenominal growth as well as its unchanging flourishing.

The latest addition has been the building for bottling. Since the demand for bottle beer has continually grown over the last years, this division received the most attention, and it is equipped with the latest and best equipment, certainly the best available, and exceedeed by none, so that the brewery continues to be Cleveland's finest, justly proud in its resistance to the trust.

The brewmaster of the Isaac Leisy Brewing Co. is Mr. Carl Faller, who was born in Buchheim near Freiburg, Baden. He enjoyed an outstanding education, and when he had completed his schooling, he took apprenticeship in the Schwarzbauer Brewery in Freiburg in order to learn brewing. He came to America in 1886 and settled in Cincinnati, where he worked at the Schaller Bros. brewery for four years as brewmaster. From there he took the same position in the Senne & Ackermann Brewery in Louisville, Kentucky, where he worked for ten years. From there he came to Cleveland in 1900, and since then he has been the brewer in the Leisy brewery. The fact that he is capable in his business is shown by the fact that he took his first position as a brewmaster when he had been in the country barely three months, and that he has remained a brewmaster ever since.

Mr. Faller is a founder of the Concordia Lodge of the Freemasons and president of the Brewmasters' Association. He married in 1876 to Miss Magdalena Gauweiler. Three children came from this marriage, of which one has sadly died, but the other two, a son and a daughter, are still living.

The Gund Brewing Co.

The Gund brewery takes a first rank as a model brewery uniting all the latest achievements in the technology of brewing.

Founded in 1861 by Jacob Mall on Davenport Street, where Cleveland's first brewery was located, it was taken over by Georg F. Gund in 1897. It was first incorporated under the name of the Jacob Mall Brewing Co., but it was later changed into The Gund Brewing Co., which is its name today.

The president and treasurer of the business is Georg F. Gund; the secretary is Jacob Fickel; vice president Georg Kärcher.

The new form and the great rise in business of the brewery is due to its takeover by Gund. The brewery now consists of a group of imposing buildings, of which the largest is the brewery itself, with an annual capacity of 150,000 barrels. The second building has the bottling plant, and the third is the stables.

As was already said, the brewery is extremely modern, and its operation is on a grand scale.

In the new construction, which was completed in 1906-7, there are 38 steel tanks, each capable of holding 265 barrels. These are glazed according to the latest invention.

The beer is put in barrels according to the latest "Golden Gate Filler Patent" procedure.

The bottling division of this vast Gund brewery demonstrates how innovation has reduced work to a game, and how far technology has gone. The beer which is to fill the bottles is kept in the so-called "government tanks," of which there are four, each with a capacity of 250 barrels. A government official seals these tanks and opens them again after the amount is noted and a tax of $1 per barrel paid. From there the beer passes by an underground pipe to the filler machine. This fills the bottles and brings them automatically to the corking machine. Once filled and corked, the bottles pass to the pasteurization machine, so that the beer will not deteriorate. The brewery's famous Crystall beer uses only the best Bohemian imported hops.

There are two electric motors in the machine rooms of the brewery, one of them of 75 horsepower, the other of 40, two ice machines with a respective capacity of 75 and 150 tons, along with two boilers of 300 horsepower each. To suppress smoke, which also contributes to cleanliness, there are new smoke dissipaters in use.

It is almost obvious that such an establishment has electric lighting, even the stables, in which there are automatic feeders and fire alarms.

Georg F. Gund, the president and chief owner of the brewery, was born in 1855 in La Crosse, Wisconsin. His parents had immigrated from Germany. He received a good schooling, at the age of 15 he entered the Batavia Bank in La Crosse, where he held various positions until he was 21. Then he gave up this employment and took up that of the brewery his father had founded in La Crosse in 1854. In 1880 the business was changed into a stock company with the name of The John Gund Brewing Co., and it was the largest brewery outside of Milwaukee. For ten years, until 1890, Mr. Gund held the position of a secretary and treasurer, but in 1890 he sold his shares. Through 1891 he was one of the directors of the Batavia Bank, where he had begun his training. Further, he was one of the incorporators and directors of the streetcar line, and he was involved in several other enterprises in his home town. There he was also an active member of the city council, the chamber of commerce and the Jobbers' and Manufacturers' Union. At the end of 1891 he moved to Seattle, Washington, having bought in May Claussen's shares in the Claussen Brewing Co., holding the position of secretary and treasurer until all the breweries in Seattle were consolidated under the name of The Seattle Brewing & Malting Co. in 1893. Except for his position as trustee, he took no further part in the management of the syndicate, but in the end he was unable to decline election as president, an office which he kept until he left Seattle. It might be mentioned that the Seattle Brewing & Malting Co. is the largest brewing company in the state of Washington, with a basic capital of $1,000,000.

At the end of 1897 Gund came here and took over the office of president of the Jacob Mall Brewing Co., as mentioned, which was later changed into the brewing company with his own name.

It may be assumed that Mr. Gund is a businessman through and through, but besides that Mr. Gund is an extremely amiable and tactful man who cannot fail to make himself beloved and to make the success he has achieved appear well earned.

The brewmaster of the Gund brewery, Mr. Georg Zimmermann, is a Badener. He was born in 1861 in Meckenheim near Heidelberg, where his parents had a farm. He attended the school of the locality and learned the craft of cooper in the Rhenish Palatinate. Then he passed over the the brewing craft, doing a two-year apprenticeship in Hoffenheim, district of Sinsheim. He then worked as a journeyman brewer in various places in Germany until he came to the idea of going to America, and he carried the idea out in 1881.

In Buffalo, where he settled, he soon found employment in the local breweries, and here he worked his way up to brewmaster in the course of years. He was in Buffalo for 17 years, for the last six years as brewmaster of the Broadway Brewing Co. In 1898-90, after leaving Buffalo, he attended the Wahl and Henschius Brewers' Academy in Chicago to improve his technical knowledge. After graduating from the Academy he moved here, and since then he has been the brewmaster of the Gund brewery.

Mr. Zimmermann is as capable in his specialty as he is loyal in treating the personnel. Even outside the brewery, Mr. Zimmermann is generally loved. He was already active in society life in Buffalo, where he joined the Odd Fellows. In the Brewmasters' League, to which he belongs, he holds the office of secretary, a proof of the preference he has with his colleagues. Mr. Zimmermann also belongs to several singing societies. Anna Storm, born in sea-embraced Schleswig-Holstein, became his wife in 1884, and this happy marriage has produced four children, three daughters and a son, all of them grown and healthy and the pride of their parents.

The Cleveland Home Brewing Co.
The Cleveland Home Brewing Co. is a company of the most recent date, but only in name, and now, in 1907, with a stock capital of $500,000, it has a new organization, but the brewery was established in 1875 by Joseph Beltz at the corner of 61st Street and Outhwaite Avenue.

At the head of the new company is the locally beloved and respected brewing director Ernst Müller. Joseph Beltz, the founder of the brewery, is vice president, Carl F. Schröder secretary and treasurer. Sales management is done by Adolph Müller.

The brewery consists of five buildings with an area of 1.5 acres and equipped with the most modern facilities. Important changes in the construction have been undertaken to raise the productive capacity from 50,000 to 100,000 barrels, hence doubling its output.

Ernst Müller was born in 1852 in Alsenz, Rhenish Palatinate, but he came with his parents to Cleveland while still a child, in 1856. After working for years in the malt business, in

1887 he took over the Schmidt & Hoffmann brewery, making it into the Cleveland Brewing Co., changing it into a flourishing business through his extraordinary ability. The beer which the brewery produced after the takeover was known as the best Cleveland beer, and its fame persists.

There is no doubt that the Cleveland Home Brewery will rise to great popularity under Ernst Müller's leadership.

Since this brewery is precisely the one which understood the situation and decided to resist the brewery syndicate with German stubbornness and persistence, to preserve its birthright, it seems proper to get to know those who lead this company and fight for it.

The actions of Ernst Müller in the last few years in well known, particularly that from 1897 on, when the breweries faced with consolidation, including the Cleveland brewery, formed the brewery syndicate, the Cleveland & Sandusky Brewing Co., in which he was active and was essentially responsible for its success. He was first of all second vice president of the syndicate, but after he had become important in the board of directors, he became president in 1898, and remained that until recently. His positions were anything but easy, since the temperance groups used the emergence of a beer syndicate to promote the Jones Law and other laws in the legislature to "dry up" several districts. His position was also rendered difficult by the intrigues, in the last phase of which he was not reelected as president despite conscientious service. It is well known that he did not smart long over this but organized his new operation.

The fact that the sympathies of German circles were on his side is shown by the fact that he had always given great aid to all German organizations. How much he contributed to their well-being is shown by the fact that he played a role in the foundation of two of them, the Social Turners and the Vorwärts Turners, and that both of them regard him as one of their principal members. Ernst Müller is also recognized as one of the most respected members of the Cleveland Singing Society.

Joseph Beltz was born on 21 February 1840 at Heidesheim near Mainz, and after learning cooperage he came to Cleveland in 1867. He immediately found employment in the Dangeleisen brewery, but later he worked exclusively at barrel-making, and in 1871 he established his own cooperage. He ran this until 1877, when he began brewing wheat beer, and from that small beginning came the Beltz brewery, which has now received a new name, underlining Mr. Beltz' modest withdrawal from leadership.

Carl F. Schröder is also a well-known personality in this city. He was born in Frankfurt in 1852, and in 1868 he came to Cleveland. The son of a well-known German teacher, F. P. Schröder, he dedicated himself to the profession of a merchant, and for years he held the position of bookkeeper at the Phoenix Brewing Co. After consolidation of the breweries in the syndicate he received a responsible position in the management, and during the last years he was secretary and treasurer of the syndicate. His exit together with Ernst Müller shows the relationship between the two men. Mr. Schröder is musical, and for several years he plays several instruments. He was one of the most outstanding members of the old philharmonic orchestra, and not just that he founded it. He has belonged to the orchestra of the Cleveland Singing Society for years, as well as the Concordia Lodge, F. A. M. He is married with Miss Clara Krause and father of three talented children. Erna, his oldest daughter, teaches in the Public Schools. Clara, the second, attends the Women's College, and Walther, the son, is an employee in the Murphey Iron Works in Detroit, which makes smoke dissipaters.

Rudolph Müller was born here in 1853 and has been involved in the brewing business for 32 years. He was once with the Phoenix brewery in Akron, but he has been here in Cleveland without interruption for 20 years.

For many years he was collector, and he was manager of the Cleveland Brewing Co. until coming to the Cleveland Home Brewing Co. He is a cousin of Ernst Müller, and like that man he is generally beloved and belongs as well to several German societies. The brewmaster of the Home Brewing Co., Mr. John J. Beltz, is a son of the founder of the brewery. He was born here on 9 June 1874. After attending public schools and attending a business college, he entered his father's brewery. In 1897-98 he took two courses at the Brewing Academy in Chicago in order to train himself in the theory of brewing. Although Mr. Beltz was already a capable brewer and leader of a great brewery, his attendance fulfilled all the requirements currently expected of a brewmaster of a large brewery, which is that he be both theoretically and practically trained.

Mr. Beltz married Miss Bertha Kübler, the daughter of Kübler the brewmaster, and two children came from that marriage. He is a member of the Aurora Lodge of the Harugari, the Eagles, the Cleveland Singing Society, Germania Turners, and the Brewmasters' League.

Lawrence Beltz, collector of the Home Brewing Co., was born on 10 August 1876, a brother of the brewmaster. He was active in his father's brewery for nine years before he took his present position. In his younger years he also attended business college. He married Miss Barbara Heintz, and he is a member of the Germania Turners, the Harugari Men's Chorus, the Harmonie and of the C. M. B. A.

The Pilsener Brewing Co.

One of the independent, autonomous breweries is the Pilsener brewery, standing on Clark Avenue and 65th Street. Since its property covers more than 5 acres, the brewery has room for expansion with the needs of the time, which happens from year to year.

In August, 1893, the brewery was established under the name of the Medlin Pilsener Brewing Co. The founder, Mr. Wenzel Medlin, led the company until 29 December 1894, when the name was changed to Pilsener Brewing Co. During the last few years the brewery has expanded by adding new cellars and a modern new brewing house, bringing capacity up to 150,000 barrels a year. The growth in business has compelled the management to add new buildings and supply the most modern machinery. Hence a new kettle house 50 by 100 feet in area and 150 feet high has been built. At the same time came a fireproof stable with an area of 10,000 square feet, as well as a wagon building, a new cellar division, with 13 giant vats, each with a capacity of 280 barrels. The filling room has been considerably expanded, and a particularly fine machine hall has been erected. In it there are two large ice machines, and the new one is the largest vertical machine of its type in Cleveland.

This also applies to the brewing kettle, since it is the largest copper brewing kettle in our city. Here the famous Extra Pilsener beer is brewed from the best Bohemian hops and select American malt. The painstaking cleanliness in all departments excites the astonishment of all visitors, who are always welcome and will be courteously guided through the entire brewery.

The bottling plant in particular deserves the attention of anyone interested in progress in this field. The bottling division was put up in May, 1906, since there was intense demand in private circles for Extra Pilsener beer. A large, separate building buiding on the heights of a roomy courtyard was equipped with machinery of the newest sort, and the newest branch of this growing business sprung from the ground. Extra Pilsener bottled beer is now all over the city, and it is loved everywhere both because of its exceptional flavor and because of its richness in nutrition.

The Standard Brewing Co. is one of Cleveland's newest breweries, and it is managed by the united strength of German and American brewers.

The imposing new building stands on the southwest side on Train Avenue, and it was placed in operation in 1904. Before the completion the business was located on Sackett Street.

The company is incorporated with a capital of $250,000, and most stock was subscribed by tavern owners. As a peculiar creation of its time, the Standard is the brewery of tavern keepers; one recalls that the first brewers were also tavern keepers, only abandoning it when they had enough business as brewers, so in the contrary direction enough tavern keepers banded together to build their own brewery.

The Standard brewery is second to none in terms of the business or its extremely modern equipment. On the contrary, its effort is to make Standard the best in the city, and in view of increased demand capacity has been set at 100,000 barrels a year, and demand is rising so much that this will soon be reached.

The Standard brewery is under the leadership of S. S. Creadon as president; Chas. Renz is vice president, secretary Tom C. Fischer and John F. Feighan treasurer.

The Excelsior Brewery was called to life by Jacob F. Haller, and it is one of the upwardly-striving brewing establishments in the city. Incorporated in December, 1904, with a stock capital of $30,000, the Excelsior Brewing Company began operating as a brewery in May, 1905. It stands on Sackett Street. The complex of buildings has a front of 270 feet and a depth of 65 feet. The brewery, equipped in the most modern fashion, built for a capacity of 30,000 barrels, is expected to be expanded soon, since demand has risen to an extent far beyond expectations. It sold 10,000 barrels in the first year, and this figure has easily doubled since the first year.

The officers of the Excelsior Brewing Co. are: Louis Kurzenberger, president; G. J. Maurer, vice president; Jacob Haller, secretary; Jacob F. Haller, director.

Jacob F. Haller, the director and founder, was born on 20 December 1859 in the Swabian country town of Hausen ob Veranau. His father was a propertied farmer and he was the eldest boy. Jacob attended the school of the village and then went to the Schlüssel brewery in Spaichingen in order to learn the craft. After two years of training, he became a brewing journeyman in various towns of Württemberg, last of all in the famous and large Wulz brewery in Stuttgart until his entry into military service, which he did with the 7th Württemberg Infantry Regiment No. 125. Since his father had died, after his release he went home to help manage the family farm, since his youngest brother had just been called to arms. When the brother was finished, he followed his resolution to emigrate to America.

Coming over in 1885, he first settled in Cincinnati, finding his first occupation with the Wiedemann brewery in Newport. Here he worked until 1891, when he took over the job of first cellar master at the Buckeye brewery in Toledo. He held this for four years, and during this time he enjoyed the general respect of his superiors and subordinates. He then resolved to complete his theoretical knowledge and took a four month course at the Chicago Brewers' Academy, and after graduation he took the first position as brewmaster in Middleboro, Kentucky. He held this position for 2 1/2 years. From 1898 to 1901 he was in Chicago in the Mullen brewery and in St. Louis in the Stiefel brewery.

Then Jacob F. Haller came to Cleveland. The position as brewmaster in the Diebolt brewery, which was his first job, did not please him. He bought Goodfellow Hall, and after running the tavern there for 2 1/2 years he founded his own brewery, Excelsior. It has been seen what success he had, and he is well known here and in brewing circles, but most of all in the Excelsior brewery.

The Cleveland & Sandusky Brewing Co. was formed in the years 1897-1998. In the last year the consolidation begun at the outset had become complete. This is the brewing syndicate to which the following larger breweries in Cleveland belong: Cleveland, Gehring, Baehr, Columbia, Phoenix, Union, Star, Bohemian, Schlather and Fischel.

The first officers of the syndicate were F. W. Gehring, president; W. H. Chapman, secretary and treasurer; Jacob Kübler, first vice president, Ernst Müller, second vice president. In 1900 Ernst Müller was elected president, and in 1907 Fischel took Ernst Müller's post.

Several of the breweries were founded as true German breweries which have played their part in making beer at home in this country.

Chapter 6
Outstanding Manufacturers and Business Firms

Theodor Kundtz

Without doubt one of the greatest industrial enterprises in Cleveland is the factories created by Theodor Kundtz for manufacturing cabinets for sewing machines as well as for making bicycle tires. The cabinet factory is found on West Center, Washington and Winslow Street, and the tire factory on Winslow, Main and Center Street. The first of these was established in 1875 and is today the sole factory of its type in Cleveland. The main building, with a height of four or five stories, already makes an imposing impression from afar, and impression which is only increased when one enters the building. About 500 workers are active around the year under their own leadership making sewing machine cabinets destined for White, Standard, Davis, Eldridge, New Home and smaller sewing machine factories. The factory area is supplied with all the innovations of the time, such as electric lights, and even natural gas is used. Three large steam boilers keep the hundreds of machines in motion. Also used in the Kundtz factories is the automatic sprinkler machine invented by Mr. William Neracher, which has proved so effective in stopping fires. The consumption of wood is of course colossal, since almost all varieties of wood are used. The wood arrives during the summer by ship, with each load amounting to between 200,000 and 400,000 board feet, while in the winter it comes in by railway. The wood is brought first of all to the sawmill, is stored for 14 days in the drying house, and then put to use. In the factory created in 1895 to make bicycle tires, the technical leadership also lies entirely in his hands, and Mr. Theodor Kundtz has managed through his own innovation (inserted tires) to make it unique in all the land as well. Mr. Kundtz's iron energy, his tireless hard work and above all his technical knowledge to thank for the prosperity of his businesses. Two additional factors are his business solidity and his care for the well being of his workers. More than half of the employees come from Mr. Kundtz' homeland narrowly defined, and most of them have managed to buy a home of their own. In order to make the experience during the working hours as pleasant as possible and to provide them with inexpensive meals, Mr. Kundtz called into being a special kitchen and dining hall where the employees may eat. The enterprise flourished for several years, but it failed in 1896 due to indifference on the part of the workers.

For the advantage of the workers in the factory itself, there is a Theodor Kundtz Support Society. Every employee pays in 1/2¢ on every dollar of wages, but in exchange receives 10% of their monthly pay as a support when ill, and in the case of death each employee pays 25¢ to those left behind.

Mr. Theodor Kundtz was born in 1852 in Untermetzenseifen, Hungary, where his father was a respected furniture maker. He attended the local primary school and learned his father's craft. Due to the early death of his father, he was compelled to take up the business at an early age, for he was the oldest son and had the main concern to take care of the family. The young man proved up to the responsibility; even at an early age his will was stiffened and his autonomy developed in the hard struggle for survival. At the age of 21 Mr. Kundtz decided to emigrate to America, which promised to be a good place for his craft, a feeling which never deceived him. In May, 1873, he arrived in Cleveland, completely stripped of all resources, for the trip here had cost him every cent. Fortunately he was able to find employment at once in a furniture shop on Leonard Street. Here he worked for a year, then the company moved to St. Clair Street, where it soon failed. Now Mr. Theodor Kundtz took over the collapsed business with two other employees, and soon it so blossomed that they had to rent larger quarters on West Street. And just as with most small enterprises of this sort, the want of money soon made itself palpable, the partners fell out, with the final result that the business was divided. Each of the three partners now began working for himself, and while one partner remained on St. Clair Street and the other on West Street, Mr. Kundtz took over the ruined business of R. T. Holden on Center Street. The three new businesses prospered for years until competition grew so intense that all of the sewing machine companies in Cleveland, six in number, went out of business one by one.

A few years later he bought from Georg Gebhardt his factory on the corner of Center and Washington Street, which he expanded through new additions and improvements. During this time Mr. Kundtz had the misfortune that his factory located on Elm Street went up in flames, so that he saw himself forced to work day and night to fill orders. He never rebuilt the burned factory but only expanded the existing factory to meet needs.

In 1895 Mr. Kundtz, whose business grew by the day, bought the structure at the corner of Winslow, Main and Center Street, where there had been a bucket factory for a long time. The first factory was given over completely to the manufacture of cabinets for sewing machines, and today the products of this factory has a high reputation in all sewing machine factories of the country.

At the same time that Mr. Kundtz was extremely active in business, he was no less involved in finances and social matters. He was interested in all the intellectual activities of his countrymen, and all humanitarian and charitable efforts found in him a warm and active supporter and founder. His name was always first in the establishment of newspapers, the building of a Hungarian hall, etc., etc.. He did not forget his home town of Metzenseifen, and he invested large sums for noble purposes. Mr. Kundtz found his eldest son to be a major support in his many business undertakings, and his son received a good practical education.

A few years ago Mr. Kundtz built a large home, where he could enjoy a peaceful family life in the midst of his relatives after a hard day's work, and he always enjoyed it when his friends sought him out and he could practice hospitality with them.

The King of Hungary, in recognition of his services, named Mr. Theodor Kundtz a Knight of the Order of Franz Joseph, a distinction which Mr. Kundtz certainly deserved and which many friends and countrymen greeted with joy and satisfaction at a splendid banquet.

On its foundation, he granted the German-Hungarian Women's Society a gift of $500, and he is still that group's true friend and benefactor, just as he zealously supports other associations of his countrymen and their efforts. Mr. Kundtz has also supported German efforts in general with the liveliest interest.

The Cuyahoga Rendering & Soap Works

In the Cuyahoga valley, close to the C. C. & S., C. L. & W. and the Valley lines, there is the establishment of the Cuyahoga Rendering & Soap Works. The business has been in existence for some years, and the enterprise has been accompanied with success. The history of the development of the factory is also interesting, since it shows that hard work, energy and solid practice can still lead to the goal and accomplish something. Elsewhere in this work a biography is dedicated to Mr. A. W. Stadler, the creator and owner of this, the largest Cleveland soap factory. As is stated there, he started out as a young, 20-year old man to make himself independent after working for a time with his father, and he started with very modest means. For a year he delivered wares to other fat melting operations in the city, and he finally rented his father's establishment for a year on a weekly basis. In 1876 he began his factory on Denison Avenue on the Cuyahoga river. In 1889 he added an entire soap factory employing 28 workers. The monthly production ran to an average of 12,000 to 15,000 boxes of soap, some of select varieties, including the famous brand of "Housekeeper's Delight," a soap which is thought the best brand of soap, very popular and available at all grocers. The "Sailor" (floating) soap for dressing room and bath has no equal, made of pure vegetable oils, and then the renowned

"German Mottled" soap, together with other varieties of washing and toilet soap, which always find a good market.

A walk through the factory is rewarding. At once one is surprised by the extraordinary cleanliness of the place. In the "Rendering Department" there is a series of giant tanks filled with tallow, serving to render the tallow. The rendered tallow goes to the soap department, also in large tanks, where it is boiled along with other oils and fats which are needed to make soap. Boiling goes on for four days. Then the mass remains standing for two or three days, when it is run through pipes to wooden frames. There are about 175 such wooden frames, each with a capacity of 1400 to 1500 pounds. The frames are then moved to another large room, where the contents are formed into bricks or bars.

In order to do this, the sides of the frames are opened. The soap is then cut into pieces using a very clever device, and then it is brought to a table for a further cutting process. Then the pieces pass to a drying room, where they are placed in racks stacked up and left until they achieve the necessary solidity.

Near the drying room is found the wrapping department. Here the individual pieces pass through a stamping machine and are wrapped by experienced persons. It is truly astounding how rapidly the wrapping takes place. A single person can fold 3000 covers a day. A complex system of pipes come from the "power house" to provide power and heat for the entire establishment. Near the power house is found the glycerine department. The precipitate from lye is transformed into glycerine in specially-constructed kettles.

The entire establishment has an area of 4 acres. The main building, which is filled with an outstanding soap storage, measures 104 by 80 feet. Despite the significant size of the establishment, the need for more space becomes more pressing with every passing day.

The stables are located by the residence of Mr. Stadler, 1422 Denison Avenue. One can get an idea of their extent when one sees that besides having room for 32 horses, there is space for 14 wagons and several buggies, as well as a ton of hay and great quantities of oats and other fodder and straw. Two and a half tons of hay and 150 to 200 bushels of fodder are consumed every week. Every modern accommodation is to be found in the stables, and the cleanliness of a parlor prevails.

Mr. H. C. Stringer functions as manager and bookkeeper. He was born here; his parents are Germans. Stringer has been with the company for twelve years.

Mr. W. L. Stewart has been active as superintendent and chemist of the factory for 16 years. He came from the state of New York, and in his double capacity has contributed much to making the enterprise a success.

J. A. Roll, the first salesman and city representative, was born in Pennsylvania, and he has been employed by Mr. Stadler for the last 17 years. He is the man who takes care that the wares are marketed, particularly in this city.

Mr. F. F. Theobald has been employed for twelve years as a traveling salesman, and he is much respected by his customers in northern Ohio. His talent and experience in sales have continually expanded the circle of customers.

Mr. C. E. Ord is chief machinist, and he has been with the company for 18 years. He is an expert in his field, which is well demonstrated.

Mr. Fred Bluhm is chief stable master. He was born in Mecklenburg and came to America when he was 22. His employer holds him in high esteem.

The Langenau Manufacturing Company
One example how German fortitude can make headway on little or no means and prevail despite all storms and problems is W. C. Langenau, the founder of the establishment on the N. P. Railway at Franklin and 84th Street.

Born in Dietz, Nassau, in 1848, he attended the school of his birthplace and learned locksmithy. After the completion of his apprenticeship, he emigrated to America in 1867, settling first in Erie, then in Sharden, Pennsylvania. Compelled to work with his hands, and since he could find no work in his own craft, he at first earned his living as a day laborer building roads, as a brick maker and as a farmhand, until he managed to find work as a locksmith and machinist. In Cleveland from 1869 on, he married here in 1870 and became independent a year later by starting a small workshop making models and metal patterns, with a basic capital of $128, with $450 lent by friends. He had hardly begun when the crisis of 1874 came, forcing him to close the doors of his workshop, since he was unable to meet his obligations. He started anew, with no capital at all, and the lathe which he used then is still in his factory. He paid off the debts of his first enterprise dollar for dollar. He invested all his energy until he was able to make the manufacture of small ironwares his specialty. In 1898 the business was incorporated with a stock capital of $50,000. He eventually bought back all the stock, and the business boomed, the factory was expanded several times, and today the factory is one of the greatest of its type.

Mr. Langenau leads the business end of his firm, while his son Frank is superintendent of the factory. All departments are equipped with machines of the most modern type.

Mr. Langenau is father-in-law of the former mayor, McKisson. He has also risen to the highest rank in social life, and although his involvement with business, he preserves his German character and gives the warmest support to German efforts.

The Fuller Company

The Fuller Cleaning Company was founded in 1903 with a stock capital of $40,000. The company has a lovely factory location at 7607 Carnegie Avenue and is equipped with the latest inventions. It is astonishing when one enters this establishment and sees how the cleaning and reconditioning of carpets using technical aids and processes are done, all helping this company to prosperity. Characteristic and convincing of a German hand is the cleanliness and order reigning in the entire operation, which has astounded many who find the opposite to be the case in similar places. Among the many and various processes found there the most interesting is probably that which turns old carpets into new small rugs. The process by which these rugs are produced is patented, and the rugs thus produced differ from all the rugs produced by other factories. The Fuller Company is also the only carpet company in Cleveland with the exclusive franchise to use this process in the county, and these rugs are a major object of their special manufacturing carried out alongside their cleaning.

The Fuller cleaning institution was originally located on Quincy Street. The facilities there were expanded several times. Steps were taken to move to Carnegie Avenue and to build a new factory suited to increased demand at the time of incorporation in 1903.

The operation of the business rests primarily in German hands, which is of essential importance. The president and manager is John H. Dremann, the son of a German pioneeer, born here in 1854. His father fought bravely in the Civil War and was one of the first to respond to Lincoln's call to rally around the threatened flag. Through 1868 we find the young Dremann active in various positions, in which he distinguished himself through hard work and ability. In 1868 the opportunity presented itself to obtain the Fuller Company, and his energy and business sense have since made it what it is today.

Mr. Dremann is a very amiable man in conversation, disposing of a wide circle of friends. He is a member of the Tippecanoe Club and belongs to a Lutheran support society.

The secretary and treasurer, Friedrich Bodenstein, is also the child of a German pioneer family of old Cleveland. His parents settled here in the 1850s. His father comes from Saxony, and his mother was born in Vienna. Mr. Bodenstein attended parochial school, then entered Concordia Seminary in Addison, Illinois, where he trained to become a schoolteacher, a profession he followed for 14 years until he entered the Fuller Company four years ago, in which he proved himself so capable that he received the responsible post already named. He is happily married with Miss Rittman of Akron, Ohio.

Concerning the business it should be mentioned that outstanding citizens of Cleveland belong to the directors of the Fuller Co., such as Judge G. Schwan, Ed. Matthias and V. W. Marble.

The business connections and the circle of customers of this business, heaped with orders, reach far beyond the city and its borders even into other states.

The Zipp Manufacturing Co.

The Zipp Manufacturing Co., 747-751 Woodland Avenue S. E., takes a leading position in the area of fruit and spice essence manufacture. The business manufactures fruit extracts and juices for bakers, sodawater manufacturers, pharmacists, soda fountains, as well as for home use.

The important market for Zipp products is shown by the fact that no fewer than ten traveling salesmen are needed for the states of Kentucky, Indiana, Missouri, Illinois, Michigan, New York, West Virginia, Pennsylvania, Maryland and Ohio to serve the steadily increasing clientele.

John Zipp, the founder of the business, was born here on 13 December 1857 as the son of one of the first German pioneers of Cleveland, who was active here for years as a masonry contractor. He received his education in the Brownwell Street School, and for ten years he was bookkeeper with John H. Gause & Co., where he had occasion to gather experience in the area of exract specialties. He made himself independent on 1 September 1885 by starting the manufacture of extracts as well as of baking powder in a small shop at 64 Woodland Avenue, the old number. The success he had was complete. After steady growth of the business, Zipp Manufacturing Co. moved in 1903 to the imposing building on Woodland Avenue in which are located their factory and storage rooms. Incorporation of the firm took place in 1895. Officers are: John Zipp, president and treasurer; L. D. Zipp, vice president; W. F. Zipp, manager; W. A. Kappler, secretary.

Mr. John Zipp is married and the happy father of two children. He is a member of the chamber of commerce, the Cleveland Singing Society and of various lodges, and he enjoys general popularity and respect not only in the social world but also in private circles. He also remains piously attached to Germans, since he found the area in which his success was established among the German element of Cleveland. This area of activity now stretches far beyond the limits of the city. German efforts have a willing supporter and sacrificing promoter in Mr. Zipp.

Riester & Thesmacher Co.

The Riester & Thesmacher Co., manufacturers in sheet metal, was founded by August E. Riester and Georg F. Thesmacher in 1900 and incorporated in 1904, and in the few years of its existence it has grown to be an important business. More than a hundred workers are employed by it. The place of business of the company is located at 1510-1526 West 25th Street.

August E. Riester. president of the company, was born in Cleveland on 29 August 1873, and is the eldest son of Mr. Engelbert Riester, who emigrated here from Stetten, Baden, in the 1850s. The mother of Mr. August E. Riester was born Koch, also from Stetten; she came to this country as a young girl. August attended the Catholic parochial school until he was twelve, and then went to C. W. Hauck to learn wire-drawing. He was employed with that person as well as other firms for twelve years, until he founded his own company with Thesmacher in 1900.

Mr. Riester is happily married to Miss Paulina Gallowitz, born of German parents in Hungary. He is a member of the society of the Knights of Columbus.

Georg F. Thesmacher, secretary and treasurer of Riester & Thesmacher, was born on 22 September 1873 in Oldenburg, Germany, and came as a small boy to Cleveland. He also learned wire drawing, and he joined with August E. Riester in 1900 to form the company they lead.

Mr. Thesmacher is a member of the executive board of the Building Trades' Employers, as well as past commander of the Order of the Maccabees.

He married Miss Martha Hippler, and his son Milton Albert is currently ten years old.

Messrs. Riester and Thesmacher are among the businessmen of Cleveland who are generally respected as a result of their energetic business ability, and they cannot fail to dominate the field in their specialty.

Bakody & Berger

Emlen Bakody, of the noted photographic firm of Bakody & Berger, was born on 16 August 1865 in Akron, Ohio. His father emigrated from Temesvar, Hungary, in the 1850s after playing a prominent role in the revolution of 1848. For years his father ran a wholesale jewelry business, but about ten years ago he withdrew from business and now passes the evening of his life in Youngstown, Ohio, surrounded by a circle of friends, at the venerable age of 80.

After Emlen completed his primary and secondary schooling, he chose photography as his profession, and in this he has achieved perfection, as his works show. His first studio was in Chicago, and then he was established in Louisville, Kentucky, for a long time. From there he came here, and for the last two years Mr. Bakody is in partnership with Henry E. Berger. The Bakody & Berger studio at 612 Euclid Avenue is already generally known.

Mr. Bakody is a member of all Masonic orders. He has been happily married since 1897 with Adela Milar of New Philadelphia.

Henry E. Berger is a partner in the photographic firm of Bakody & Berger on Euclid Avenue. As the name itself says, Berger is of German origin. His parents had Cleveland as the goal of their emigration to this country, and his father, Louis Berger, is active as a railroad employee.

H. E. Berger first saw the light of day on 6 November 1867 on the West Side. He attended the Orchard and Detroit Street public school, taking service with the once-noted photographer John C. Ryder in order to learn the art of photography. Endowed with natural ability and special talent, he trained himself so well that he moved from apprentice to chief operator in the business. He was active there until 1905, hence all of 22 years. On 1 April 1905 he became independent and founded his own studio with Bakody at 612 Euclid Avenue. Customers came from the highest circles, which had seen his work and knew how to judge it.

Mr. Berger married Miss Lulu French. His two sons, Loran and Harold, are now 15 and 12 years old.

He is a member of the West Side Helicon Lodge of the Freemasons, and due to his fine appearance and intelligent conversation is as respected as he is beloved by those who come into contact with him in the course of his work.

The Remington Typewriter

What office today does not have a typewriter? Who receives a business letter these days which is written by hand? And yet it is no more than a quarter century that this useful invention, sparing time and trouble and increasing clarity, was developed, and the first typewriter in the West was delivered. It was the Remington typewriter.

Other "inventors" shot out of the ground like mushrooms, but the mother of the idea held its ground and continuously improved the machine it had invented, so that it has triumphed over its followers and imitators.

No typewriter in the world can beat the mother of the invention, the Remington Typewriter, in solid construction, practical design and productivity.

The local establishment of the Remington factory is 514 Prospect Street. The machines may be obtained with ribbons of choice, even with two colors, and in various models, according to their purpose, and with a taste as diverse, or for any language, normally costing a hundred dollars. They may be bought in installments or rented.

Koch and Henke

One of the largest businesses in Cleveland whose growth and prosperity is due entirely to German hard work and German energy, is doubtless the large furniture business of Koch and Henke on Lorain Avenue, corner of West 30th Street.

Located in the middle of the most German part of our splendid Forest City is the grandiose store of that company, in one of the loveliest palaces of trade in the city, the mecca not only for buying Germans but for buyers of all nationalities who have discovered that they will find a selection there and they will always be well served.

Georg D. Koch, the senior partner in the firm, was born on 23 December 1850 in Schwäbisch-Hall, the son of a turner. His parents emigrated to America in 1854, bringing the little Georg directly to Cleveland, one of the best places where a man could find some elbow room to occupy himself in keeping with his energy and capabilities and find a place in the sun. This is where the aged father of Mr. Georg D. Koch now passes the evening of his life, surrounded by children, grandchildren and great-grand-children. After graduating school the young Georg entered the furniture business of J. Vincent as an apprentice, learning the art of laquering and finishing furniture. In 1872 the 21-year-old Georg established a small furniture business in partnership with Mr. Fleming under the name of Fleming & Koch at the corner of Penn and Lorain Street. Older residents of the West Side will recall that shop. A large part of the furniture of older residents of Cleveland come from that business. Only a year after foundation the business had expanded so much that a branch was opened at Detroit Street, with Wm. Toni as a partner. The firm was now Fleming, Koch & Co. Both businesses were later consolidated, and the company moved both warehouse and store to the corner of Pearl and Lorain Street, in one of those buildings which were later broken down to make room for the Westside Market. The firm dissolved in 1875, and in fall of the same year Mr. Koch took over the interest of Mr. Puls, business partner of Mr. Franz Henke, so that Mr. Koch became partner of Mr. Henke. In 1881 Mr. Henke bought the property on Lorain and West 30th Street where their imposing place of business is now located, which in the course of years has been repeatedly expanded in keeping with sales.

Mr. Georg D. Koch married Bertha Berno in 1875. From this happy marriage came four children. The eldest son, Georg Koch, Jr., born in 1876, now a member of his father's firm, is a capable, amiable salesman and has the capability to win new friends for the company. He married Miss Elsie Mader, the daughter of a respected family from Bucyrus, Ohio, and a daughter, Norma, has come from this extremely happy marriage. Mr. Koch, Jr., takes a lively interest in all charitable and public matters. He is a member of the Chamber of Industry and the chamber of commerce, and he belongs to the Elks and the Cleveland Grays.

Franz Heinrich Henke, founder of the business, was born in 1824 in Hanover. He emigrated to America in 1844, coming directly to Cleveland, which has the energy of people like the old Henke to thank for its prosperity. In autumn, 1872, Mr. Henke opened a furniture store on Detroit Street east of Pearl in partnership with Mr. Puls, later moving it to Lorain and Penn Street. Two years later, when Mr. Koch bought Mr. Puls' share, there was the foundation of the company of Koch and Henke, whose business at first continued at the same place. In 1892 Mr. Henke completely withdrew from business in order to pass the rest of his days in peace and leisure. His sole son, Henry August Henke, who had thoroughly learned the business at his father's side, and had demonstrated that he understood how to use the business talent inherited from his father, took the burdens from his father's shoulders. Unfortunately, it was not granted to the old gentleman to enjoy his well-deserved retirement for long. He died in 1906, to the deep sorrow of his relatives and his many friends and acquaintances.

Henry August Henke, who took over his father's share in the firm of Koch & Henke in 1892, was born in 1861. He obtained his training in the public school and business colleges. The financial leadership of the firm is his special trust, and in the best of hands. Mr. Henke, Jr., is not only a thoroughly capable businessman, but also a very amiable gentleman with whom everyone wants to speak. He married in 1888 with Miss Louise George, daughter of the noted iron goods dealers of the West Side. This thoroughly happy marriage has produced eight children, five daughters and three sons.

One of the great public "business secrets" of the company of Koch and Henke is the absolute harmony of the partners, who always show mutual respect and trust. This, besides the promptest and most solid service of all customers without distinction of persons, is the main reason why this company has risen to phenomenal success from modest beginnings in a relatively brief time.

Dr. A. E. Hitch

Dr. Hitch is one of the most outstanding dentists in Cleveland. Born in 1859 as a child of Cleveland, Dr. Hitch has resided here his entire life, and as a result, though a relatively young man, he is one of the longest-serving dentists in the city.

Dr. Hitch had his office on Public Square for thirty years. and many of the most respected citizens of Cleveland have visited him and asked for his services. His working area has always been supplied with the latest inventions in keeping with the newest technical means.

Dr. Hitch's studio is now located at 1303 E. 110th Street N.E., equipped with all the acquisitions of science, and since Dr. Hitch's reputation as one of the most accomplished dentists in the city is more than well-deserved, patients turn to him without hesitation when they need dental operations. Dr. Hitch takes care of all type of work involved in his business, including extractions, filling and replacement of teeth, and in so amiable a way that he is visited with pleasure, and he enjoys a large circle of friends as well as customers.

Chapter 7
The Unveiling of the Schiller-Goethe Monument

Hail to thee, brave Germans, beyond the great flood!
You bore with you hither an irreplaceable good
In your German fidelity and your German sense,
Which wins for your new homeland a splendid profit:
Then do your duty and keep your trust, for that is the German way;
You have kept it in the New World as in the Old,
And our great poets, whom you honor so worthily,
Have taught you such a virtue both there and here.
(Felix Dahn, Breslau, on the dedication of the Schiller-Goethe Memorial.)

Without a doubt the grandest event in the history of German-Americans in our splendid Forest City on Lake Erie was on Sunday, 9 June 1907, the solemn unveiling of the Schiller-Goethe Memorial, which found its provisional location in the shadowy Wade Park, a paradisiacal piece of earth in the summer. Later, when the main buildings are completed for the Group Plan of public buildings, it is supposed to find its place in the park in the main part of the city, to remind the larger population of the significance of Cleveland's Germans. The preparations for the realization of this plan, so honorable to Cleveland's Germans, to erect on the shores of Lake Erie a monument to the finest of the many poets of the German language, took several years. They finally came to launching through the incorporation of the Schiller-Goethe Memorial Society, aimed at realizing the desires of Germans to honor the memory of their two heroic poets. The goals given in the articles of incorporation were as follows:

1. The erection of a monument to the poets Schiller and Goethe in the city of Cleveland on public or private grounds with the purpose of giving it to the citizenry as a gift. In this way the donors would state their high estimation of the permanent revelations of the spirit of lasting benefit to mankind by these great German poets and thinkers, as well as the unbreakable dependence of the donors to the free institutions of their adopted fatherland.

2. The creation of a German library which should be donated to the library of the Western Reserve University as a gift so that it would contribute to the knowledge of the origins, the relationship by blood, and the development of the nations of German origin among the students.

3. The raising of the necessary means should be achieved for the Schiller-Goethe Memorial Society through the issuance of certificates to members, as well as through receiving voluntary contributions and donations.

4. The society should have the right to obtain land and be empowered to give the land along with the memorial either to the city of Cleveland or to an art gallery.

Now they went zealously to work to collect money for the considerable costs of an adequate monument, determining that this could only be a casting of the double statue of Goethe and Schiller by Ernst Rietschel, of which the original is in Weimar. And the Germans were happy and willing to make their contibution for such a work, which honored them all. Already, a half-year after the incorporation of the Memorial Society, the date could be set for the unveiling of the statue. At first it was thought possible to consider to do the unveiling already in October, 1906, but an unexpected injury to the pedestal made it necessary to delay the festivities, to guarantee that popular participation would not be restricted by bad weather, until the start of the month of roses in 1907.

Sunday, 9 June 1907, was the day of unveiling of the double monument, and at the same time doubtless the finest holiday in the history of Cleveland Germans. Graced by splendid spring weather, all the Germans in the Forest City participated in the celebration, which fell into to major portions, a parade from Willson Avenue to the memorial square in Wade Park, and the actual unveiling in Wade Park.

About 10,000 persons participated on foot, horseback or on carriages in the imposing parade, which ran along the long route of march to the cheers of tens of thousands of non-Germans. The number of persons who were witnesses of the actual unveiling in Wade Park was estimated at 65,000. On this day they were all standing together, the Clevelanders of German language, wherever their cradle had been in the old fatherland, for Schiller and Goethe belong to all Germans, all people of German tongue, without any regard for social class or political allegiance.

The dedication itself of the monument ran without disturbance and it was worthy in every sense. The enthusiasm of the participants was genuine, and each supported with a full heart the festival speaker, Professor Ernst Voss of the University of Wisconsin, who said, "May this splendid monument, the incarnation of a healthy idealism on realistic foundations, ever remind us how true and constant men must do in great and small what duty and honor bid them, which is to be brave and true to the death. But also, in keeping with our fathers' song, we should have joy in this lovely world and enjoy this sweet life with the swing of a sword and the sound of a harp, the beauty of a woman and noble wine. And, renouncing frivolous wishes, to dedicate ourselves piously to the eternal power which continuously awakens in us new life."

The festival speaker who pointed out the significance of this gift to the Americans in English was Professor Robert W. Deering of the Western Reserve University. His speech was a spirited exposition of that which Goethe and Schiller have to offer the Americans today. He sought to bring to consciousness what the American nation today owes to the two great Germans, and how Goethe and Schiller cross the limits of this community of people and became the great apostles of all that is truly good in modern life, and whose spirited leadership may be accepted by Americans as a related people with the same justified trust as by the Germans themselves.

The dedication had two moments of extraordinary enthusiasm. The first was when the monument was released from its surrounding cover and golden sunlight fell on it for the first time. The sight was dramatic and will remain unforgotten by all onlookers. The image of the sculpture with its background of the vernal green trees of the park, with a decoration of flowers and the decoration of the many wreaths placed at the feet, besides the forest of flags of seventeen societies, the platform with the singers male and female in festival clothing, finally the celebrating multitude and the whirl of trumpets in the music, all of that made a great impression.

The second moment of extraordinary joy came with the reading of a message from the German emperor, who could not restrain himself from making a public statement greeting this German deed of Cleveland. "To the Citizens of German origin in Cleveland," the emperor cabled, "I send my best greetings on the dedication today of the Schiller-Goethe Memorial. Its erection and the estimation of German ideals expressed thereby is a joy to me." The musicians played the German national hymn, "Heil Dir im Siegerkranz" ["Hail to Thee in Victor's Crown"]; loud hurrahs filled the air. The head of the memorial committee cabled Emperor Wilhelm in response, "Emperor Wilhelm, Berlin. Goethe-Schiller Memorial unveiled in presence of 65,000 persons. In this sacred hour American citizens of Cleveland of German origin respectfully thank Your Majesty for his good wishes. Memorial Society."

As said, the day of the unveiling of the Schiller-Goethe Memorial shall remain a day of honor for the Germans of Cleveland. The arrangement of the celebration was in the hands of messrs. W. J. Siller, president; C. A. Mueller, vice president; J. H. Gerlich, secretary; Ernst

Mueller, treasurer; Emil Ring, festival director, and other gentlemen, of whom sketches are contained in this work.

Part IV
Biographies

A decade has passed since the publication of our first work on *Cleveland and its Germans.*

At inspecting that first book we are reminded clearly of the saying, *Tempora mutantur* [times change]. How differently Cleveland is formed and organized, and what changes have taken place in the composition of the population! If we have to register with deep sadness the departure of so many who embodied the Germans of those days and stood out among them, we have the consolation that the unquenchable source of German life has not ceased to produce new life destined to fill the gaps when we look into the Germans and seek new members representing German hard work, energy and honorable, persistent effort in powerful Cleveland today.

With the rise of other nationalities in the Forest City it is proper for Germans to call for the recognition of their own virtues. While we mourn the passing of so many whose life and work filled our first volume, in this volume we will make a collection of those who guarantee the continuity of Cleveland and are representatives of Germans in Cleveland today.

These examples demonstrate that Germans have not simply continued to contribute to the progress of Cleveland, but that in the German element are to be found those who contribute to it essentially and stand now as before at the pinnacle of its progress and prosperity.

Just as we have, in the meantime, raised a monument to both of our spiritual heroes in Wade Park, so we have created here a worthy hall of honor for the worthy representatives of German labor, German hard work and striving. Many tracing origins back to Germany might not be found there because they have so distanced themselves from Germans that their membership is no longer obvious or announces itself. The brave band of those proud of their German origins and who announce it proudly and assert it is registered on our pages. They are the kernel of the Germans preserved today in Cleveland, and may their images persist without fading when the black crepe is hung over them with the passing of time, and nothing is left of their deeds but our sketches.

Stephen Buhrer

In Stephen Buhrer, who has already reached his 81st year in full possession of his powers, Germans of Cleveland can see one of their most worthy and ripened representatives. Thanks to his constantly-proven loyalty and uprightness, he received the high honor of twice being elected as head of the municipal administration.

Stephen Buhrer is a German man of true substance and material. Although born here, he has preserved German customs and ways into his old age, and he stands in high honor in the eyes of the most various elements of which the city on Lake Erie is composed.

Stephen Buhrer saw the light of day on 26 December 1825 near the picturesque little town of Zoar, famous as a colony of the idealistic communist sect of the Separatists. His parents had immigrated from the Grand Duchy of Baden in 1817, first settling in Pennsylvania but then at Zoar on the advice of friends. The area was then like a wilderness, and it took many years of tireless labor by the settlers to make Zoar's environs what they now are, a garden overflowing with fruitfulness and productivity. Unfortunately Stephen's father did not experience the success of the settlement; an illness took him away in 1829, leaving a troubled widow and two small children to bewail the death of a spouse and father.

According to the strict but philanthropic principles of the Separatist congregation, to which the deceased Caspar Buhrer had belonged, the congregation took over the education and support of the children until they were capable of earning their own bread. Young Stephen had to watch the sheep of the community at the age of nine, and he lived as a shepherd for three years. When his physical strength was adequate for hard labor, he was apprenticed in the shop of a cooper, and he worked there for the following six years, although he often enough expressed concern that his visibly weakened body was not up to the labor. Still he survived this period of apprenticeship without injury to his health, and so at the age of 18 he arrived in the city of Cleveland, where he worked another year as a cooper's helper.

Finally, however, he came to the conviction that he would not prosper if he continued in a cooper's career. He thus hung up his craft for the moment and went into service with a mercantile firm as a traveling salesman, in which capacity he traveled through western Ohio, Michigan and Indiana. The journeys enriched his experience and sharpened his naturally clear vision. Unfortunately swamp fever, which was then more common and more virulent than today, soon put an end to his activities. Sick and consumed by disease, he returned via Detroit to Cleveland, which he always regarded as home. The aid and support of a true friend brought him solace in his difficult situation, for the consuming disease and the lack of work had long since used up his small savings. His old craft, cooperage, was taken up again, providing him with an income and a strengthening of his health.

Finally, in 1848, he was able to see the realization of his longing and desire and establish a house and home. He married Miss Eva Maria Schneider, with whom he lived in happy marriage. She bore him three fine children. Two years later, Buhrer was in the position to expand his cooperage and associate with a partner.

This is perhaps the place to consider Buhrer's schooling. From what has already been said, he was not supplied with a fine education among the brethren of Zoar. The boys and girls were very early sent to work without much concern for their lack of education. "Pray and work" was the proverb of the congregation. Yet the young man did make good use of his free hours, so far as he could, and through self-directed study he sought to fill the gaps in his knowledge. So it came about that the young, ambitious citizen drew the eyes of the wise upon himself, so that he was elected no less than three times to the City Council with the trust of his fellow citizens. As there were then no professional politicians, this was a high honor and a demonstration of the respect in which the elected one was held by his fellow citizens. In 1853 Buhrer founded a company to distill spirits, and he won considerable success with it. He continued this until 25 May 1907, when he entered a richly deserved retirement.

His first election to the city council took place in 1855, and his reelections in 1863 and 1865 fell in the midst of the terror and upheaval of the Civil War. Buhrer was a zealous friend of the liberation of slaves from the beginning, and he supported the party that had written on its banner the indivisibility and permanence of the Union. Only a physical debility denied him his desire to serve in the ranks of the fighters to put down the slave-holding South. Yet he made use of his position in the city council to improve the lot of the wives and children of the defenders of the Fatherland who had gone into the field. His popularity improved more and more, and when he saw himself elected to the city council the third time unanimously, his many friends were already decided that he was the man who deserved the highest civic office, "as the worthiest citizen of Cleveland." Hardly was his service in the city council at an end than he received unanimous nomination for the office of mayor, and he was elected with the same unanimity by his fellow citizens. Mr. Charles Miller and his cousin Fletcher were the ones who convinced him to stand for election to such a responsible office, which he opposed to no small degree.

Through his conduct in office, Buhrer demonstrated that the election had not fallen on one unworthy of it. The office demanded a whole man of tried loyalty to duty and tireless energy. This is because the mayor was head of the entire municipal administration, and the division into various departments was not yet the fashion. The mayor was not only chief of police and responsible for their conduct, but also had the fire department under him, as well as the control of municipal finances. These involuted and overextended duties were fulfilled by Mayor Buhrer to the satisfaction of the entire citizenry, and he was concerned only with the general good, completely ignoring the demands of party. So his name was put at the head of the ticket once more in 1869, with the success that he was elected by the citizenry in April by what was then the enormous majority of 3000 votes. This was despite the fact that his party, the Democrats, were quite unpopular at the time. His fellow citizens trusted the brave citizen Buhrer, not the party man.

Although the Democratic party nominated him again for mayor, this happened over his own opposition. He felt too weakened and tired for a further fulfilment of his duties, which had grown dramatically with the expansion of the city. In 1874 his party convinced him to participate in the elections for city council once more. As a member of the finance committee and of the improvements council, he was one of the first to support the construction of the present viaduct over the deep-cut bed of the Cuyahoga River to bind the west side with the east side. He was always the warm friend and supporter of institutions favoring the common well-being. He never sought for himself an office which involved a salary. His public activity was only dedicated to the well-being of his fellow citizens. He is a true representative of antique virtue of a citizen, for which our modern progress seems to have no more room. May the worthy old man have many more years of untroubled health in the circle of his own and his fellow citizens. His manly and dignified attitude to the howling of the temperance fanatics during the so-called crusade against taverns will always fill his liberal friends with thanks and high respect.

Stephen Buhrer has belonged to the Masonic Order for 45 years, and he holds the 32d degree in the Scottish Rite. Since 1845 he has been owner and manufacturer of the famous Buhrer's Gentian Bitters. In the last 12 years he has made an annual trip to the great West all the way to Mexico, usually accompanied by his second wife. His first wife died after a long illness in 1889, during which she received the finest care, and a year later Mr. Buhrer married a Clevelander, Miss Marguerite Patterson, whose origins are in New York. The latter lady is a member of the Methodist Episcopal Church and is distinguished by her quiet philanthropy and simple, inner piety. She is a straightforward lady of significant intelligence, with a strong inclination to family life and a winning personality. The family life of the Buhrer couple is the most happy imaginable. Unfortunately it remains childless.

Prof. Dr. Gustav C. E. Weber

On his quiet country estate in Willoughby the man now passes the evening of his life in retirement who for many years drew the attention of the public to himself, particularly in the circle of physicians. For there are few men of this science to practice the art of medicine with such self-sacrifice as he, or who have as many splendid accomplishments to show. We mean Dr. Gustav Weber, who may serve as the prototype of the true German man of science, who may be celebrated as such with justified pride.

Dr. Weber saw the light of the world on 26 May 1828 in Bonn on the Rhine, where his father was at the university there and had been active there since its foundation in 1818 as a surgeon and had won a name as the author of a series of outstanding medical works. His son Gustav received an outstanding education. After he had completed the *Gymnasium* in Bonn, he went to the university there, studying medicine, and in fact he was a fellow student with

Carl Schurz, who was studying law at the time. The agitation of the revolutionary year of 1848 did not permit the fiery youth to rest. It expelled him forcefully into the wider world, and he could no longer stand to dwell on the banks of the father of German rivers. So he emigrated the next year to America, where he settled first near St. Louis to take up agriculture. But Weber could not get a taste for that, and his longing for his beloved Rhine and the desire to increase his knowledge drove him back to Europe, where he brought his medical studies to an end in Vienna, Paris and Amsterdam. From this moment on, he gave himself totally to his profession and has remained committed to it ever since.

In 1853 Dr. Weber returned to America, where he became a partner of his brother, also a physician, living in New York. The brother died young, however, and so Gustav took over his practice, which expanded in such a way that he temporarily had to withdraw due to overwork. On a journey to recover he visited Cleveland, among other places. His reputation as a physician and surgeon had reached that far, and he was asked to make his permanent seat here. He received a professorship at the Cleveland Medical College, which he kept from 1856 until 1863. When the Secession War broke out, Governor Todd named Weber physician-general of the militia of the state of Ohio, in which capacity he did such outstanding work on the battlefields that the war minister Stanton declared his appreciation in a hand-written letter. But service in the field, the visiting of battlefields, the unending activities, all undermined Dr. Weber's health to such an extent that he had to resign. So he returned once more to Cleveland and took up his practice again. His reputation as a physician was so significant that he soon had a substantial practice. Patients came to him from near and far to be handled by this important surgeon. This moved him to found the Charity Hospital Medical College, to which he dedicated all his efforts. Later this college was combined with Wooster University. Dr. Weber had an enviable reputation as an operating surgeon, a reputation reaching across the country. Full of wonder, the entire medical world listened to the daring and fortunate operations he did in the course of the year with patients sent to him as beyond healing. Physicians who know Dr. Weber claim that no surer hand has ever held the scalpel. The hundreds of students who have been trained to be physicians under his control can witness to the fact that they could not choose a better teacher. With his sure hand and his practiced eye, Dr. Weber combines a calm and *sangfroid* which amazes the medical world.

Dr. Weber has made two discoveries. The first is a new method for closing arteries during operations and preventing bleeding. By that method the entry of alien materials into the blood is prevented, which would easily have blood poisoning as a result. The second discovery is a new method of removing tumors from the esophagus.

Up to the present day, Dr. Weber enjoys the highest reputation with his colleagues, who listen to his opinion in critical cases as if from an oracle. This man also has a large, noble heart that beats for his fellow man. He is a philanthropist in the best sense, a man, as Goethe says, "noble, helpful and good," and the many poor he has helped for free will remain thankful to this man. Even when his body has fallen to dust, yet his great name will live on.

May Dr. Weber long be preserved to us as a man and as a practiced physician. The many friends of the bold man and fighter in the service of science will certainly join in this wish.

In July 1897 Dr. Weber was named by President McKinley as United States consul in Nuremberg, which post he held with high honor until he returned to his adopted fatherland.

Since then Dr. Weber has withdrawn increasingly from the public, taking account of his years, since he soon will pass his eightieth birthday, certainly a high age for one who has been so active until recently.

It is well known how modest and unambitious Dr. Weber has been concerning his services, and if anyone he was one of those Goethe mentioned who are noble, helpful and promoting the well-being of mankind. His name will live after his body has long since fallen to dust for the many poor people he has treated without compensation.

C. A. Muerman

The "crazy years" of 1848 and 1849, which German-Americans in general and our Forest City in particular have to thank for so many worthwhile people and to which Cleveland largely owes its economic, political and social prosperity, also brought our well-known citizen Mr. C. A. Muerman to the hospitable shore of the United States and eventually to Cleveland.

Mr. Muerman was born on 20 February 1829, in Petershagen, near Prussian Minden. He attended the elementary and the highly regarded civic school, and with a passing grade qualified for entry into the *Secunda*. After his confirmation he decided to work in a soft leather tannery, although and perhaps because his family, an old merchant family, wanted him to enter a mercantile career. In 1847 he completed his apprenticeship. At once he went to an old childhood friend, whose father ran an important export business in shoe-sole leather, in Benzheim, Hessia-Darmstadt.

In the meantime 1848 approached. There was ferment everywhere. The students, the Turner -- Mr. Muerman included -- and young hotheads took to the field for the "holy cause of liberty," and when the story ended in military force, most of them, if they did not fancy prison at hard labor or worse, sought their safety in flight. Among them was the object of this story. After long wandering, continually pursued by agents and always harrassed, an inconquerable longing drove him back to his home town. But the authorities, then deeply involved in sniffing out demagogues and in persecuting young people who had an episode of opposition during their adolescence, had forgotten nothing, and Muerman's visit to his parents' house lasted only six hours. He arrived at 4 PM, and at 11 PM he returned to the road with a handkerchief wrapped around some linen. He managed to get down the Weser to Bremen by stowing away on a boat, a young man with a sentence of three years and a thousand *Taler* on his head.

In Bremen he turned to a business friend of his father, who gave him some tips about doing without a passport. Love of Prussia was not so great in Bremen or in the provinces that a young man could not argue his way out of trouble with the passport-checking gendarmery and convince them that they should not stand in the way of someone going to America.

Mr. Muerman was fortunate enough to get to America on the steamer *Washington*. He remained in New York for a year, where he operated as marketer for a tannery employing 123 workers, despite his youth. In 1853 he came to Cleveland, finding a position in the leather company of Bratenahl Bros., where he later served as a partner. He remained there for years, interrupted only by a time when he took over a tannery in Deerfield, Portage County, which he later gave to his two brothers. He also founded the leather shop of Muerman, Hartness and Weitz, and when Hartness left, he remained with Joseph M. Weitz until 1876 in the same shop on Water Street. Later he invested himself totally in an insurance company, which he heads to the present day. His office is located at 259 Arcade Building.

Mr. Muerman has always been a convinced Democrat by conviction, never a spoils politician nor an office hunter, but always ready to bring sacrifices for his convictions. In 1862 Mr. Muerman married Miss Emilie Pennigrott, a young lady whose parents were neighbors of the Muerman family and which had made a journey across the ocean for reasons of health. The happy marriage produced three children, two daughters and a son. Mr. Muerman has always been involved, not only in political life but also in social life. He is a member of the Concordia

Turner Society and the Cleveland Singing Society, was always a primary supporter of the Casino, is among the founders of the Concordia Lodge of Freemasons, is a member of the Pioneer Society. He was a member of the tax adjustment office for six years. He is known everywhere as a strict businessman, an outstanding citizen, a good joiner and an honorable man who is esteemed by all. It should be mentioned that Mr. Muerman has an extraordinarily developed artistic sense and a good understanding of art. His collection of paintings and pen drawings, as well as his library, are rich, and among the drawings are a number of extremely valuable original works, as well as rare sketches and illustrations of important worth.

Rt. Rev. Ignatius Friedrich Horstmann

Bishop Horstmann, the third bishop of Cleveland, an outstanding pillar of Germans and the warmest and most influential promoter of their interests, was born in Philadelphia, or more precisely in the district of Southwark, on 16 December 1840. His parents had previously emigrated from Germany, and his father was a respected businessman in the city. Ignatius, who was devoted to the clerical estate, was at first sent to the private academy of Mme. Charrier and her daughter, Mlle. Clementine in German Street. From there he passed to the Mount Vernon Grammar School, which he graduated with distinction, passing then to the Central High School, which he passed with outstanding final examinations in 1857. Then he was taken in by the Jesuit-led St. Joseph's College, and he later attended the seminary at Glen Riddle. Bishop Wood was so pleased with his talent and efforts that he sent him as one of the first students to the newly-founded American College in Rome, which he completed after winning many medals and prizes for literary and oratorical competitions, and he was ordained on 10 June 1865 by Cardinal Patrizzi. He continued his studies in the Eternal City for another year, winning the title of Doctor of Theology at the end. Returning to Philadelphia, he was made professor of logic, metaphysics and ethics, as well as of German and Hebrew, at St. Charles Borromeo Seminary, where he taught the subjects through 1871, before being moved to Overbrook, Pennsylvania, where he held the title of professor until 1877. In that year he came to St. Mary's Church in Philadelphia as pastor. He served there not quite eight years, and he not only won the hearts of his congregation, but he drew a great public into the holy house to hear his elegant and interesting sermons. The financial profit this brought to the church can be seen by the $19,000 the church brought in during the period of his service. In Sepember, 1885, he was named chancellor of the diocese by Archbishop Ryan in view of his demonstrated abilities, an office he led with great ability until his elevation to bishop in 1892.

During his activities as chancellor, he had more time for literary side-activities, to which he was always inclined, and as a tireless collaborator in the American Catholic Quarterly Review he provided continuous contributions, expanding his efforts to an unlimited sphere. He was also spiritual head of the Catholic Club in Philadelphia and chaplain of the Notre Dame cloister, where three religious communities had their seat. His 25th priestly jubilee was celebrated in one of the most impressive festivities ever held at Philadelphia's cathedral. Archbishop Ryan presented the jubilee sermon. At the reception in the Club which followed, lay supporters presented Horstmann with a gift for $4200, which he gave at once to the St. Vincent's Home.

Rt. Reverend Ignatius Horstmann was ordained bishop on 25 February and installed as successor to Bishop Gilmour, who died in April, 1891. The celebration of his installation, which is still generally remembered, was a true festival of all residents of Cleveland. Bishop Horstmann has long since demonstrated that he has the ability to lead the large and significant diocese of Cleveland, and he has attracted veneration and respect from all quarters. A proof that German interests have a convinced supporter in him is shown by his speech at the meeting in the new St. Michael's School under the auspices of the Roman Catholic Central Club on behalf of the preservation of the German language, a speech which excited the interest not just of Cleveland but of the entire country. In this speech Bishop Horstmann declared his support of the Germans, and declared that he would act to support their dignity and efforts insofar as he had the power.

Rt. Rev. George F. Houck

Father Houck, one of the most outstanding Catholic pastors and ecclesiastical officials here, chancellor of the episcopal chancery for years and since 1904 papal chaplain, was born on 9 July 1847 in Tiffin, Ohio, to German parents. His father, Johann Houck, had immigrated as a boy with his parents from Baden. His mother, born Ottilie Fischer, came to the country at the age of 10. His parents' marriage took place on 16 February 1846. Rev. Houck's father died in 1889 after working at a shoe business for almost 50 years. He had to work there for many years, until he was 20, and in fact he took over the store for two years during his father's illness.

On the one hand these activities restricted his studies and delayed his entry into the priesthood, but there is no doubt that these practical and business activities provided the episcopal chancellor with an insight which was not without use, and it is probably due to these circumstances that he went so far.

Rt. Rev. Houck received his first education in the St. Joseph's parochial school in Tiffin. Later he attended Heidelberg College there for two years. Although he desired to become a clergyman from his early youth, he had to assist his father, as mentioned, and it was only at the age of twenty, in September, 1867, that he was able to enter St. Mary's Seminary in Cincinnati to dedicate himself entirely to study and prepare himself for ordination. He remained in the seminary until June, 1874, when Bishop Gilmour called him to complete his studies in the seminary of the Diocese of Cleveland, to which he belonged legally. On 4 July 1875 he was consecrated priest in the cathedral here. Bishop Fitzgerald of Little Rock, Arkansas, then represented the ill Bishop Gilmour. Four months after his consecration he was installed as pastor of St. Joseph's in Crestline, Crawford County, and he remained there until July, 1877, when Bishop Gilmour named him secretary of his chancery. He also made him chancellor, though his naming was only officially declared at the synod taking place in May, 1882. He has held both offices since then, and he was confirmed in those offices by Bishop Horstmann after Bishop Gilmour's death.

Father Houck is widely admired in the Catholic ecclesiastical world because of his capable administration and tireless spiritual activity, and under his leadership the diocese of Cleveland is a model for all, since administration has been businesslike and orderly. Besides his official duties, Father Houck has functioned since 1877 as the chaplain of St. Vincent's Hospital, and alongside this he has been spiritual advisor for the last 18 years to Catholic inmates of the Workhouse. In 1878 he was named head of Catholic cemeteries here, and he functioned in that role until 1903. The purchase of Calvary Cemetery and its modern landscaping and equipping are primarily his doing.

Alongside all the claims on his time, Father Houck has still found time to do historical research and to publish the results.

One of these is a biography of the first bishop of Cleveland, Rt. Reverend Dr. Rappe. A further is entitled, *The Church in Northern Ohio*. His most important work, however, is *A History of Catholicity in Northern Ohio*. This covers 300 pages and is both an inestimable good for the Church and its descriptions are a monument for the state and its history. The work has already appeared in four editions.

When considering his many-sided and significant services as well as his zeal for office and his rare ability, Father Houck was named papal chaplain by Pope Pius X with the title of Monseigneur, as was mentioned at the outset.

Wm. Backus, Sr.

One of the most outstanding and well-known German-Americans of this city is always willing to take center stage for the promotion of German interests is without a doubt Mr. Wm. Backus, Sr. Born on 8 April 1834, the son of bourgeois parents in Neubamberg, Rheinhessen, he helped his father in agriculture after leaving school. Monotonous country life soon became boring to him, a man of lively nature, and at the age of almost 18 he emigrated, coming straight to Cleveland. He worked for two years, spurning no labor here or there, pursuing work on the road and ending finally in Chicago. There he remained until 1856, when he returned to Cleveland. Shortly after his return he married Miss Lina Strobel, a marriage that produced three children, of which one son is still living, the noted lawyer Wm. Backus, Jr.

Responding to the call of President Lincoln for volunteers in service of the North, he enlisted in the 20th Ohio Battery under Capt. Smithnight as a private and marched to war in 1862. As a result of his abilities, soon recognized by his superiors, he rapidly moved from level to level, so that in December 1864 he was named captain of his battery by Governor Brough. He served in the Army of the Cumberland and the Tennessee under Generals Thomas, Sherman and Grant, taking part in most of the battles and distinguishing himself with his bravery.

On 9 December 1906, in the Sunday supplement of the "Wächter und Anzeiger," Mr. Backus published his fascinating war memoirs, which a meeting of his former comrades after 41 years in Chattanooga, Tennessee, called freshly back to memory. The article, "War Memoirs. Experiences and Observations from the Campaign of the Army of the Cumberland. Essay by Capt. William Backus," which was read with general approval, since they give a particularly lively portrait of exciting battles with a remarkable recall of detail which one might only expect of a professional writer.

After the end of the Civil War he was made a governmental harbor inspector, taking over another governmental position in 1868, that of an inspector of cigars and tobacco for the Internal Revenue Service, a position that was abolished by an act of Congress in 1869.

In 1871 Mr. Backus received the position of municipal market inspector, which he held for several years. He was known until then among his friends as the strictest Republican, and his transfer to the Democratic Party, which he shared with so many others dissatisfied with the dominant Republican Party, aroused considerable attention, and he worked hard to try to elect Horace Greeley as president.

In 1883 he became a member of the city council from the old ninth ward, and in the same year he took considerable interest in the campaign to elect Governor Hoadley.

What made him beloved of his fellow citizens of whatever political party were his loyalty of convictions and the uprightness of his actions, which could never be altered by any pressure. In 1876 he took over the responsible position as manager of the brewery of his brother-in-law, Mr. L. Schwager.

At every opportunity when he could break a lance for the Germans or the common good, Mr. Backus was to be found in the first rank. He is a respected and perennial member of the Social Turner Society, *Harmonie* and other German societies.

The simplicity of his appearance, free from affectations, and his readiness to give advice and help when it is called for, have won him many warm friends in all levels of the population.

Conrad L. Hotze

We cannot avoid listing the lawyer C. L. Hotze, consular agent of the German Empire in Cleveland.

Mr. Hotze was born on 1 September 1839 near Mainz, Rhenish Hessia. He descends from a respected mercantile family and received an excellent education. He attended the *Gymnasium* in Innsbruck, the Tyrol, and later a private school in Wiesbaden. In his later education, which he carried forward without interruption, he went his own way, so that his career of studies was more extensive and longer than most. He passed several years in Paris. Unlike many visiting the French metropolis, he avoided its enjoyments so that he could take mercantile positions, and he used the evenings to take scholarly courses and pursue his studies. Doing this, he took the direction of an autodidact, which he continued until he had reached his goal. After his period in Paris, he visited his brother Peter Hotze in Little Rock, Arkansas, in 1860, with no more expectation than to make the visit and then go home. But the country and its conditions so appealed to him that he stayed. He pursued rigorous studies, and at the same time he was a support to his brother. In 1864 he was taken on as a teacher of history, French and physics in the Hughes High School in Cincinnati. His reputation as a teacher of extraordinary training and ability, which is what he proved to be, soon reached Cleveland, and in 1867 two members of the local school board called him to Cleveland to teach chemistry and physics at Central High School. Many would have been happy as professor of these two subjects for life, but Professor Hotze was ready for even more education, and after studying jurisprudence, composing two textbooks along the way, First lessons in Physiology and First Lessons in Physics, he passed the bar examination in 1878. After this accomplishment, he decided to do his homeland the honor of a visit of five months after an absence of 18 years. Following his return, Mr. Hotze began his career as a lawyer, on 1 January 1879. He soon distinguished himself in this capacity and won many clients.

The rare ability of such a significantly educated man could not fail to draw upon him the attention of circles with an interest in winning such men, and both the Austrian-Hungarian government and the German government turned to him to serve as consul. On the basis of his 25 years as an attorney for the Imperial German consulate in Cincinnati, he was named consular agent in Cleveland on 4 October 1906 with approval of the German Imperial Chancellor. Whoever comes into contact with Mr. Hotze in this official capacity will confirm that no one is more friendly or readier to help with advice and deed than Mr. Hotze, who has the highest respect in those circles which have come to know him over the years.

In 1882 Mr. Hotze married Linda, the highly-educated eldest daughter of Judge J. B. Stallo of Cincinnati. The marriage was very happy, but it only lasted 8 years, since Mrs. Hotze died in 1889. A widower since this time, Mr. Hotze, who is not far from the age of 70, remains physically and mentally fresh and elastic like a man in his best years. The office of the lawyer C. L. Hotze is located at 434-435 Williamson Building, corner of Public Square and Euclid Avenue.

Franz Edward Cudell

Among the number of Germans who have left a memorial of their ability and labor before the eyes of Cleveland in an immutable and palpable form, the architect F. E. Cudell rises as an example.

Born on 11 May 1844 in Herzogenrath near Aachen, educated in his home town and at the technical college in Aachen, Cudell came to America in 1866. He immediately found employment in New York with the noted architect Eiblitz, but he moved to Cleveland the next year and has remained here ever since. At first he was also active here as a draftsman, but he established himself independently in 1871. The first time the city became aware of him also made his reputation, which was in the erection of the triumphal arch on the Square for the victory celebration in 1871. The Haltnorth Block, the Odd-Fellows-Hall on the West Side, the Jewish Orphanage, the Excelsior Club, the Perry-Payne Building, the McBride Bros. Building, the Worthington Block, Blockman Block, the Freemasons' Temple, the Germania Hall, St. Joseph's Church, Church of Christ, St. Stephen's Church, and many other prominent buildings have had in Franz Cudell their spiritual creator and building master, and they stand as a row of witnesses of the architectural art placed in the service of America by German schools.

Cudell withdrew from architecture in 1890 to dedicate himself to the manufacture of the "sewer traps" he had invented, and since then this has been his main concern. He also laid out Müller Avenue and Cudell Street, named after him, in the West Side. He is also invested in Wachsmann Malting Co., whose establishment he leads.

To the present day Cudell has the strongest interest in all public activities, and he is not only one of the primary supporters of the Group Plan, he drafted a plan for it which is regarded as the most practical and beautiful by those technically qualified. Although Cudell has invested considerable money for the achievement of this plan, his designs have not received their deserved adoption.

Mr. Cudell has been twice married. His first wife, Marie née Hessenmüller, died in 1887, and after her death he married Emma Müller, the daughter of the pioneer and former Lieutenant Governor Jacob Müller.

Mr. Cudell has lived for years in the earlier Governor Müller mansion on the West Side.

Ernst J. Siller

Mr. Ernst J. Siller is an outstanding promoter of Germans, and as the president of the Weideman Co. he numbers among the most important burghers in the city.

Born on 19 May 1847 in Hattenhofen, Württemberg, he attended the schools in his home place as well as those in Kirchheim bei Teck. He then committed himself to the mercantile career, receiving a position as a commission salesman in the noted ironware dealership of Nopper in Stuttgart, where he remained for a year and a half. Then the awakened sense of the young man moved him to the larger world, and in 1866 he chose America as his second homeland.

He found his first occupation in Canal Dover, Ohio. In 1868, two years after arriving in the country, he settled in the city of Cleveland, which has been his home ever since. He also remained true to his business all the years he has been here, the same business he entered on arrival and within which he has risen step by step. In those days the company was called Weideman-Tiedemann & Kent. It was already a wholesale grocery business, and he began as a porter. After only 4 months he was promoted to the office, and 4 months later he held the position of bookkeeper. His energy and talent made him ever more effective, so that on 1 July

1874 he entered into the business as an associate. When the company was transformed into a stock company in 1899 [1885?], it was only natural that no one but Mr. Siller be treasurer, and he continued as such until the death of Mr. Weideman in 1900, when he became president of the company, the position he holds to the present day.

Mr. Siller undertook extensive travels, both professional and for his recreation and to expand his personal knowledge of the world. So, for example, he visited China and Japan, the Philippines and India. His library is certainly one of the largest private libraries in Cleveland, a proof that this man, who rose from the bottom to the top of the commercial world still has a need to keep himself at the heights of the knowledge of his time.

Siller is an outspoken character with significant energy and a stubborn nature peculiar to German blood. In the view of all dealing with him in business or personally, he has penetrating understanding, uniting foresight, prudence and breadth. Without these he would not have come so far. On top of this he has a broad heart and humanity which is not falsified. Although he does not deal directly in public life, he still thinks in social terms, and a guest finds great help from him. Whoever has obtained his friendship and proved worthy of it possesses it for the long haul and without restriction. Much Siller has done to support public efforts is not known and shall never be known, for he is no friend of notoriety.

It should be stressed that the realization of the recently-dedicated Schiller-Goethe Memorial in Wade Park began with his efforts. He was elected president of the Goethe-Schiller-Society, and as such he brought the matter underway and led it from the outset.

He was not present at the dedication, since he was stricken by an illness contracted during a visit to his old homeland, which delayed his return.

Mr. Siller's services at supporting the Schiller-Goethe Society as president to give Germans a suitable monument were stressed by the press in its treatment of the dedication and were recognized in the most thankful way.

Dr. Martin Friedrich

Dr. Martin Friedrich was born on 11 May 1855 in Listen, district of Klingenbrunn, in Lower Bavaria. His parents were Joseph and Therese Friedrich. In 1867 he entered the Latin School in Passau, and in 1871 the *Gymnasium* there. He graduated in 1875 and then studied philology in Munich. In 1878 he made the acquaintance of Miss Ottilie Bousson of New York and married her. Early the next year he went to Paris to study French literature, working there in the Bibliothèque Nationale Béné Richelieu. In autumn, 1889, he passed via Le Havre to New York, from whence he went to Pennsylvania for his health and lived in the countryside. Here died his dear and true companion in life, who was buried in New York. In 1892 he came to Cleveland to study medicine, passing his examination for the doctorate in 1894. He immediately received a place in City Hospital, but he only remained there until the next year and then returned to Germany.

In Frankfurt a. M. he studied under Ludwig Edinger and under Neusser for further training and his assistant Orthner at the General Hospital in Vienna. Then he attended the Berlin summer course and returned to Paris, where he studied nervous illnesses in the Hôpital La Salpetrière under Dr. la Tourette and skin diseases in the Hospice St. Louis under Fournier. In 1898 he returned to America and settled down as a physician in Cleveland. Since 21 June 1901 he holds the office of the premier health official in the city. Dr. Friedrich is Professor of Internal Medicine in the College for Physicians and Surgeons in Cleveland, a member of the American Medical Association, of the National Association for the Prevention of Tuberculosis, a member of the National Health Association, as well as a member of the Academy of Medicine in Cleveland.

After the loss of his wife, Mr. Friedrich lived for his children alone, who gave him much joy and beautified a lonely existence. These are his son Karl Alfred as well as his daughter Dolly Emily, born in Paris. Both graduated from West High School, and while his daughter heads the household, his son is attending the Case College to study mining engineering.

C. A. Müller

Among the best-known of the German citizens of Cleveland, known not only within a narrow circle according to their business but respected generally, one is certainly Mr. C. A. Müller. He was born on 25 February 1851, at Egenhausen, Bavaria. He attended his father's school until he was 14, when he chose the career of a merchant and apprenticed himself with the merchant Anton Wuerth in Brueckenau, Bavaria. After completing his apprenticeship he entered service as a traveling salesman for Mr. Adolph Kempf in Frankfurt am Main, where he remained until 1871. In May of that year he decided to emigrate and came to the United States, where he stayed for a time with an aunt in Columbus, Ohio. He was employed in Columbus for five years as a traveling salesman in the large cutlery business of the firm Osborne & Kershaw, until he moved to Cleveland in 1876 and settled here permanently. Since arriving here, Mr. Müller has been involved in several commercial enterprises. For 16 years he was in wooden goods of Arnold & Hord, and when the company became a stock company, he became co-owner. He resigned his active role in this company on 1 February 1897, in order to enter the fire-insurance firm of Faulhaber, Müller & Co. This company is incorporated under the laws of the state of Ohio and enjoys a good clientele. The firm provides insurance and real estate services and also retains a notary public. Mr. Müller has always been actively interested in German efforts in this city. On the occasion of the celebration of German Day in 1890 he was vice president and one of the most active members of the arrangements committee. He spared neither time nor money to make these events a success. During the great North American singing festival in 1893 he was a member of the festival committee as well as chair of the quartering committee. Here as well he took up his mission with earnestness and energy, doing everything imaginable for the success of the festival. When the North American Singing League was being reorganized in Pittsburgh, he was elected as a member of the executive committee. Mr. Müller also does not neglect to work ardently for Catholic groups. Fifteen years ago he represented the St. Joseph's Support Society No. 1 of St. Joseph's Church in all the general assemblies of the Central Union of North America. He held for six years the office as president of the Widows' and Orphans' Fund of North America. Bishop Horstmann chose him as a representative of the Catholics of Cleveland to the Catholic Congress, which met at the time of the World Exposition in Chicago. For years he has also been vice president for the state of Ohio representing the Central Union, and he was secretary and then president of the Catholic League of Ohio. As vice president of the Goethe-Schiller Memorial Society, he was a zealous coworker in bringing the monument into being, and he contributed much to making the dedication a success. He presented the monument to the city of Cleveland in the absence of president Siller. It was he who persuaded the Catholic societies to participate in the parade. Mr. Müller is treasurer of the Catholic Federation, to which 67 Catholic societies presently belong. Further, he is a member of the Cleveland Singing Society and its president, member of the Bavarian Support Society No. 2 and member of the Germania Bowling Club.

In 1872 in Columbus he married Miss Rosa Wagenhäuser, born in Rieden, Bavaria, where her father was the teacher. From this happy marriage come five children, four girls and a boy. Mr. Müller owns a lovely family home in the 46th Street S.E., and he enjoys the best of health and general respect.

G. H. Schwan

Judge Georg Heinrich Schwan was born on 27 March 1860. His father, Heinrich Christian Schwan, was the noted Lutheran pastor who was president of the Synod of Missouri, Ohio and Other States, who looked back on a long career. Prior to his emigration to the United States, Pastor Schwan was a Gymnasium teacher, pastor and for years a tutor to a German planter family in Brazil. His wife, Judge Schwan's mother, is the daughter of a German Brazilian planter who came to know his father there, and who still lives as a sturdy old woman.

Judge Schwan is the first German-American to be elected to the important position of Judge of Common Pleas in this city and in Cuyahoga County, and it is a striking proof that German manner and German ability can accomplish something here.

Judge Schwan, in distinction to so many Germans who were born overseas and come here in order to strip off everything German as rapidly as possible, is a model of someone born here who keeps the faith with everything German. Although he has no particular need to, Judge Schwan speaks German at every opportunity. He commands the language like a born German.

G. H. Schwan received his first education in local schools and from his father, higher education at the *Gymnasium* in Fort Wayne and at St. Louis University. After graduating the last school he went into practice as a lawyer. He first entered a public career when he became assistant to the police attorney in 1887. Four years ago he became Police Judge, and since December, 1904, he holds the office of Judge of Common Pleas. He is a Republican.

The fact that Mr. Schwan is one of the most capable and conscientious judges is well known, just as he has shown himself capable of his earlier offices and had a great practice as a private man as well. He was well known and patronized as a German lawyer.

In 1887 he married Miss Flora Schade, and from the marriage came three children, Georg Walther, Flora and Thea. As was the case with himself, these children have also received a true German education, for the mother is also of German origin.

Judge Schwan has the opportunity to bring Germans support and honor in several political societies to which he belongs. The same is true of the East End Men's Chorus, to which he belongs.

Leopold Einstein

When one comes to speak of our German businessmen, one must include Mr. Leopold Einstein, partner in the significant wholesale business of Ullman, Einstein & Co. He holds an outstanding position not only in the business world, but also in social circles. Born on 24 May 1843 in Buchau a. F. in Württemberg, he attended the local *Realschulen* and the preparatory school before apprenticing to a mercantile company. After completing the apprenticeship he became a bookkeeper and later traveling representative. In 1865 he came to America, settling in Youngstown, Ohio, and receiving at once a position with Ullman Bros.. Six months later he was a partner, with the company name altered to Ullman Bros. & Co. Two years later, on 1 January 1868, the company closed there and moved here on Michigan Street, where it quickly bloomed, with a further change of name in 1880 into Ullman, Einstein & Co.

Besides his activities in his own business, Mr. Leopold Einstein has been able to involve himself in many other societies and enterprises. He is one of the directors of Ullman, Philpott

Manufacturing Co.; is director of the Germania Hall Co.; is trustee of the Jewish Old People's Home, and for many years was the director and for a while vice president of the most respected Jewish society in Cleveland, the Excelsior Club. He was earlier vice president of the Willson Avenue Temple, and he belongs to the building and finance committee of the organization. He is a member of the Cleveland Singing Society and of the Germania Turner Society. Further, he is a Freemason and belongs to the financial committee of the North American singing festival held here in 1893. As a wholesale beverage dealer he holds the office of vice president of the State Liquor Dealers Association of Ohio, as well as with the National Liquor Association, and he is also one of the executive officers of the local Wholesale Liquor Dealers Association. He is also a member of the chamber of commerce.

In 1875 he married Miss Bertha Rauh from Dayton, Ohio, born in Germersheim in the Palatinate, who emigrated with her parents as a young girl. The family had three children, two sons, of whom the eldest son is a traveling salesman with the firm. For several years the business has been located in the large building 2222 Fourth Street, opposite the new Market Hall.

Professor Joseph Krug

There is hardly a nobler, but also hardly a more difficult profession than that of a teacher. We entrust to the leadership and care of teachers the most precious thing we have, our children, and we bestow on them the largest part of the mission and future of the country to create useful and honorable members of human society. This is a difficult but also fulfilling duty that unfortunately is too often taken too casually and also too little esteemed. If the Biblical saying, "Many are called, but few are chosen," has application in any area at all, it is among teachers. Dr. Joseph Krug, the noted Cleveland pedagogue, is among those few who have been called, both as a practicing teacher in our schools and through his essays on progressive teaching methods published in the leading pedagogical journals in English as well as German. In these articles he energetically combats stereotyped institutions and stresses the necessity for developing the pupil's intellectual capacity and ability to think. He has distinguished himself in the service of American schools, which has been readily recognized by many seen as authorities.

Dr. Krug was born on 18 June 1848 in Bellamont, Biberach district, Württemberg, where his father ran a notions shop and also held the office of tax collector. Through his twelfth year he attended his local school, and here the ground was prepared and the seed ripened for his later profession.

Mr. Krug speaks even today with love and esteem of his teacher, Mr. Ehrhardt, who was himself a true scholar, a rarity among German village schoolmasters, and whose name was respected in wider circles. His parents had intended Joseph, who early demonstrated great intellectual gifts, for the clergy, and he attended the *Gymnasia* at Biberach and Rottweil. Theological studies turned out not to be his taste, and in addition there were the cost and the young man's desire to dedicate himself to teaching. So he entered the state seminary of the Kingdom of Württemberg and prepared to be a teacher, and he also took a special course in the Deaf and Dumb School. Despite splendid grades, it was not possible for Dr. Krug to get a position as a teacher, as there were no vacancies, so that he took a position as a teacher in the Institution for the Weak-Minded in Mariaberg, where he demonstrated special talent in the deaf-and-dumb division in teaching these unfortunates. In Mariaberg he also met his later wife, who worked as a Kindergarten teacher.

Mr. Krug remained in this institution until 1868. There it soon became too restrictive, and he had prospects of a position in the state institution for the deaf and dumb. But he soon grew tired of waiting and decided to emigrate to America, hoping, like so many others, to find a wider circle in which to work. On 17 September 1868, he landed in New York, stayed there for six weeks, as he was not able to find an adequate position, and he then went to Buffalo. Here he married his bride, who had followed him to America, and through an uncle of his wife, a Mr. Marschall living in Buffalo, he found his first position as a teacher in the Evangelical Protestant St. Paul's Church, commonly called the Burger congregation. The school was attended by between 150 and 200 children, and his duties as teacher were not light. After two years and ten months he followed a call as a teacher to the St. John's Church in North Buffalo.

When the then superintendent of Cleveland public schools, Mr. And. Rickoff, came to Buffalo in 1872 to seek German teachers after the introduction of German to the public schools, Dr. Krug was presented to Mr. Rickoff by the Besser brothers, German booksellers. Rickoff won Krug for the local schools as a teacher. Immediately after his arrival on 8 April 1872, he was installed as a special teacher, teaching in turns at the Sterling and Mayflower schools. In 1877 he received the position of teacher in the German-German department of what was then the East High School. After completion of Central High School, the German-German division was given to Pastor Kimmel, and Dr. Krug took over education in the German-English classes. Later he was named assistant to the principal of Central High School.

After the introduction of the reorganization of the schools required by the Federal Plan, the school superintendant A. Draper made Dr. Krug supervisor of German instruction, which office he held from 1892 to 1895 with outstanding success but which he resigned due to reasons of health. His wish to take up his earlier position at Central High School, which had become vacant, was fulfilled at once, and Dr. Krug is once more engaged as a teacher of German at Central High School. Genuine activity as a teacher is more interesting to him than serving as a supervisor, and he only kept the office for a further year on the pressing request of Mr. Draper. He feels more satisfied in his present activity.

The following is the best proof that Dr. Krug is one of those teachers who completely commit themselves to their profession. First of all, he is a member of the Pedagogical Association of Cleveland, whose constitution he drafted, and he is a member of the Northeastern Ohio Teachers Association, a member of the Society for Modern Languages of the State of Ohio, and the National Education Association of North America. Further, he belongs to the Cleveland Singing Society, he was a member of the Germania Turner Society for 14 years, and he is a member of the Concordia Lodge of German Freemasons.

The articles published by Dr. Krug here and overseas have drawn the the attention of experts to him, and other articles published in newspapers under the pen-name of Pencil Vania show that he can accomplish something outstanding in the literary area. Mr. Krug has also presented numerous, informative lectures in Turner Societies and teachers' organizations.

Four children were born of his happy marriage with Kath. Magdalena Weinhardt, born in Württemberg, three boys and a girl. The oldest son Wm. Heinrich, who studied chemistry and was hired by the federal government in Washington, and who also possessed musical talent, died in 1905 in New York. The second son of Dr. Krug has established himself in New York as a specialist in eye and ear diseases. The sole daughter Emilie is active as a German teacher in Central High School, and the youngest son Franz is still a pupil at Central High School. Dr. Krug is known as a conscientious, finely trained, modest citizen, and he enjoys the respect of his fellow citizens and the esteem of all of those privileged to grow under his tutelage.

Emil Ring

Emil Ring is a German-Austrian, born at Teschen on the Elbe in the lovely region of the Saxon Switzerland. After attending the local *Volksschule*, he began developing his musical talents. At the age of 11 he was taken into the Royal Court Chapel Boys' Institute in Dresden, where along with *Gymnasium* courses he committed himself with full zeal to music under the leadership of the Court Chapel Master Karl Krebs and the composer Edmund Kretschmer. After three years he went to the conservatory in Prague, finishing a six-year course in 4 years, and he was regarded as a model student, graduating with honors. As a one-year volunteer he performed his military duty in the Austro-Hungarian army, passing the officer's examination and becoming a reserve lieutenant. As a member of the Mansfeld Chapel in Dresden he came to know Holland and much of Germany, spent a summer in England and was two years as a solo horn player in the Conzerthaus Orchestra in Berlin. There he received a call to the Boston Symphony Orchestra, and as a result he set foot on American soil in March, 1887. In 1888 the Philharmonic Orchestra in Cleveland called him as director, and since then he has lived in Cleveland. His ten years as director of the Cleveland Singing Society have been praiseworthy, particularly his great concerts, such as the performance of Hoffmann's *Fairy Tales of Fair Melusine*, Bruch's *Fritjof*, and *Cross of Fire*, Krug-Waldsee's *King Rother*, Hegar's *Manasse*, Bruch's *Glocke*, Mozart, *Requiem*, Rheinberger's *Christophorus*, and others remain in the memory.

The 27th Singing Festival of the North American Singing League, which took place in Cleveland in 1893, was under his musical direction. Mr. Ring also serves as a teacher of the Musical Conservatory, and he is the singing teacher at the Jewish Orphanage. In the Order of Freemasons, Mr. Ring holds a prominent position, and he is also a member of various other social societies.

In 1898 Mr. Ring married Miss Edith Bohm, daughter of the noted Justice of the Peace Bohm.

Mr. Ring is not only at home in the region of music, but also well grounded in the sciences and very well read. His library is one of the best private libraries in the city.

Thomas P. Schmidt

Mr. Thomas P. Schmidt was born here on 8 October 1874 as the son of the late Mr. Gustav Schmidt. His father was in partnership with the late Lieutenant Governor of Ohio, Mr. Jacob Mueller, in the noted legal firm, Mueller & Schmidt. The two men were also related by blood, insofar as Thomas P. Schmidt was the nephew of Mueller.

Thomas P. Schmidt is thus the descendent of a high-ranking Forty-Eighter, now all passed away, as is the case with the old pioneers of our city, whose ranks grow ever thinner. The noted Hans Thieme was also an uncle.

Thomas P. Schmidt received his education first of all in the grammar school, then the high school and lastly the University of Michigan, from which he passed the bar in both Michigan and Ohio. He began his law practice under his father and his uncle. Several years later an illness and increased business obligations compelled him to suspend his activities at Mueller & Schmidt, and when he resumed practice in 1903 it was as a partner of the noted lawyer E. L. Hessenmueller.

Without doubt Thomas P. Schmidt is one of the most active young men playing a role in the life of the city. He is director of the Forest City Street Railway Co. (known as the "three-fer"), president of the Cleveland Chamber of Industry and also one of the directors of Depositors' Savings & Trust Co.

In autumn, 1905, he was elected into the state senate on the Democratic ticket, as part of a "Reform and anti-Boss" campaign, and he was one of the youngest if not the youngest members of the senate. His brilliant qualities immediately made him a power in the legislature, and his personality stood out in the sessions. He showed himself to be a capable speaker, promoting a political program with a broad basis, but also as a decided enemy of corruption and abuse of privilege. The result was that when the senate named a committee to investigate political misdeeds in Cincinnati and Hamilton County, he became not just a member but the secretary. It is well known how capably and with what astonishing results the investigations proceeded. In view of his stunning political debut, Thomas P. Schmidt may be predicted to have more important political roles in the future.

Mr. Thomas P. Schmidt is a member of various German societies and associations, and hence a shining example for other descendents of immigrant Germans, who unfortunately often do not follow the ideals of their fathers in remaining as true to German education and German efforts as he has, who has joined in the social life of the Germans.

On 10 October 1906 Mr. Schmidt married the daughter of Hermann Mueller, also one of the older respected German citizens of this city.

Charles W. Maedje

Mr. Charles W. Maedje, the present leader of the _Wächter am Erie,_ was born on 30 July 1856 to German parents in Cleveland. He received his first education in the Salinski private school, as well as in the German Free Men's school, after which he attended public school. After a year in high school, he applied himself to the career of a merchant. He found a position as entry clerk in 1873 with the wholesale notion business of the firm of M. Halle & Co. in Water Street, which post he gave up within a year in order to work as a helper and courier in the Cleveland _Anzeiger._ Thanks to his gifts, he quickly moved to cashier and bookkeeper. Later he took over the advertising agency of the business and when the _Anzeiger_ Publishing Co. was incorporated, he became secretary of the company. He remained with the _Anzeiger_ until 1889. In October of that year, he obtained the controlling majority of the stock of the _Wächter am Erie_ Publishing Co., reorganizing it and becoming its manager and president. Through his great business experience, the _Wächter_ soon took on new life. With its amalgamation with the _Anzeiger_ in 1893, under the title of German Consolidated Newspaper Co., he was elected the technical and business manager of the enterprise, which position he still carries on with undoubted success. He was also secretary for years of the Cleveland Singing Society, and once its president. He is still a member, as well as a member of the Germania Turner Society, the German-American Club and the Chamber of Commerce. During the last singers' festival of the North American Singing League in our city, Mr. Maedje was one of the liveliest and most zealous officials as controller of finances. He has always remained true to his mother tongue, and in him German activities have a zealous and upright spokesman and promoter. In 1888 he married Miss Emma Heimerdinger, and the marriage has produced three children, two daughters, Irma, 17, and Hildegarde, 7, and a son, Carl, 12. In April, 1898, he went to Europe for several months to get acquainted with the various political and social institutions of Europe through his own experience.

Edward Belz

The genial and personally amiable Mr. Edward Belz, secretary of the most important abstract company in this city, was born on 23 December 1844 in the town of Philippsburg, Grand Duchy of Baden. In its time Philippsburg was a federal fortress, and it was bombarded by the French in 1799. The house in which the Belz family grew up was one of the few to survive that bombardment. Only one extraordinary episode deserves to be mentioned. A plow standing before the house was struck by a French shell, and half the plow was thrown onto the roof by the explosion. The owner left it there as a remembrance, and it was not removed for 30 years. During his childhood Mr. Belz attended all the classes of the school of his native town and obtained a rather solid education. After leaving school at the age of 18, he helped his father Heinrich Belz, Sr., who worked the land. Then he entered the Philippsburg district auditor's office as a scrivener, but later moved to Bruchsal, where he passed the actuary examination.

From Bruchsal he went to Rastatt, functioning from 1866 to 1867 as an actuary in the police office; then went to Freiburg, serving in the district court, then to Gernsbach, where he held the office of district actuary from 1869 to 1872. The salaries then paid to actuaries in Baden were not high, so Mr. Belz decided to seek America's hospitable fields as a better theater of operations. So he arrived in the United States in December 1872 and settled in Cleveland. Soon after his arrival he managed to receive a position as scrivener in the office of Justice of the Peace Kolbe, which he held from 1873 to 1874. After the end of the Mr. Kolbe's term in office he entered the office of the abstract company of Cozad, Thomson & Co. and worked for a time.

Belz did not find the longed-for improvement of his situation, and it got worse, for America was no longer the land once described in the old fatherland where one only had to bend over to pick up the dollar bills off the pavement. He had very hard times. But even under the worst of circumstances, he did not allow his wings to hang useless. His good humor and his young hopefulness still kept him in the sunny air that an inborn genius keeps as a means of surviving any problems. And the wings did indeed swing cheerily and with powerful, self-assured intensity. He made a decision and became a subscription collector for the *Anzeiger*, but even this was not enough, and he took -- even today he trembles when he thinks of it -- a position as a sub-agent for the life insurance agency of Goldman and Jankau.

Yet all had an end, and Mr. Belz finally managed in 1877 to find his place that suited his talents. He dedicated himself to examining the legal titles for landed property, and his inborn precision, which is called for in the examination of legal titles, made him an expert in his specialty. Today he holds the title of secretary of the abstract stock company, The Cozad, Belz & Yates Abstract Co.

On 3 July 1882 Mr. Belz married Mrs. Matilda Fish, née Wicken, who died on 21 January 1904. He married again on 26 December 1904 with Miss Bertha Friederika Schlossstein of St. Louis, and his married life is, as was the case with his first wife, the happiest imaginable.

At the beginning of the 1880s Mr. Belz was secretary of the United Singers of Cleveland, and he loves to look back on his activities then with pride. On the approach of the Singing Festival of 1881 he created the plan with Mr. Jacob Mueller to have a preparatory festival in Cleveland, drawing in the singing societies from surrounding towns. Haltnorth's Garden teemed that splendid summer Sunday with the singing brethren and their friends, and the success was not just a matter of song but also financial, so that the profits could send all the Cleveland singers to Chicago without their having to pay a cent from their own pockets.

At the burial of President Garfield it was once more Belz who suggested that the United Singers march from the Square to the Lake View Cemetery, where they were given a place of honor, singing the impressive *Integer Vitae*, which did not fail to reflect credit on German-Americans.

Mr. Belz stood for election in 1894 and 1900 as a candidate for County Recorder on the Democratic ticket. He ran considerably ahead of the ticket in both elections, but he lost to overwhelming public sentiments in the other direction. That was bad enough that Mr. Belz declared himself happy to spend the rest of his life inspecting legal titles. It is the wish of his every German countryman that this life be a long one, and it is shared by a circle of friends consisting of more than his countrymen.

Ernst Königslow

Among the citizens of the city who have honorably won a name of importance and respect, who have known how to combine idealistic efforts with industrial ability and to obtain a position of social popularity, Mr. E. Königslow belongs in the first rank. He, the son of the famous pioneer H. Königslow, from an old Danish family, was born in Cleveland in 1852 and went with his father to Germany in 1860, where the father built a machine factory where the young Kšnigslow received his technical training. After attending several German schools and receiving theoretical training, he came back to Cleveland in 1870, working first as a bookkeeper, and later establishing himself by creating an industrial specialty of his own. The success of his undertaking shows that he did not deceive himself.

It was opened in 1890, undertaking to prepare and produce small metal wares, machines, stamps and forms from models for inventors and patented articles. The number of articles manufactured by him, and their variety is so great that there is no room to describe them. Thus, for example, almost all the small savings banks large banks distribute are produced by Königslow Stamping & Tool Works. The variety of things produced is enormous, and the company receives orders from all parts of the country, for tree sheers in California, sheep chutes in Montana, patented hammers and can openers from Connecticut and the New England states, etc. The factory employs 50 workers and is in continual expansion.

Mr. Ernst Königslow earlier took an intense part in idealistic efforts. He was a member of the Casino, and when the "Frohsinn," one of the most accomplished singing societies Cleveland ever had, came into being in 1879, he joined it, and he was its president for several terms. His open, free sense, his jovial nature, his enthusiasm for art and science, and his efforts for the intellectual efforts of our times are so well known that it is not necessary to enumerate them.

Jacob B. Wieber

Mr. Jacob B. Wieber, founder of the most important local clothing business, who died here in 1870, was one of the old and respected German pioneers of Cleveland. He was born on 18 March 1835 in Friesenheim, Grand Duchy of Baden. He was apprenticed as a tailor and emigrated to America in 1854, settling in Cleveland. From 1855 to 1859 Wieber worked for the tailor business of Moley at the corner of Pearl and Detroit Streets, then established himself by buying the business from his earlier employers and creating his business house on Detroit Street in 1862, where his palatial building now stands. In 1856 Mr. Wieber married Miss Solonsa Zipf, who was born on 18 November 1836 in Friesenheim, Mr. Wieber's place of birth, and who came to Cleveland in 1854. Five children came from this marriage, of whom a boy died in infancy. The other children are Carl L. J., Mrs. Ludwig Keiper, Mrs.ÊAlbert May, and the late Mrs. Joseph G. McClurg, who died in 1903. Mrs. Saloma Wieber, born Zipf, was born on 18 November 1836 in Friesenheim, at Mr. Wieber's birthplace, and came to Cleveland in 1854. After the death of her husband the amazing and capable businesswoman kept the business going for 20 years with visible success. Now Mrs. Wieber lives in turn with her various children, and despite her advanced age is very active and competent. She was one of the first residents of the Altenheim, and she is very generous and helpful to the poor. She is not only deeply beloved and respected by her children and relations, but also by a wider circle of friends.

Carl L. F. Wieber

The sole son of Mr. Jacob B. Wieber was born on 15 February 1861, in Cleveland. He attended the German school of the Stempel congregation until he was 13, then the Spencerian Business College. After graduating he entered the tailoring business established by his father, which was being run by his mother. His father died when Carl was only nine. Aware and intelligent, Carl soon became a talented and reliable support for his esteemed mother, and he learned the business in all its branches. Since 1888, Mr. Carl L. F. Wieber has been the sole owner of the huge custom tailoring business. Under his leadership it has enjoyed a great increase, so that it is regarded as the leading tailoring business not only in Cleveland, but in the entire West. On 8 January 1889, Mr. Wieber married Miss Martha E. Dietz, daughter of the old pioneer Mr. Geo. Dietz. From this happy marriage have come three children, a son and two daughters.

Despite the fact that, the enormous establishment of Mr. Wieber demands much time and attention, 100 persons are continually employed, Mr. Wieber also gives considerable attention to various other enterprises. He is president of the Detroit Street Investment Co., director of the Forest City Savings Bank Co., and director of the Detroit Street Savings & Loan Co. Mr. Wieber is a member of the Halcyon Lodge F. and A. M; Thatcher Chapter; and Forest City Commandery, as well as the Shriners. Further, Mr. Wieber is a member of the chamber of commerce and of the German-American Club.

Mr. Wieber lives in a splendid home in Lake Avenue and enjoys the respect of a great circle of acquaintances.

J. P. Urban

J. P. Urban was born on 8 February 1839 in Ungstein near Dürkheim a. d. Haardt, Rhenish Palatinate, and he came to Cleveland as a boy in 1847. Here he attended the public and private schools, and after the end of school took an apprenticeship with a pharmacist. The fact that he found a profession suited to his inclinations is shown by the fact that he remains with it to the present day. For years he has headed the well-stocked pharmacy located at 58-60 Ontario Street.

At the outbreak of the War of Secession Mr. Urban volunteered to defend his adopted fatherland, and he entered the heavy artillery, in whose ranks he spent the entire war.

Taking a practical part in public life, he was twice elected by the Republican Party as police commissioner, from 1884 to 1886, with a large majority, and he held this office with general satisfaction.

Mr. Urban has always preserved his German character despite immigrating as a boy and receiving an entirely American education.

After passing sixty years on American soil, the old man enjoys the greatest respect among the seniors of the German-Americans.

Mr. Urban married Miss Hattie Thomson in 1864. He had as much happiness in this marriage as he has had success in public and business life.

A. F. Salzer

One of the grandest successes in the tailoring, fashion and men's haberdashery branch is that of Alois Ferdinand Salzer, since no fewer than three shops of this branch were created by him in Cleveland, the first at 973 Woodland Avenue, the second at 637 Willson Avenue, and the third at 8811-8813 Quincy Avenue, all three with the largest circle of customers.

Hard work and persistence, thorough knowledge of his specialty, an open sense for business, an entrepreneurial spirit and a good manner are qualities which have made A. F. Salzer a success.

Born in Prague in 1845, he came to Cleveland in 1867 at the age of 22 to Cleveland and worked his way up in his business step by step. The result of his ability and labor lies congealed in his three shops, which he owns and whose operations he leads with youthful energy and freshness despite his sixty years. Mr. Salzer speaks English, Czech and German.

Along with his businesses, Mr. Salzer also founded a flourishing household. He married in 1874 with Miss Settchen Hassmer, daughter of an old German pioneer family, producing four children, two sons and two daughters, all of which have married.

Further, this entrepreneurial and successful businessman and fortunate father of the family takes an intense interest in society life, is a member of the Concordia Lodge of the Freemasons, of the Harugari, of the German Mutual Support Society, of the Knights of Pythias, an active member of the Goethe and Schiller Society, and there has been no undertaking worthy of support which he has not aided.

So Mr. A. F. Salzer is in the first rank of those men to which the Germans of Cleveland may point with pride, both as promoters of trade and exchange in the city and as outstanding participants in its expansion. They are also among our fellow German speakers and compatriots who are called to win local German life for themselves and raise it in estimation.

Otto F. Schmidt

Mr. Otto F. Schmidt is one of those Germans who are the real pioneers of German culture in this country and of which the Germans here may be proud. He was born on 8 April 1869 in Apolda, a factory town in Saxony-Weimar, famous for its weaving and knitted-goods industry. The young Schmidt dedicated himself to the latter branch of production after the completion of his schooling. He studied knitting in his home town, and then he went to Berlin to work for two further years and attend technical school. From Berlin he went as a relatively young man as work master in one of the largest knitting goods factories in Vienna. Thoroughly trained in all the area of knitting, he came to America in 1892. At first he resided in Philadelphia and visited the largest cities of America, including Cleveland. Here he sought to introduce the shawl industry, producing this article by machine. But then came the crisis year of 1893 and Schmidt let the matter slide, going to Chicago, attending the exhibition and staying there until the following year. Then he returned to Cleveland, causing the knitting industry to bloom, spreading from Cleveland to the entire country, with a current market of several million dollars. What French Protestants were in Germany, who fled there after the revocation of the Edict of Nantes, bringing the knitting industry with them, Otto F. Schmidt was to the United States. Next he worked for years with the company of Friedmann & Co., which produced the first true shawls. In 1896 Schmidt and two capable traveling salesmen of that company created the N. J. Rich & Co., which produced all varieties of knitted goods with phenomenal success. Mr. Schmidt quickly saw with his insight that another field in his branch was as yet unoccupied, which was the production of fancy wares, which led to the creation in 1901 of the Standard Knitting Co. to fill this gap. The company, whose president is Mr. Schmidt, was incorporated with a stock capital of $25,000, with 80% of the capital in his hands. The company had such success producing these fashionable wares that after the passage of only 6 years they need the immense Hercules Building for production and offices, employing over 100 persons with a turnover of $300,000 and an outstanding reputation in the United States. The success is due to Mr. Schmidt, since he produces all the models. The various machines, both in the N. J. Rich & Co. and the Standard, are produced in Germany by the company Adolph LŠtsch & Co., of which Mr. Schmidt is a primary owner.

With all his extensive interests, Mr. Schmidt still finds time to give his attention to idealistic undertakings. He is an ardent promoter of gymnastics and a member of the Germania Turners, the Cleveland Singing Society and other societies. Mr. Schmidt has been married since 10 November 1897 with Miss Martha Thšme, which has produced a daughter, now in her seventh year.

F. W. Stecher

F. W. Stecher is one of the most successful inventors in Cleveland. His invention does not lie in the area of industry but of pharmacy. After long studies and experiments, Mr. Stecher succeeded in making a preparation which aids the skin and which was given the name of "Pompeian Massage Cream." The preparation has a double value of making the skin soft and healthy while nourishing it. Everyone today is convinced of the importance of skin and its right function and health as the most important organ of the body, and the cases are many where complaints of every sort are resolved as if by magic when adequate attention is paid the skin, permitting it to function and to relieve the internal organs, restoring them to their natural function. Stecher's invention is hence of the highest medical value, deserving to be more widely known. Pompeian Massage Cream has already reached the world market, and it is used in the furthest corners of the world. It is no less esteemed in the place of its invention, subverting the old saying that a prophet is without honor in his own land, in that everywhere in Cleveland, wherever rational skin care is being done, similar preparations are used, including the inevitable imitations. The inventor of course keeps the formula for Pompeian Massage Cream to himself.

Mr. F. W. Stecher was born to German parents in this city, and he began as a modest pharmacist. Today he employs a large number of persons in his establishment, at the corner of Prospect and Third Street, and his product is sent to all parts of the world in large amounts.

Max Alexander Silz

An undertaking worth the sweat of the noblest, and which will in fact demand it, has been taken on by Max Alexander Silz, and for this reason he is to be raised to the top. Silz is secretary of the German School Society, which has made it his duty and which came to life to protect the German language, the highest of all goods, against the nativist and anti-German, and to win its proper place, its full recognition and its proper teaching in our public schools through the application of united German power. The fact that Silz took on this job shows that he has a zeal for a just cause and is worthy of the thanks and recognition of every German, even worthy of the respect of his enemies. This is all the more so in view of the fact that he sacrifices his free time, and that he does not expect much pay for the effort. Max Silz has long been known as an active singer in all singing societies, as a Turner in all the Turner Societies for some time, for he has been a singer and a Turner almost as long as he has been in Cleveland, which is 16 years. Otherwise, his natural modesty does not allow him to go before the public, though he was always enthused for the interests of Germans and for progress, but he preferred to work in the background. Max A. Silz was born in Berlin on 10 April 1869 as the son of a long-time citizen, Friedrich Adolph Silz, and he was educated in the best Berlin schools. At first committed to a different profession, as a result of the sudden loss of his father as well as of property, he was thrown on his own at the age of 14. He found support as a worker, which supported him for four long years. After surviving this, he undertook to wander, and on foot he walked through northern Germany, the Rhineland, Hessia and South Germany, working all the way. In Gšppingen, in lovely Swabia, he had to do military service, and this sent him to Ulm on the blue Danube, where he served in Dragoon Regiment no. 26. As a result of his good education he was able to be assigned to the regimental chancery, and he had the further good fortune to meet and fall in love with his present wife, Miss Frida Lieb from Gaildorf in Württemberg, who was then serving as an educator of the children of his commander. After the completion of his military service he had her come to Berlin, and in 1890 they formed the bond for life. A year later the Old World had grown too small for them, and they shipped off for the their new homeland and moved to Cleveland. This happy marriage has produced two children, Hertha and Walter. As already mentioned, Mr. Silz is a Turner and a singer. In the Social Turner Society, where he is still an active member, he had made a name for himself organizing large presentations. It is certainly less well known that he was for four years the national secretary of a workers' organization and at the same time the editor and publisher of its central organ, *"Volks-Anwalt,"* a social-political weekly which once appeared here, which he led through the panics of the 1890s until he gave it up to save his health, since he pursued it alongside his work as a pattern maker.

Mr. Silz works even today as a pattern maker. The office of secretary of the German School Society was taken up by him with great readiness, since he saw its creation as the means to unite the divided Germans under one flag "due to necessity and not due to their own inclinations." Mr. Silz has been enthusiastic about this undertaking. It will take notoriously long and only in the face of mortal peril that the German lion will awaken. Mr. Silz has undergone considerable preparation in his earlier organizing activities. Possessed from birth with the courage of a lion, he is entirely the man to bring actions underway at a time when the existence of German in our schools is in question, and which we should demand in view of German rights and as a recognition of our services.

Rudolph Albrecht Küpfer

Mr. R. A. Küpfer was born on 15 September 1857 in beautiful Switzerland, in the capital city of Bern. Mr. Küpfer passed his youth in his home town. He attended the Realschule and as an intelligent and capable pupil he obtained the knowledge which prepared him for his profession, which was mercantile. He had already developed in his profession to some degree when his homeland became too narrow for him, and he bad his home town of Bern farewell along with the shimmering Alps and the green pastures of Switzerland in July, 1881, and passed over land and sea to the promised land of the United States. Choosing Cleveland as his destination, Mr. Küpfer had connections with compatriots and a job in the Forest City on the Erie. He was active in several large businesses, in the last instance working for seven years as first bookkeeper in the Gund brewery, before making himself independent as an auditor.

Always a friend of song, Mr. Küpfer joined the Cleveland Singing Society as well as the Society of the United Singers of Cleveland. He also functions as the secretary of the last group. He is also a member of the German-American Central League and its first vice president. The extent of the estimation for Mr. Küpfer's work for Germans is shown by the number of times he is chosen as part of the committee of honor on festive occasions.

Mr. Küpfer married Marie née Märkle on 21 March 1883, and a single child, Pearl G. E., has been born. Mr. Küpfer enjoys general and great respect as an outstanding bookkeeper and ready promoter of German causes, and his open-hearted Swiss manner makes him many steady friends.

Fred. Kohler

There is no dispute that Mr. Fred. Kohler is a self-made man in the truest sense of the word, the man who now sits at the pinnacle of the security of the best-governed city in the country, and he is the right man for the job. This compliment was made to our capable police chief by no less a personage than President Roosevelt, head of the United States, on a visit to Cleveland. Starting from small beginnings as a patrolman, he rose through the conscientious fulfillment of his duty to his present height. Born in Cleveland in 1864, the son of an old respected German pioneer family, he attended our public schools, learning German there, a language which he can speak quite well to the present day. In 1895 he was hired as a patrolman in the office of the police secretary, and in the same year he was made sergeant. In 1896 he became lieutenant, in 1900 captain, and on 20 July 1902 he was promoted to chief of the secret police, and on 2 May 1903 to Police Chief of Cleveland in recognition of his invaluable services as well as because of his outstanding personal qualities. Mr. Kohler holds this high office to the satisfaction of our fellow citizens better and more conscientiously than any other could, or perhaps has ever done. Under his leadership the city has become an imposing metropolis where peace and order are kept and the well-being and security of the citizens are guaranteed in every way.

Rev. Nicolaus Pfeil

Rev. Nicolaus Pfeil, who was named by Bishop Horstmann as permanent rector of St. Peter's, Cleveland Diocese, on 10 May 1897, is a child of Cleveland. He was born on 4 November 1859 on the West Side in his parents' house at the corner of Chatham and Penn Streets. His parents -- his father born in Königheim and his mother in Gissigheim, Frankonian villages in the so-called Taubergrund area -- emigrated from Baden in 1847. He received his first schooling in the school of St. Mary's on Jersey Street. This school, under the pastorship of Rev. Stephan Falk and under the direct control of the Brothers of Mary of Dayton, enjoyed an excellent reputation as an educational institution. With the continuous growth of parishoners, the creation of a new congregation was mandatory. For that reason, at the age of 11 he was moved to St. Stephan's School on Courtland Street, and he remained there until his first communion in 1872. Rev. Pfeil says, "Every day I had to go to school, although the way was very long and the dirt so bad, but I am thankful to my parents even today for that."

In the fall of 1873, the talented young Pfeil was sent along with a younger brother to further training at Canisius College in Buffalo, New York. This institution had been founded a few years before by Jesuit fathers who had been driven out of Germany as a result of the May Laws [during the Kulturkampf of Bismarck against the Catholic Church]. Under the leadership of these intellectual, highly educated teachers, he began classical studies, completed in 1878 with a brilliant exam. This qualified him to be a pupil in the episcopal seminary (St. Mary's

Theological Seminary) on Lake Street in Cleveland. Here he dedicated himself with zeal from 1878 to 1880 to the philosophic study of the scholastic method, under the leadership of the famed writer Father Irenaeus Birnbaum, O. S. F., and his fellow Franciscans, Father Ewaldus Fahle and Bernardus Döbbing. The following three years were dedicated to the study of theology under the leadership of the late Dr. Hecht and the present president of St. Mary's Seminary, Dr. W. A. Moes. Totally prepared for the spiritual order, he was ordained by the Most Reverend Richard Gilmour, D. D., on 1 July 1883.

Rev. Nic. Pfeil held his first position as pastor of St. Patrick's in Hubbard, Trumbull County, Ohio. After seven months of work there he was moved by Bishop Gilmour in February, 1884, to Avon, Lorain County, where he held the pastorate at Trinity Church for 13 years, winning the love and esteem of his congregation in the highest degree as pastor and advisor. They were sorry to see him part from them. His more than ten years as pastor of St. Peter's is seen as entirely successful, and Pastor Pfeil not only the respect of his congregation, but he is extraordinarily beloved and respected by all the nearby Germans.

Pastor Casimir Reichlin

Reverend Casimir Reichlin was born in Steinerberg, a pilgrimage place for St. Ann in the canton of Schwyz, Switzerland, on 16 December 1843. He hardly had any chance to know his parents, a pious, God-fearing pair, since he lost both in his earliest youth. His mother died when he was two and his father when he was five. They left five sons, of which the two youngest entered the clerical order. The other three sons soon followed their parents in death. Already as a boy, the young Casimir Reichlin felt himself drawn to the clergy. In autumn, 1859, he went to Einsiedeln, where he commenced classical studies, but the state of his health compelled him to return home in early 1860. After a severe illness he recovered, and in autumn, 1860, he went to the famous spa of Engelberg in the canton of Unterwalden, a splendidly located high valley in Switzerland at the foot of the Titlis (10,000 feet high), which he chose chiefly out of health concerns. Here he remained in the abbey of Engelberg until 1866, completing his *Gymnasium* studies.

In autumn, 1866, he went to Brieg, an ancient town splendidly located on the Rhône at the foot of the famous Simplon, canton Haute Valais in Switzerland, where he studied theology for a year. About this time the late Bishop Amandus Rapp, the first bishop of this diocese, was in Europe seeking young priests and theologians for his diocese, since there was a great shortage of priests. He held an address in the St. Lucius Seminary in Chur, canton Grisons, at which Casimir's older brother, Leonard Reichlin, decided to emigrate with Bishop Rapp. The eminent bishop of Chur refused permission, and so the seminarian Casimir Reichlin decided to go with Bishop Rapp in his brotherÕs place. For this he applied to Bishop Rapp, who was then staying in Paris, and he announced his intentions in writing. He shipped out of Le Havre on 23 August 1867 on the French steamer "Napoleon III" and arrived in New York on 13 September. He was in Cleveland already on 14 September, where he resumed his studies in the local St. Mary's Seminary.

He received the lower orders from the hand of Bishop Rapp on 8 September 1869; on the 30th of the same month he received consecration as subdeacon and on 1 October 1869 consecration as deacon. He was ordained a priest on 19 April 1870 by the late Bishop Luers of Fort Wayne, Indiana, since Bishop Rapp had gone to Rome.

The newly-made priest celebrated his first mass on Sunday, 21 April 1870,
in St. Peter's here, whose pastor was then the Most Reverend P. Gloden, now pastor of St. John's in Defiance. The new priest then received placement as pastor of the new St. Stephen's Church,

where he celebrated the first mass in the building on 1 May 1870. His further career is closely connected with that congregation. One might add that it is a rarity that a priest and congregation should begin their career together, passing through so many harmonious years together, and to have the opportunity to celebrate the Silver Jubilee together, which was done on 1 May 1895 with imposing festivities.

Mr. Reichlin distinguishes himself through his excellent culture and his commitment to Christian love, his conciliatory attitude to those of different faiths, which secures him respect and love among all coming into contact with him.

Pastor Erich Becker

Pastor Erich Becker was born on 23 January 1864 in Danzig, capital city of West Prussia in Germany, the eldest son of the pharmacist Paul Becker. He attended the Gynasiums in Danzig and later in Königsberg in Prussia, in the latter of which he took his graduation examination, after which he went to Kiel to study machine engineering in the Imperial German Navy. A financial misfortune which devoured the greater portion of his father's property forced him to give up his studies and ripened in him the decision to go to America, in order to stand on his own feet as quickly as possible.

His deficit of knowledge of English and his complete lack of any connections in America hindered the young man's advancement. Still, he did not give up, and he went straight ahead anyway, so that after four weeks he could renounce any further support from home. For more than a year he struggled for existence through hard but honest toil, until he came into touch with theological circles which moved him to dedicate himself to the study of theology. After a successful examination, he was formally ordained a minister in the German Evangelical Protestant Smithfield Church in Pittsburgh, Pennsylvania, and he was called at once to the Evangelical Protestant congregation in Tarentum, Pennsylvania. After serving several smaller congregations with great success, he was elected unanimously from seven candidates by the large German St. Paul's Church in Belleville, Illinois, near St. Louis, Missouri, which he brought to unparalleled prosperity in 5 1/2 years of conscientious effort. For climatic reasons and because he had always wanted to work there, he followed the call issued in autumn, 1905, by the local congregation "The Little Bark of Christ." The Belleville congregation was extremely sorry to see him go, and both Belleville and St. Louis papers wrote praises. Pastor Becker has been married to Miss Emma Matthes since 28 October 1891, from the Kingdom of Saxony. Four children ranging in ages from 9 to 15 years are the pride and joy of the family.

Pastor Becker is no friend of narrow-minded efforts as a representative of progressive theology, but his relations to other denominations is entirely friendly, but his position as pastor is independent, and as a person he takes a vital interest in all questions touching Germans in general.

Pastor Becker is very happy in Cleveland, and he hopes that he will be able in the course of time to bring the congregation of the Little Bark of Christ to new prosperity and do his bit to see that German ideals are always treasured in Cleveland.

Rev. J. H. C. Röntgen

Pastor J. H. C. Röntgen, D. D., was born on 19 June 1844, in Elberfeld, Rhenish Prussia as the third of the five children of Ferdinand and Henrietta Röntgen [née Hüser). The mother, Henrietta Catherina Hüser, born 18 January 1806, died on 28 January 1860 in Emmerich on the

Rhine. The father, born on 10 August 1804, in Lennep, Rhenish Province, came with his two children (three had died young) to America in 1872, at first living in his daughter's home, who had married Pastor Julius Grauel, then of Mosel, Wisconsin, and later with his son in La Crosse, Wisconsin, where he died in 1882. Pastor Röntgen at an early age felt the call to be sent as a missionary to Madagascar. He was seized by this conviction when he participated in a gathering of youth in Op Hemert, Holland, and heard Baron Makay, then the prime minister of the Netherlands, speak. His words enflamed him with enthusiasm for missionary service. Yet the way hither was long closed until the Lord cleared the way in 1872 and led him to his desire. On 28 May 1872 he left the old homeland together with his father and sister, and in September of the same year he entered the missionary house at Sheboygan, Wisconsin, to prepare himself as a preacher. Here he studied under professors Mühlmeier, Bossard, Kurz and Rütenick. He graduated there, and on 11 October he was ordained by the Sheboygan district, entering service with a missionary congregation in La Crosse, Wisconsin, leaving there on 2 January, 1883, when the congregation became autonomous.

From La Crosse Pastor Röntgen passed to Cleveland, Ohio, where he received a call from the First Reformed Church. This provided him with a great field of effort and a constant opportunity to prove himself. Alongside his service of a large congregation he was active for years in education within his church. From 1885 to 1892 he was teacher of religion at Calvin College and for years a member of the administration of this school, and he was also for ten years a member of the visitation authority of the theological seminary in the mission house. In June, 1892, he was given the doctoral title by the theological faculty of Franklin & Marshall College in Lancaster, Pennsylvania, in recognition of his theological abilities.

When Christian care of the poor and the sick became a concern in 1892, R. took it upon himself to found a deaconess project for this purpose. It became his favorite project, to which he dedicated a great deal of his time. From very modest beginnings the project developed into ever increased blessings for the suffering. Here he preferred to spend his time and effort. When the work became too much, he laid down his congregational office he had held for 18 years and dedicated himself full time to the deaconess work as superintendent and minister. Conditions compelled him to resign his office on 30 September 1903, which he did with great distress of heart. The Deaconess House in Cleveland is the first of its kind in the Reformed Church and could be called the mother house of the order.

Another activity opened itself to him in the Hungarians without a preacher. They came from the Reformed Church of Hungary. R. came into correspondence with some officials here as well as there, and as a result of his efforts a Hungarian preacher was called here, and it was in his church that the first Hungarian congregation was organized. Since that time there have come to be about 20 or 25 Hungarian congregations in the Reformed Church. Since 1903 R. has taken over the work at the Seventh Reformed Church in Cleveland, where he is happily at work.

Professor Ršntgen married Miss Marie Luise Friederika Walther of Sheboygan, Wisconsin, on 15 December 1874, which marriage was blessed with four children: Louise, Heinrich, Dorothea and Arthur. The first died at the age of 11. Besides these are living his sister, the wife of Rev. J. Grauel, Indianapolis, Indiana, and his sole cousin, Dr. W. C. Röntgen, the professor made famous for his discovery of X-Rays.

The intense interest of Pastor Röntgen for the preservation of the German language and its instruction in the public schools should be mentioned particularly. It is not just that he was one of the first to protest against the suppression of this subjects in the schools, but that he fostered the establishment of the German School Society. He is one of the directors of the society and also holds the office of financial secretary.

Rev. Franz Koloszewski

Rev. Koloszewski is a clergyman tried by the storms, a man who became a priest by his own efforts and who gave autonomy to a flourishing congregation. Born on 5 September 1851 in Elzbietow in Poland as the son of a master builder, he received his first education in the local school, later in the Gymnasium in Siedletz. The family was driven out by war and revolution in 1864. The deep scar on Rev. Koloszewski's face dates from this time and is a momento of the Battle of Kutnow and the blow of a lance received from a cossack. The family was then driven to the Black Sea. With the restoration of more peaceful conditions they returned to Poland. His father fell ill in Warsaw, and Franz was placed with a gardener. When the father recovered, he found a job near Warsaw, and later moved to Ostrow, and it was in Ostrow that Rev. Max became pleased by the voice and nature of the young Franz in his choir and told him he should become a clergyman. Yet he lacked the means. The pastor arranged that Franz could study with him in the evenings, and he worked during the day. Rev. Koloszewski recalls those times even now, when he would stand on the filter at a sugar factory and review his evening studies. That lasted two years, and the reverend would have sent him to Rome for further studies, but a greedy sister who was not fond of Franz would not permit it. Rome never turned out, then. It hurt Franz so badly that he gave up and left. He traveled to Lotz and found a place in a machine factory. After 2 1/2 years he was declared a journeyman. When his father heard this, he was so overjoyed that he came to visit him. Franz worked a further 3/4 year as a machinist journeyman before going on the road and going to Germany. He saw the cities of Berlin, Potsdam, Danzig and Stettin. He was working in the last of these cities when his father emigrated to America in 1873, and they met in Stettin. Franz was supposed to return to Poland to support his mother, which he did.

In the following year, however, Franz emigrated to America himself and joined his father in Cleveland. He found his first employment in Charley Rau's wagon factory on the West Side, later going to Detroit and then to Wisconsin. In Green Bay, with a last piece of bread in his pocket, he entered the Ave Maria Church and fell, exhausted, into a deep sleep. Three times he heard a voice telling him that he would find work where the great chimneys were. After waking up to the voice the third time, he stood up, went to where he saw smokestacks, and there he found a brewery where he found the work his dream had promised him.

With this a new star had arisen on Franz's horizon, and he was soon in the position, after cleaning barrels and caring for machines entrusted to him, to take private instruction after the end of the work day, to study, and above all else to learn English. Once again the desire awoke in him to become a priest, and he determined not to relent until he had reached this goal, which seemed to promise him everything. It cost him great labor and trouble, but that was something the young man did not shy away from. He lived cheerfully and happily in the Green Bay and worked at the brewery until he had mastered the language enough and had gathered the money to return to Cleveland, since it was in Cleveland that he wished to reach his goal. His mother and the rest of the family had by now gathered in Cleveland.

On returning to Cleveland, he became acquainted with Father Kilian at St. Joseph's Church, who had just returned from a journey through Europe and was interested in founding a society for youth. Franz Koloszewski became the first member. At first he earned his support once more at Black's wagon factory on Broadway, and in the evenings he studied with the Franciscan father. Now he had a connection to the clerical world. It was not a full year before he was taken into the cloister, and now he could live and study there in exchange for his labor. In two years he worked through five classes. When he had advanced sufficiently, he was sent to the mother house in Teutopolis near St. Louis. There as well his studies went excellently, and he also found occasion to show his mechanical expertise by making an armoire with 64 doors for the brothers. After finishing the sixth class he returned to Cleveland in keeping with his parents' desire. At that time St. Joseph's Church was consecrated, and Father Kilian presented the promising young man to Bishop Gilmour, who took great interest in him. He was referred to Dr. Quigley, and he referred him to Professor Maal at the priests' seminary on Lake Street, and after passing a thorough examination he was taken into the seminary. The seminary kept him for five years, and then he achieved priestly ordination. That was on 1 July 1883. With his ordination as priest began the efforts of Rev. Koloszewski for which his entire life had been a preparation and for which he was the right man. The hardest struggle lay ahead. The Polish colony in Cleveland then consisted of 45 families, of which barely a dozen were in the area foreseen for a new church, and the others were scattered widely. The church he undertook to found is the present St. Stanislaus Church, the most beautiful in all Ohio, whose decoration cost $150,000. In the course of time the number of families in the area multiplied, which made the construction of the church possible.

The flourishing of the congregation filled clergy with jealousy, and a movement arose against Koloszewski which finally moved him to flee persecution and enmity by going to Syracuse, New York, where he remained for a while, founded a new congregation and built a beautiful church. Other members of the church who supported him wished to have him back, and he finally gave in and returned. But then the old intrigues began once more, and in the end there were trials and even an excommunication of Koloszewski. After the clergy had gone that far, Koloszewski's supporters turned to form a congregation of their own, which numbers no fewer than 600 families. It obtained a fine building lot, 320 by 280 feet, on Fremont Avenue, where they built a new church, the Church of the Immaculate Heart of the Blessed Virgin Mary, surrounded by a pretty park, and next to it a fine house for the brave pastor, who can continue his spiritual work and leisure in undisturbed peace. He is assisted by a capable young clergyman, Andreas Ryczek, who received a theological and philosophical education at the University of Krakow. Besides the church, the congregation owns a cemetery of its own on Marcelline Avenue with an area of 10 acres. That is Koloszewski's work. Although he stresses that he is a Pole, he was long enough in Germany and takes such an intense interest in German efforts, and further the interests of Germans and Poles so closely connected in this country that we give him the place in this book which he deserves.

Adolf Kromer

Professor Adolf Kromer, who holds the important position of teacher at the South Side High School, doing great honor to the German name thereby, and who is always ready to support German causes, was born on 23 June 1861 in Wahlberg in Baden. At first he attended only the Catholic primary school of his place of birth, but he so stood out through hard work and ability that his parents decided to get him a better education. The parents were fortunately able to do this, and he was able to attend the Realschule in Ettenheim and later that in Leipzig.

In 1881-82, after he had chosen to do service for a year as a volunteer, he served King and Country with the Guard Regiment no. 108 in Dresden, though he needn't have, since the next year he emigrated to the New World, the United States, which became his second fatherland. Cleveland was his goal from the outset. To complete his studies, after his arrival he attended the Catholic teachers' seminary in St. Francis near Milwaukee, but after he had finished his studies within a year, he returned to the Forest City, and he has remained here ever since. In February, 1885, he was appointed a teacher in the public schools. After nine years of service, he was promoted to the high schools in recognition of his outstanding education and pedagogical ability in 1894 and placed in South High School, where he has worked without interruption ever since.

Prof. Kromer sees the calling of a conscientious high school teacher to be a responsible profession, and he invests his entire strength to develop the talents of his pupils and to make them capable of later progress.

As mentioned at the outset, Professor Kromer takes a strong part in the promotion of German interests. He rightly regards that as part of his duty, which he has not neglected in the case of his compatriots.

He is one of the most prominent members, as well as a director, of the Schiller-Goethe Memorial Society, and he held the German festival oration at the first spadeful. He is a great orator, and his powerful presentations on that memorable day excited the greatest applause and the highest enthusiasm.

Beyond German circles, Professor Kromer is regarded by his colleagues as well as his pupils as embodying the true character of a teacher. Many pupils retain a fond memory of him long after leaving his classes.

Julius Heinrich Gerlich

Julius Heinrich Gerlich was born the youngest of five sons of the court locksmith and ironwares dealer W. Gerlich (died 1871) on 29 November 1855 in Mainz. He received the best possible education and graduated the Gymnasium in Mainz, and in 1874 after completing his military service as a one-year volunteer he emigrated to America. Soon after his arrival he began his career as a journalist as a reporter for the "*New Yorker Staatszeitung,*" the largest German newspaper in America. In 1881, after several years of work he took a journey through the principal states of Europe, dedicating two years to this. In 1883, on his return to America, he entered the editorial staff of the *"Westliche Post"* in St. Louis, and he was employed there until 1893. Then Mr. Gerlich sought to make himself independent by taking over a weekly newspaper in Stevens Point, Wisconsin, which proved to be a bad financial speculation. In hopes of bettering himself, he bought the weekly in Duluth, but he just went from the frying pan into the fire and suffered significant losses through these undertakings. That was also the reason he gave up the latter newspaper in April, 1901, and took his position here at the *"Wächter und Anzeiger,"* where his journalistic abilities could have full development without financial risk. Besides his activities as a journalist, Mr. Gerlich has also taken a significant role in promoting German interests. He was the first to promote the erection of the Schiller-Goethe Memorial, on the occasion of the meeting held on 7 September 1904 in the Cleveland Singing Society Hall preparing for the Schiller Festival taking place the following year. In the following period he dedicated himself totally until the monument was actually in being, which demanded the best efforts of the friends of Germans.

As a result he was elected to the board of directors of the Schiller-Goethe Memorial Society, taking the demanding job of secretary. As a result he composed a complex and thorough history of the Goethe-Schiller Memorial, with its preludes in the Goethe celebration and the Schiller festival, gathering a plethora of useful historical material along with the proceedings and actions of the Memorial Society.

Since 22 February 1876 Mr. Gerlich is married. He won the hand of Olga Nowakowska, the daughter of Mrs. Fanny S. Jenks, the wife of Prof. John Howe Jenks of Washington University in St. Louis. This happy marriage has produced five children: Elsa, 18; Fannie, 16; Albert, 13; Harry, 11; and Thekla, 4.

Gottlieb Johann Leopold Fecker

Mr. Fecker is one of those Germans in Cleveland who appear little in public, and who are as a result little known, but who do Germans all the more honor in their area of activity.

Little is known even in his own circle of the origin and education of this genius, the main force behind the considerable company of Warner & Swasey, and who could know that the discoverer and constructor of the famous optical and astronomical instruments which go from that company to the observatories of the world is a German?

This ingenious countryman and fellow citizen was born on 23 February in the palace garden in Karlruhe, Baden, the second son of the Grand Duke's chief gardener Leopold Fecker and his wife Karoline née Bacher. At the age of eight, he was sent by his father to the Keifer Private School, where he remained until confirmation. After graduating as the first student, he wished to train as a wood sculptor, but his father's will was stronger, and the boy had to bury his desires and follow his father's desires and become an apprentice in the mathematical-mechanical institute of the court mechanic Karl Sickler. At Easter, 1873, we find him as the best pupil receiving a diploma of honor as the best pupil. Then he attended lectures for a year in experimental physics as a scholarship recipient at the Grand-Ducal Polytechnic under Prof. Sohnke. At Easter, 1874, he was found to have a lung ailment which only responded to the efforts of his mother and of physicians, and he spent two months at the Black Forest clinic in the Kinzig Valley, requiring him to abstain totally from all the pleasures young men require. Only in October was he able to resume. In June, 1875, we find him at the Polytechnic Institute of Starke and Kammerer in Vienna. This institute, with its rich treasures of art, its collection of physics and astronomical instruments, and its meteorological observatory, opened his horizons and showed him how much remained to learn, and he thoroughly studied all these collections in the course of his three years in the Imperial city.

Following the demands of learning, he returned to his homeland and took the position of a project overseer. But this is not what drew him back, but rather the stillness of the forests, of the beautiful palace garden, in which the troubles of the world and the city vanish, and we find him working eleven hours day and night, studying under the leadership of Prof. Dr. K. L. Bauer to learn mathematics, physics, but most of all optics.

During six years of private instruction a mutual reinforcement of theory and practice had the result of the finest new constructions of physical devices which significantly benefited the business, but the turning point came with the moving of the Grand Duke's observatory from Mannheim to Karlsruhe, leading to his acquaintance with its director, Prof. Dr. W. Valentiner.

After completing the erection of the old Steinheil refractor and creating a meridian gauge from Reichenbach, in the course of which the stone pillars erected by the construction office proved unreliable, Prof. Valentiner asked G. Fecker to deal with the matter himself, but only on the condition that he guarantee the pillars. As a result, Fecker worked with masons to build the wall, foundation and pillars, creating the setting for the balance lever himself, winning Prof. Valentiner's enthusiastic support. Thus Valentiner excited Fecker's interest in astronomy. He passed six years in private instruction with these men of science, and there is no doubt they were not the hardest of his life, for his talent developed as a result of his great strength of character. With his study of history, of astronomy and optics, dealing with the biographies of the greatest mechanics, such as Reichenbach and Fraunhofer and their great achievements in creating astronomical instruments, he became ambitious to make the greatest telescopes in the world, so he conceived the idea of travelling the world to apply his unique preparation with an iron will and patience without equal.

His way led him to Wetzlar, where the microscope industry was then centered, and he soon became a participant in what was then still a small industry. During this period small transportable instruments were made to export to England, as well as the great refractor for the Karlsruhe observatory and chronographs for several German observatories. Hundreds of visitors gathered in the cloister garden of the old Imperial city of Wetzlar to marvel at the masterpieces of this young mechanic before they were sent off, and young and old enjoyed marveling at the rings of Saturn through the giant tube.

It was precisely in this period that the inexpensive manufacture of magnesium and aluminum was discovered, and the creation of the first magnesium lamp led to many orders, but the great hopes soon proved in error and the business closed. In July, 1887, he bade farewell to the old homeland and followed a call to Washington to participate in the creation of astronomical instruments, and here again his influence was so positive that he received a diploma at the World Exposition in Chicago on the direct nomination of his superior. It is in this period that his great equants, meridians and ephimerides instruments went from Washington to various observatories, such as to the U. S. Naval Observatory, the Catholic University, the Jesuit University in Georgetown, in Providence, Rhode Island, Denver, Colorado, and even the 20-inch equitorial built for the Spanish in Manila. It was during this period in Washington that Mr. Fecker came to know the director of the Georgetown College Observatory, and it was the time of the creation of the photochronograph by Mr. Fecker.

In August, 1895, Mr. Fecker became superintendent of the astronomical instrument division of Warner & Swasey in Cleveland, which was a fulfillment of his dearest wish to apply his art to the greatest telescopes in the world. In Washington he had made the position micrometer for the 36-inch Lick Telescope, and then for the 40-inch Yerkes Equitorial. Only in Cleveland could his talents unfold fully so that they would either triumph or fail. The most important undertaking was to create a precise calibration for the automatic measuring device in keeping with the demands of both bosses, creating something which is the best possible, and Mr. Fecker resolved the assignment in the briefest time and according to an entirely new method, but also with a precision exceeding the best life's work of the greatest mechanics before him by 57% (report of Prof. Morley).

When one considers that a human eye is not permitted an error of more than six millionths of an inch in work lasting about twelve months, then it is no wonder that Mr. Fecker had to put aside all pleasures for the last two years to recover from the intellectual exhaustion created by this labor and to come back to his old self. One must ask what desire enthused this German soul to exceed efforts which had received the attentions of the finest minds in science for almost a hundred years.

It is easy to see that the finest harmony prevails between messrs. Warner and Swasey and their superintendent. These gentlemen trust him, since they know his work over the years and treasure it, and in the true sense of the word, theirs is a matter of united strength. The complexity and richness of this construction of astronomical instruments is shown by the fact that not just theoretical and mechanical knowledge is demanded, but also experience in optics and clockmaking, since it incorporates all of these. The instruments Mr. Ficker constructed and designed in Washington were presented by his former boss marked "Constructor G. N. SaegmŸller," and Mr. Ficker is amazed that there are people who are not ashamed to puff themselves up with his own ideas.

The extraordinarily fine and precise calibrations achieved in automatic measuring machines have not only fortified the reputation of Warner & Swasey and placed our America in the first rank of manufacturers of the finest measurement equipment for astronomy, the Queen of Sciences, but the U. S. Naval Observatory, which has two of the finest instruments of W. & S. made by Mr. Ficker, has risen to the rank of the first observatory in the world, so that Mr. Ficker has contributed significantly to the promotion of art and science in his adopted fatherland.

In Winter, 1870, the exhausted boy knelt in the snow after working eleven hours, with two hours of study yet to go, and begged his creator to give him strength and health to become one of the finest mechanics, and with the help of God he has made this a fact. He did not pray for wealth, only for strength and health, and he learned on his own. Almost every observatory in America has instruments which have passed through the master's capable hands.

Since large telescopes must follow the daily movements of the stars, the telescopes must be moved from east to west at the same rate as the world moves from west to east. Clever clockwork is necessary to accomplish this so that the telescopes make a circle around the pole once every 24 hours with the same precision as the earth itself, and since the only concern is not only to make small portions of the sky visible but to measure even smaller portions, large telescopes are equipped with a series of marvelous little measuring devices. In order to assure the comfort and precision of observation, even the largest refractors weighing thousands of pounds are provided with the same machinery so that it follows a star steadily, so that one thinks he is looking at a motionless sky.

Mr. Fecker married Miss Emma Boecker, daughter of the court secretary there, on 14 October 1886 in Wetzlar on the Lahn River. A boy has been born of this marriage. Mr. Fecker is a corresponding member of the German Society for Mechanics and Optics of Berlin, and he belongs to the Bavarian Artistic Crafts Society in Munich.

Hermann Anhäusser

Hermann Anhäusser was born on 15 November 1846, at Oberndorf in the Rhenish Palatinate, the only son of a prosperous wine merchant owner of a grain and saw mill, Mr. Georg Anhäusser. In his youth his father sent him to the famous watering place of Kreuznach, Rhenish Prussia, to its noted mercantile school and *Gymnasium*. He certainly did not miss a good education. After his father's death in 1868 the property, which had been passed down within the family for 278 years, passed to the son. Seeking greater success, Anhäusser suffered reverses that finally compelled him to sell his property. For a while he retained the wine trade, but he soon learned that in the old Fatherland, one who has suffered disaster has no other choice to avoid being endlessly belittled, but to shake the dust of the place from his feet. Although a brother-in-law, a Protestant clergyman, wanted to advance him a large sum of money if he would drop his plans, he could not be talked out of a decision once made. Before he took his step he wrote to a prominent German here who was known to him, letting him know of his plans and asking advice. In the most forthcoming and friendly manner, the gentleman in question wrote a long epistle, whose apex was that this country was large, splendid and rich, but that it only had a future for those who had strong hands and good backs, but nothing for those used only to hunting and other pleasures. The last passage was naturally aimed at Anhäusser, as he had never done physical labor of any sort. Mr. Anhäusser did not allow himself to be scared away by this; rather, he said to himself, "If nothing more is needed than strong fists, you have them!" So he emigrated to beautiful America with his wife as a result of a quick decision in 1884. His wife, born Hepp, is from Hamburg. Born in Zweibrücken, she met Anhäusser in Langenkandel, where her father, Mr. Georg Hepp, was an Austrian estate overseer.

Mr. Anhäusser is a man who has traveled the world. Before he came to America he had made extensive journeys to Germany, Switzerland, Italy, Spain and France. Arriving in America rich in experience but poor in money, he went directly to Cleveland, finding a job in the malt house of Hermann Müller & Co. and working two years for this firm. He then became foreman in the Löffler malt house in Massillon, Ohio, where he remained for ten months, returning to Cleveland. He accepted an offer from Mr. Oppmann, then the owner of the Phoenix Brewery, as collector, a position he held until 1900, when he became manager of the brewery. He held that responsible position until 1905. After giving that position up he intended to take a trip back to his old fatherland, but he passed on that plan due to the obligation he had taken up to raise two orphans, girls of the age of 14 and 16. In the first period of his residency here, he sent several essays to the _Kölner Zeitung_ dealing with American conditions that stood out for their fresh humor and biting satire. These were read in Germany with great pleasure.

Mr. Anhäusser has long been a member of the Cleveland Singing Society and of the Social Turner Society.

Simon Hickler

Simon Hickler, the editor of the "_Wächter und Anzeiger_," has held this position since 1896. He came from Milwaukee, where he had been for several years, including four years at the "_Herold_" there, in response to a call. At the "_Herold_" he was both a political reporter and a local editor.

Besides Miwaukee, he was active at various papers in Baltimore and Chicago, at the "_Journal_" in Baltimore and in Chicago at the "_Arbeiterzeitung_," the "_Press_" and the _"Personal Rights Advocate_," the weekly organ of the Personal Rights League. In all of these jobs he distinguished himself. He is an autodidact from head to foot, but he can boast of his knowledge in many fields, but particularly economics and politics, two fields which play a particularly great role in modern life. So far as his capabilities as a journalist, his editorials in the paper speak for themselves. Without exaggeration, one may say that under Mr. S. Hickler the _"Wächter und Anzeiger"_ has become one of the leading German dailies in the United States.

He was originally a merchant, but he shifted professions in America because he had more enjoyment writing in newspapers than in trading. He has been in America since 1881. He came from Gross Gerau, Grand Duchy of Hessia, where he had lived for seven years. He was born on 20 July 1859 in Messel, two hours from Darmstadt, in the same Grand Duchy. Since 1895 he has been married to a German-American born in Milwaukee, the former Miss Gunz, who was a German teacher until her marriage in the public schools of the German Athens. A son has been born to the marriage.

John C. Groll

On 24 August 1894, an old and well-known German pioneer, John C. Groll, died at the age of 65. He was born and raised in Kulmbach, in the Bavarian district of Upper Franconia. As a man with liberal views, he was pulled into the maelstrom of the freedom movement of 1848, and the result was that he had to leave his homeland the next year. He emigrated to the United States and settled in 1854 in Cleveland. In the same year he married Miss Anna Margaretha Schubert, a highly educated lady who had been born in Margenreuth, near Kulmbach, and who had received an extensive musical education in her youth. Four children were born of this happy marriage, of whom three still are living, all of them receiving rich gifts from nature. His son Georg is a talented local drawer and painter. The daughters are Mrs. W. C. Parson and Rita Elandi, the famous singer.

Mr. Groll was owner of the Cleveland Sponging Works at the time of his death, and his departure saddened a considerable circle of friends.

George C. Groll

Among the young Clevelanders who have earned a significant reputation in the art world, one of them is indisputably Mr. George C. Groll, born to German parents here on 2 August 1861.

Already as a student in the Brownell School, he attracted general attention with his talent at drawing, and so after leaving school he entered the noted lithographic institution of W. J. Morgan & Co., corner of Wood and St. Clair Streets, to learn the art of lithography.

In 1889 he made an extensive study trip through Europe, studying under the most important artists in Paris and Holland and visiting various other parts of the European continent to make landscape sketches when there was opportunity, sketches which have received a high rating from connoisseurs. After his return, rich in experiences gathered in the area of art, he reentered the service of W. J. Morgan & Co., and he soon held the office of superintendent of the great lithographic institution. Enthused by rare energy, Mr. Groll, who had done considerable in the area of water colors, had time not only to send works to art exhibits in Chicago and New York, but also sent one or two of his works to local exhibits. Mr. Groll was one of the founders of the Art Club and the society Painters in Water-Colors, and he takes a major role in both of them. He is also a member of the Cleveland Singing Society; the Cleveland City Lodge, F. and A. M.; and the Webb Charters.

Amalie L. Groll

The German-Americans of Cleveland can point with some pride to a very significant phenomenon in music in the person of Miss Amalie L. Groll, known by the stage name of Rita Elandi. She is both a born Clevelander and the daughter of a respected old German pioneer family, Mr. and Mrs. John C. Groll.

Her reputation as the best American singer and prima donna was established beyond a doubt by her performance with the Carl Rosa Opera Co. in England. Her primary success was in her interpretation of Wagnerian roles, and her entire artistic talent appears to be created to perform the most difficult parts of the master's tonal works, demanding extensive and fine voices, passionate acting, warmth of feeling and sovereign bearing.

Miss Groll received her first musical training in the Cincinnati Musical Conservatory, where she managed to win all prizes set by the faculty as a result of her natural artistic and musical gifts. From Cincinnati she went east to extend her studies, and after a brief pause there she passed on to Europe to receive further training under the guidance of the noted artist Marchesi. Marchesi at once recognized the genuinely great talent of the young artist and brought it about that she was allowed to give a concert after only six weeks of study. She made her debut as Gretchen in *Faust*. The success of her debut was phenomenal, and she then made a tour through Italy, Spain and Germany. Not satisfied with the applause and determined to improve her efforts even more, she returned to Paris to develop a musical repertoire with the famous Destrée. The longing to see her homeland again after all the applause for her musical genius caused her to take the role of prima donna in 1893 at the 27th Singing Festival of the North American Singing League. After the conclusion of the festival, she became prima donna in Hinrich's Opera Co., and later in the German Opera under Damrosch. Returning to Paris, she once more studied at the music conservatory under Prof. Duvernoy, then she took the role of dramatic soprano with the Carl Rosa Opera Co. The roles which won her particular applause from the European musical and artistic public were her performances of roles such as Elizabeth in *Tannhäuser*, which stimulated a virtual storm of applause in all the larger cities of England, as well as Elsa in *Lohengrin*, Santuzza in *Cavaliere Rusticana* and Donna Anna in *Don Giovanni*.

Her wonderful rendering of the prima donna role as Santuzza in the opera Cavaliere Rusticana in London, in Signor Lajos' Italian Opera Company, caused Queen Victoria to call her to Windsor Castle to have her repeat her role as Santuzza before herself and members of the royal family. Miss Rita Elandi was the first American singer to receive such an honor. Her personal appearance, her obvious musical talent, tied with the magic of her voice, caused the queen to wish the artist well personally and, on her departure, to give her a bracelet decorated with diamonds as a souvenir.

Miss Groll is not only an ingenious priestess of the muse, but also an amiable, intelligent and active person. She lives and moves only for art, and knows only one thought: to embody the creations of the composers in perfection. She doubtless has a splendid future ahead of her among the musical and dramatic heroines of Europe.

W. H. Crane

It would be unjust not to mention Mr. William H. Crane, one of the literally gifted artists making Cleveland his field of work. It is true that Mr. Crane is not really a German-American in the narrow sense of the word, but as an enthused supporter of German arts, a pupil of German masters, to whom he owes many of his own artistic successes, and as an upright friend of German ways and German customs, he deserves a place of honor here.

It has only been within a relatively brief time that Mr. Crane has risen to be a star in the heaven of painting as a result of his paintings of biblical subjects. There have been storms of recognition and praise by true artists and friends of art as well as astonishment by laymen who know how to value and recognize what is good when they see it even though they cannot give an informed analysis of it.

"Thy will be done," is the title of a picture by Mr. Crane which shows Jesus in the Garden of Gethsemane which drew the attention of the art world to Mr. Crane. This painting was first displayed here in Cleveland in summer, 1906, together with a collection of images of the Messiah by renowned masters, and it was recognized as one of the best pictures of that collection, which reports made the rounds of all the artistic centers in Europe and America. The picture of Mr. Crane is of heroic dimensions, and the scenery around Jesus is as grandiose as the figure itself. Rev. McGuire of the Gospel Church on Central Avenue, who contemplated that picture on several occasions, gave the following telling evaluation: "Wm. H. Crane's picture exceeds any previous version of the figure and face of the Savior I have ever seen, although I have looked at almost every painting of that sort in Europe and can make a comparison."

Recently Mr. Crane made a series of scenes from the region around Cleveland. These are masterful. The artistic critic of the local English newspaper wrote about it, "There is an extraordinary depth in the landscape paintings of Mr. Crane, a perspective, which refreshes the eye and leads us to forget that we are looking at a painting on flat canvas. One of the landscapes show a country road through a fir forest. The rays of the sun breaking through the branches of the trees achieve a lighting effect which is absolutely wonderful."

It is no marvel that Mr. Crane is such a genius. Genius is, so to speak, part of his inherited material. He was born in New York in 1862, the son of one of the most capable stage technicians, who only died about four years ago, and who throughout his entire career was always able to enchant those who attended the theater and, what is not to be ignored, to stuff the box-office receipts. Edith Crane, the famous actress and wife of the talented actor Powers, is a sister of our Clevelander Crane. It appears that artistic genius in the Crane family, widely-spread all over America, is as it were "in the blood." Mr. Crane made his first attempts at painting as a 14-year old boy under the direction of the ingenious German set decorator W. Schaefer in New York, who at once recognized the boy's talent and promoted it to the best of his ability. About two years ago Mr. Crane moved from New York to Cleveland. His studio, in which he is working eagerly on a new "Madonna and Child," is on the sixth floor of the Republican Building.

When Powers, the brother-in-law of Mr. Crane who lives in New York, saw the picture of the Savior in the Garden of Gethsemane, he at once wrote Mr. Crane to return to New York, since only there would he find development and reward for his talent. But Mr. Crane has come to like Cleveland, and we hope he is happy enough never to leave us.

Chas. W. Voth

Mr. Charles W. Voth was born on 3 April 1858 as the son of an old German pioneer family. His parents were resident in Bur, Hanover, emigrating to the United States in 1846, and after a brief residence in Erie, Pennsylvania, they soon moved to our Forest City, where they recently died in high old age, surrounded by a happy family circle. They were blessed by a fortunate Providence to be able to celebrate the rare festival of the golden wedding anniversary eleven years ago (1896). Besides Charles W. Voth, the object of this sketch, three other sons, John, Samuel and Frank, as well as two daughters, Eliza and Emma, the wife of Mr. Robert Suhr, are alive, as well as the aged mother.

Charles attended the German Lutheran school and received a completely German education there, because as is generally known, a true German spirit is instilled in such schools. Later he attended the public schools and graduated from the Spencerian Business College before entering his father's wholesale business. In 1879 he took a position in the wholesale hat business of Goodhart & Koch, and in 1883 he became a traveling salesman for this company, which he continued to do until the company gave up the hat business in 1889. He then took a similar position in a New York company, Hillburn Bros., traveling for them for 3 years.

Tired of the unstable life of a traveler and already seized by rheumatism, he accepted an offer in 1892 from the *Wächter am Erie* Publishing Co. to serve as advertising agent and gave up his position as a traveling salesman. Hilburn Bros. was very unhappy to lose him. He remained with the *Wächter* for almost two years and his open, friendly manner won him an extensive circle of friends and customers. Later, after he had worked for a time with the *Germania* and the *Deutsche Presse*, he took a similar position with the *Cleveland Anzeiger*. He bought stock, and before the merging of the two papers as the *Wächter und Anzeiger*, he was vice president of the *Anzeiger* Publishing Co. When the merger took place, he sold his interest to the company and involved himself in fire insurance and real estate under the company title of Wetzel, Voth & Co. The office is in room 335 of the Society for Savings Building.

In 1889 Mr. Chas. Voth married Miss Lena Piel of Indianapolis, Indiana, daughter of an old, respected German family there that also emigrated from Hanover. A boy, Walter Piel, now 12, came from this happy union.

Mr. Voth was an outstanding member and treasured singer of the *Frohsinn* Singing Society, is a member of the German-American Club, and is one of the oldest members of the Commercial Travellers Association. Further, he is one of the directors of the Cuyahoga Building & Loan Co.

He possesses a splendidly decorated home at 1882 E. 66th Street, and he is a guest gladly seen wherever he goes.

A. W. Stadler

A. W. Stadler, the owner of the Cuyahoga Rendering & Soap Works, was born in Mecklenburg-Schwerin in 1856, and he came with his parents to America at the age of one year. The family settled in Cleveland and remained here. The boy was educated in the local schools and then worked with his father to the age of 21, when he founded his famous soap factory in 1871, whose owner he still is, and which he has brought to such heights that it is not only one of the largest factories in Cleveland, but among the most important and premier soap factories in the country. This is more thoroughly described elsewhere in this book among the industrial establishments of the city. Mr. Stadler has always dedicated all his strength to his business, and he has never participated in politics, though he is a member of the Chamber of Commerce and has joined several societies, including the Knights of Pythias and Kirk's Military Band. Despite his important position, Mr. Kirk is as modest and courteous as only a German can be, which makes him generally all the more beloved and respected.

Mr. Stadler married on 20 July 1900 Miss Anna B. Splittdorf, a lovely and amiable lady of German extraction, of Collinwood. A son, E. Wilson, was born on 24 September 1901 and is the pride of his elders.

Mr. Stadler lives in a splendid residence at 1422 Denison Avenue, where his friends are always welcome. His liberal character has won him many generous admirers. Mr. Stadler treasures this higher than material success, which is certainly the finest and most truly German element in Mr. Stadler, so that the Germans of Cleveland may point to one of the most capable citizens and businessmen with pride.

John Georg Splittdorf

Among the German pioneers of Cleveland, to whose energy and hard work the city owes its success and good name, is Mr. John Georg Splittdorf. Born on 19 June 1850 in Schwarzenburn in Electoral Hessia as the son of the wagon-maker Christoph Splittdorf and his wife Katharina née Kleir, the object of this sketch attended the Protestant schools of his locality and, as soon as he was confirmed, he took an apprenticeship with the esteemed cabinet maker Andreas Feuerbaum in Grevenhagen. In 1867 he emigrated to America as a youth of 17, coming directly to Cleveland, where he worked for two years as a cabinetmaker. Since he did not like cabinet making, he gave it up and turned to the grocery business, which gave him prosperity. He was long ago able to withdraw from all business and take a deserved rest. Mr. Splittdorf is a respected member of the Woodmen of the World, the Sons of Hermann and the Peace Lodge. In 1871 he married Miss Elisabeth Gerst. Five children came from this happy union. The girls have all married, and they are: Mrs. Chas. W. Ehrke (Martha), Mrs. A. W. Stadler (Anna), and Mrs. Geo. TeLinde (Amelia).

Pastor A. J. Franz

Pastor A. J. Franz was born in 1865 in Steinbach in the province of Hessia-Nassau as the son of a teacher. His father busied himself with historical research, and from him the son obviously obtained his love of study and literary ability. Young Franz first attended elementary school and then the *Realschule* for two years. Unfortunately he lost his parents in 1881, as a boy barely fourteen, through death. He then came to America and found refuge with relatives living in Holgate, Ohio. Following his inclination to a profession in the clergy, he attended the college of the Reformed Church in Sheboygan, Wisconsin, for five years and then graduated the three-year theology course at the same place. After being licensed as a preacher, he took over the ministry in a small congregation in Waukegan, Illinois, 35 miles north of Chicago. In 1893 he was called to Cleveland, where he has since worked without interruption as minister of the Ninth Reformed Church. As already mentioned, Pastor Franz obtained a preference for literary activity and already has published several works. His most recent book, entitled, *Denkst Du Daran?* ["Do You Think About It?"] is of religious content and intended for confirmands. Each of his male and female confirmands receive a copy as a gift. Pastor Franz has written many very widely-read narratives as well as fine articles for ecclesiastical newspapers. Even the secular daily press has been enriched by his occasional articles.

The best proof for the ministerial activity of Pastor Franz is the fact that the membership of his congregation has risen fivefold since he took it over in 1893.

Pastor Franz has been married since 1889 with Miss Lena E. Petrie, daughter of a respected German family in Wayne, Wisconsin. The marriage has been blessed with four children, a boy and three girls.

Paul Schreiner

Mr. Paul Schreiner, police clerk, who would appear in any work about Cleveland due to his official position, is doubly worthy of mention here since he was born of German parents, on 11 August 1861, in Johnstown, Pennsylvania.

His parents emigrated to America from Oberndorf, Württemberg, in 1850, and his father worked at his trade of furniture maker in the town mentioned. In 1862 the family moved to Cleveland. Of the eleven children in that family, six are still living, four boys and two girls. Once grown out of childhood, Paul attended the Catholic parochial school of St. Joseph's, receiving a proper German education. After completing his studies he learned cigar making, and he was then active as a cigar maker for eight years. Then he accepted under Robert Cordess a position as clerk of the Police Court, holding this for three years. Then he received a post in the municipal infirmary in the Outdoor Relief Department, and he he headed it as the responsible officer under Mayor Rose, Mayor Robert Blee and six months under McKisson's administration. Then he received an appointment from Alb. Honecker as assistant clerk of the Police Court. He held this position for six years, until he was nominated by the Republican Party as Police Clerk in 1903 and won the election. He was the sole Republican to be elected that time, and his majority was more than 3000 votes, a clear proof of his great and broad popularity. This is particularly striking when one considers that all the other persons elected were from the Democratic ticket with majorities of more than 7000 votes. In the last election there were several opponents for nomination as County Clerk, but he was defeated by the strong Democratic trend, though he ran considerably ahead of the ticket.

Paul Schreiner has served well over many years in public service, and he looks forward to a secure future due to his unusual popularity. This can only be greeted with joy from the

German side, since if anyone does not forget his German origins in office it is Paul Schreiner. On the contrary, he has often acted strongly for German causes. As a result Germans have never neglected to give him full and undivided support.

Mr. Schreiner is married and the happy father of two promising children, a boy and a girl.

John Schmunk

The well-known and universally-popular police lieutenant John Schmunk is a child of Cleveland. He was born to German parents on 6 August 1855 in this city. John received a good German education, since besides an English school he also had to attend German school, and he received confirmation at the Evangelical Protestant Church at the corner of Scovill Avenue and Greenwood Street at the age of 14. Around this time John's parents moved to the country, and he helped them until he was 18, when he returned to the city and learned carpentry. At the age of 21 he entered the service of the Cleveland Rolling Mill Co., working up to foreman here, and he remained with the company until 1881. In that year Mr. Schmunk entered the local police force. Through his conscientiousness, punctual fulfillment of duty and correct perception of his profession, he could not fail to win respect and trust from his superiors, so that on 28 June 1892 he was made temporary sergeant and on 18 June of the same year sergeant. On 1 April 1894 Mr. Schmunk was already lieutenant. For sixteen years he was stationed at the Central Station as a patrolman, sergeant and lieutenant, until he was sent at the end of 1899 to the Second Precinct.

Despite the fact that he was born in this country, Mr. Schmunk has always retained a warm interest for all German efforts, has never been ashamed of his German origins, as once was so often the case. In his younger years he was an active member of the "Harmonie," and he is currently a member of the German Freemasons' lodge Concordia and a member of the Cleveland Lodge 61, K. of P. In 1875 he married Miss Minnie Arndt, and three children have come from this happy union, two sons and a daughter. Mr. Schmunk has won a great circle of friends due to his open and accessible nature, and he may justly be called one of our most popular police officers.

Theodor Janssen

Theodor Janssen, editor of the German Press & Plate Co., was born on 3 April 1853 in the village of Heppens near Oldenburg (now belonging to the Prussian military harbor of Wilhelmshaven), the son of a mill-owner. At first he attended a village school in Neuende, then the *Gymnasium* in Jever, and after graduation he spent three semesters in Tübingen, Württemberg, studying philology. Early deprived of his parents, he was compelled to break off his studies by financial conditions, and in 1873 he emigrated to America. There, after settling in Chicago and working as a congregation teacher, he began an apprenticeship as a typesetter, which served as a bridge to his later activities. He was active for one year at the *'Freie Presse'* established in 1875 in Crown Point, Indiana; then he returned to Chicago and worked as a typesetter and then as a reporter on the *'Illinois Staatszeitung.'* After working briefly for the *'Volksfreund'* and *'Arbeiterzeitung,'* he moved from Chicago to Milwaukee in 1880. There he served until 1883 as reporter and later local editor of the 'Herold,' and he married Miss Lina Doerflinger, a sister of the book dealer and editor of the *'Freidenker,'* Chas. H. Doerflinger. Following a call to Chicago, he held for many years the position of wire editor at the *'Illinois Staatszeitung,'* until after the amalgamation of that paper with the *'Freie Presse'* in 1901 he accepted a position as chief and wire editor at the *'Telegraph'* in Indianapolis, Indiana. From there he came to Cleveland in 1902, where he has worked ever since as editor of the German Press & Plate Co.

Mr. Janssen likes his present position as well as being in the Forest City best of all his previous situations, and the fact that he regards this as his final situation is shown by the active role he is playing in society life.

Gottlieb Kuebler

Mr. Gottlieb Kuebler first saw the light of day in Bartenbach, district of Backnang, Württemberg, on 28 August 1851. His parents, Ludwig and Katharina Kübler, were upstanding farmers who put their seven children to work and raised them in severe discipline. Gottlieb attended the *Volksschule* from his sixth to his fourteenth year, and after confirmation he helped his parents at their labor. The next year the young country boy entered the brewery at Backnang, remaining there for two years before continuing his apprenticeship at a brewing kettle in Hall, and he then worked until the age of 19 at the famous *Aktienbrauerei* in Heilbronn. Then young Kübler, who had been preceded by some siblings, went to America, straight to Cleveland, where he found work at first at Jacob Mall's brewery and then Gehring's. In 1879 he became brewmaster with Oppmann. Two years later we find Kübler in the same position in the Schneider brewery, where he remained until 1887, before returning to Oppmann as brewmaster. Since then Mr. Kübler has remained in this position without interruption, even when Mr. Oppmann sold his brewery to the Phoenix Brewing Co. in 1891. In 1873 Mr. Kübler married Louise Gollwitzer from Bavaria, who has given him nine children: Christ, Louisa, Bertha, Charles, Gretchen, Louis, the twins Nettie and Katie, and Hilde. On 21 May 1907 he set off on a journey to his old homeland, and since then his place has been taken by his son Louis, who was born in 1884 and has graduated the Wahl and Henius Brewing Academy in Chicago, so that he has chosen brewing as his profession like his father. Mr. Gottlieb Kübler is a member of the Brewmasters' Society, the Freemasons' lodge Concordia, the Concordia Support Society, the Swabian Society, the Brewers' Support Society, and belongs as well to the Red Men, the Foresters and the Social Turners. As may be seen, Mr. Kübler does not play a small role in social activity, and as a result of his amiable nature he is beloved in all circles.

V. Spitschka

Born on 22 August 1852 in Liebenau near Reichenberg, Bohemia, the youngest son of the glass manufacturer Vincenz Spitschka, brewmaster Spitschka received an excellent education in his youth. He attended the *Realschule* in Reichenberg, and after graduation he chose brewing as his profession. He practiced in Wimburg, Liebenau and Kleinskal. Then he undertook a great journey which took him to St. Petersburg, Moscow, Vienna, Trieste and several cities in Hungary, and in the course of this journey he collected much experience and knowledge in his specialty.

His first job was in the brewery at the Elbscloss in Leitmeritz in Bohemia, and later he became cellar master in the *Aktienbrauerei* in Aschaffenburg, and he opened a new field for his efforts by studying forestry, to which he dedicated three years, including related courses in chemistry. During this period he belonged to the student fraternity "Herzinia." Then he entered the Lehmann Brewing School in Worms, and after graduation he became assistant in that school's chemistry laboratory. His next position was that of a brewmaster in the brewery of Count Salm in Laubach, Upper Hessia, which he kept for four years. Then he took over the

Haldy brewery in Saarbrücken, running it himself for several years, until he built a brewery of his own in Fulda. After running this for several years, he gave it up, and though it still brews "Spitschka's Light" and "Dark," the founder has been in America since 1887. After landing in Uncle Sam's country, Spitschka found his first position as cellar master in the Long Island Brewery. After two years, he became the foreman in the Budweiser brewery in Long Island, then in the Rising Sun brewery in Elizabeth, New Jersey. Then, as a result of the death of young Rübsam, he became brewmaster at Rübsam & Horrmann's brewery in Stapleton, Staten Island, which he did for four years. The death of the elder Mr. Rübsam brought about changes which led him to give up his post and move to the Woodside brewery, whose president he became. This company collapsed, so that he came for the first time to Cleveland, becoming brewmaster of the Columbia brewery here.

After being active for four years here, he completed a course at the Schwarz Brewing School in New York and then was at the Anton Kopp brewery in Massillon, Ohio, for five years, after which he returned to Cleveland. First of all he was brewmaster at the Pilsener Brewing Company for three years, until the Fischel Brewing Co. was created, and he went to work there as brewmaster, where he remains today. This experienced brewmaster has also been an inventor, and he received a patent for the beer delivery system which has eliminated the early method of delivery to tavernkeepers. He also possesses several other proven patents. Despite the fact that Mr. Spitschka gives most of his attention to his job, he has always been a true supporter of Germans and a ready helper for their noble and deserved efforts, winning many friends in the process. He is a member of Schlaraffia.

C. W. Dertinger

The long-established brewmaster of the Gehring brewery, Mr. C. W. Dertinger, was born on 1 February 1847 in Calw, Kingdom of Württemberg, hence a compatriot of Gehring himself, since Württemberg in general has always provided the largest contingent of brewers and brewmasters to America.

After receiving a solid education in Swabia and learning brewing in all its branches, Dertinger turned to the land of freedom and equality in 1867 and landed on its hospitable shores filled with great hopes, which were fulfilled. He found his first employment in Kimmswick, Missouri at the Gottlieb Meyer brewery. Within two years, in 1869, he moved to Cleveland, where he entered the C. F. Gehring brewery, to whose service he has remained loyal ever since. He started as a cellar worker, but through hard work and zealous study he won the trust of his superiors to such a degree that he was brewmaster in this important brewery as early as 1871.

His knowledge permitted him to introduce important innovations, and for that reason he has been treasured by the head of the brewery, Mr. C. F. Gehring.

Truly German in his sensibilities, possessed with great strength of character and openness in dealing with friends and acquaintances, Mr. Dertinger is a universally beloved personality. An outstanding member of a number of German societies, he takes an active part in many German activities.

He married the eldest daughter of Mr. C. F. Gehring on 2 October 1873, and five children have come from this marriage, of which only three are alive. They are the pride and joy of their parents, and they esteem their German language and parentage.

Joseph Kieferle

Joseph Kieferle, a restaurateur known not only in German but also in American circles, first saw the light of day on 22 September 1846 in Mannheim. His father was the municipal building master Max Wilhelm Kieferle, who made sure the boy received a good education. As a pupil in the trades school, the young Kieferle prepared himself for the craft of machining, also learning the practical side of that occupation and later working in this specialty in Munich, Vienna, Chemnitz, Strasbourg, Zürich and other cities. Joseph Kieferle came to America in 1868 and found profitable employment in his specialty in New York. There he married Miss Marie Nasshofer, who gave him two daughters. Six years later he was once again in his old homeland, in Karlsruhe, where he remained until 1878. Then Mr. Kieferle returned to America. Arriving in New York, Mr. Kieferle made an epoch-making invention in the production of quilting machines, and he was one of the founders of the Excelsior Quilting Company, which was a great success. With small capital, since none of the partners disposed of significant money, the business was called to life. The success was phenomenal. The new company could not meet the demands of coat manufacturers by itself, so in a brief period of time the company underwent great expansion. Mr. Kieferle sold his share in the invention in 1883, which he later repented bitterly, to visit Paris and London, and at the same time he made a visit to his old homeland. Still, his visit in Europe did not appeal to him, so that he returned to America again and settled in Cleveland. Here he founded the Continental Quilting Company, a competitor of Excelsior, but due to patent disputes he had to give up the struggle and go into the restaurant business, which he has since pursued with great success. To use the common term, Mr. Kieferle is a born host. He understands as do few of his competitors how to draw guests and offer them the best of the kitchen and cellar. Currently Mr. Kieferle manages the noted restaurant, "Zum schwarzen Walfisch" ["The Sign of the Black Whale"], 119 Prospect Avenue, which is the gathering place of the better businessmen. After Mr. Kieferle lost his first wife through death, he entered a second marriage on 16 November 1881 with Catharine Repp from Darmstadt, which brought him two sons. Joseph, the elder, is manager of the wholesale furrier Checkman & Sons, and the younger, Georg, is a traveling salesman for the same firm. Both of his daughters from the first marriage are married, Fannie with Mr. Carl W. Auer, and Ida with Dr. Landmann in Berlin, Germany.

John M. Sulzmann

John W. Sulzmann was born on 4 December 1869 in this city. He is the eldest son of the German pioneer Mr. Maximilian Sulzmann from Istingen, Baden, who immigrated in 1864. The elder Mr. Sulzmann owned a factory in his homeland with 40 employees. John Sulzmann's mother is an Ansenhofer, born in Pforzheim, also in Baden. The young Sulzmann received a careful German education, attending St. Joseph's school until he was 12, then entering a cigar factory as an apprentice, and he has remained true to cigar-making to the present day. Becoming independent in 1893, he managed to build a significant business despite the panic which spread over the country in that year, and today he employs 25 workers. In 1900 John Sulzmann was elected to the city council, and in this position he has proved himself worthy of the trust the voters have placed in him. The fifth district, which he represents, then consisted of wards 13, 15, 16 and 17, and in the election he exceeded his ticket by no fewer than 967 votes. In the organization of the city council he became chairman of the appropriations and ordinance committees, as well as a member of the worker committee and the telegraph and telephone committee, and in his second year of service he was elected vice president, and when president

Dillion took a three month journey to England, he took over the presidency, and the tact he showed at sessions remains in the memory of the onlookers. Yes, the press even found it necessary to recognize him, and the *'Wächter und Anzeiger'* once noted, "The acting president Sulzmann sounds his sonorous voice to much effect. He is the first president in ten years to be able to get a hearing and who can be easily understood. The result is that the sessions have taken on a new promptness." John Sulzmann in fact has not only fulfilled his duties conscientiously and demonstrated his suitability for the job, but he has done honor to his district and to Germans generally. Mr. Sulzmann has always participated intensely in society life. He is a member of the C. M. B. A., the Eagles, the Baden Support Society, the Cleveland Liederkranz and the German Order of the Harugari. Further, he belongs to the Association of Commercial Travelers. In 1890 he married Miss Emma Reichlin, the daughter of the German pioneer, and ten children have come from this happy and blessed marriage. Both Mr. Sulzmann's and his wife's parents are still living, and they can glory in a horde of grandchildren.

John Sulzmann is in his best years, and one may not only congratulate him on his success, but also wish that he will have opportunity to serve the public again. This is because he has demonstrated his abilities to serve and because Germans have in him a brave and worthy representative.

Eugen Remy

Mr. Eugen Remy, representative of the 21st ward, was born in 1872 in Rohrbach near Landau, Rhenish Palatinate. In his homeland he enjoyed an outstanding education, attending the latin school in Landau and coming to Cleveland in 1888. Here he undertook an apprenticeship in Mr. Tielke's pharmacy, training himself thoroughly in the pharmacopoeia. Mr. Remy is currently the owner of two pharmacies, on at 677 Quincy and the other at 1496 Central Avenue, at the corner of Madison. Mr. Remy takes great interest in public affairs. In early 1903 he was elected by the Republican Party as member of the city council from the 21st ward, and he has represented the ward to the full satisfaction of his constituents, so that he has been reelected.

Mr. Remy is a member of the K. of P., the Independent Order of Foresters, and the Northern Ohio Druggist Association. Married eleven years ago with Miss Maria Tielke, the daughter of a respected pioneer family, this happy marriage has produced two children, Eugen and Josephine.

Wilhelm J. Noss

Wilhelm J. Noss is a descendent of German immigrants. His father Joseph came from Löbschitz near Königsdorf, Upper Silesia, and he first settled to practice his trade as a miller in Troy, New York, where Wilhelm was born in 1869. In 1870 the family moved to Cleveland, and Mr. Noss grew up here. He attended the public schools and then apprenticed as a cooper. In the meantime his father founded the tavern and grocery at 1906 Fulton Road. He died in 1897, and this is the business which Mr. Noss carries on. His mother, from Stettin, is still alive.

W. J. Noss is not only a businessman but a man of the public. He has always been interested in politics and municipal affairs, and he shows considerable understanding of these, to the extent that he drew the attention of his ward to himself, so that they saw him as the right man to represent them. In 1904, then, he was placed on the Democratic ticket and was elected to the city council, where he became a member of the powerful finance and park committees. Further, he is chairman of the examination committee, a proof of the regard his colleagues hold of him. He was a member of the Democratic Central Committee for eleven years, and he was treasurer three different terms. He was also once president of the Sycamore Club.

Since Mr. Noss dedicates himself to the public weal, we shall often find him on the ticket in the future, and since his election is not in doubt, we shall see him as a representative of Germans in the city council. Mr. Noss also takes part in society life. He is a member of various societies, such as the Foresters, the Red Men, the Eagles and the Stern Turners, and he enjoys great respect in all of them. Although born and raised here, Mr. Noss shows a genuine love for German things and sees himself as a German. He openly displays this to all non-Germans as well, and he bears this proudly in all settings.

In 1890 Mr. Noss married Miss Spuhler. She is also born in America, but with German parents, as the name indicates. From this happy union has come two girls and a boy. Just as was the case with the parents, they are receiving a German education and are as convinced as their parents of the value of German identity, and they are as proud as they of their German origins. The family enjoys the greatest love and respect in its neighborhood.

H. Hamm

Once one of the best-known and beloved directors of song in Cleveland is without a doubt Mr. H. Hamm, who has in recent years withdrawn from the direction of societies. Born in Dellfeld, Rhenish Palatinate, he attended the local *Volksschule* and received his first musical instruction from his father, the noted music teacher Jakob Hamm, known throughout the Palatinate. The intellectually precocious boy received private instruction for two years in German, Latin and piano from Prof. Paul in Zweibrücken. Because his father intended him to become a teacher, however, he ended his study of Latin and attended the teachers' seminary in Kaiserslautern, which was combined with an institution of music led by talented professors. Here Mr. Hamm studied piano, organ, violin, cello, song and harmonium. After passing his state examination he took another year of private instruction under Professor Berger (piano, violin and harmonium) and A. Damian (song). In 1882 he took a teaching position in Pirmasens, which he held for three years and in which he was so successful as a general teacher and music teacher that he took over the music and singing teaching in the local Latin school, as well as the direction of the leading Men's Singing and St. Cecelia Societies. Mr. Hamm was one of the founders of the Musical Society, which still exists. In 1885, in keeping with his uncle's advice and against his father's wishes he went to America, settling in the Forest City, where he soon obtained the organist position in the congregation *Zum Schifflein Christi*, also directing the singing section of the Swabian Recreation Society. The Harugari Men's Chorus elected him in 1886 as its director, and he holds that position to the present day. During this time it has managed to rise to become one of the most accomplished in the city. When the singing society called the Cleveland Men's Chorus began forming in 1886 on the West Side, gathering excellent singers who soon had trouble due to internal disputes, Mr. Hamm was elected director. In the same year he was musical leader of the great concert held by the West Side and East Side singing societies. From 1887 to 1891 Mr. Hamm directed the *Lyra* Singing Society, and for two years the Newburg Germania Men's Chorus, and for the last eight years he has been director of the Orpheus. Further, he received the musical directorship of the new *Liederkranz* Society which developed about a year ago. For the last 2 years, Mr. Hamm has been organist at St. Paul's, corner of Greenwood and Scovill Avenue. The North American singing festival held here in 1893 had Mr. Hamm as one of the assistant directors, rehearsing the massed choruses of the local societies to the satisfaction of the general director, Professor Ring. On 2 December 1886, Mr. Hamm married Miss Bertha Kleinschrodt, daughter of a local German pioneer family, and this marriage has produced two children. In 1891 he made a pleasure visit to his old homeland, visiting his old friends and acquaintances, as well as the most significant director and leader of the Teachers' Singing Society of Mannheim and Ludwigshafen, Mr. Carl Hirsch. In early 1898 Mr. Hamm attended the institute of Mr. Ferdinand Flechter in New York to train himself in practical and theoretical vocal instruction. Mr. Fechter is the authorized representative of the anatomical-physiological method of forming tones and voices, developed by Professor Julius Hey in Berlin. In 1900 Mr. Hamm returned to study the singing method of Anna Lankow in New York, and since then he has dedicated himself completely to teaching this system for voice training. His noted and popular studio is 308 Euclid Avenue, at 501 Union National Bank Building.

Prof. A. Spengler

When we review the names of representatives of music and its cultivation, we continually find names with a German sound. The name of A. Spengler and its sound have been known in Cleveland's musical world and beyond for a quarter century. Enthused with a love of music from early youth and gifted with a rare musical talent, Spengler the boy and youth already was operating at the heights of music. He then received an academic education at the conservatory in Leipzig and won his first laurels in public performances after his return to Cleveland and in other places in Ohio and Pennsylvania. The fame of Professor Spengler has been solid for some time. That of his school is just as renowned, in which the finest fruits have been produced under the sunshine and living strength of his teaching, producing glowing adoration.

The academy is located at 50 Euclid Avenue. Through his composition of a textbook embodying his original teaching method, Professor Spengler has become known far beyond the borders not only of Cleveland but of the United States, for he has found high recognition in Germany as well. Through the creation of this work he has found the means to work as a teacher over a great distance, even though he had only desired to create an aid for his students close at hand. In Professor Spengler Cleveland possesses not only an ingenious connoisseur of music of the first rank, but also a music teacher who has performed services for the expansion and cultivation of music, and to whom many owe their musical training and musical enjoyment.

J. Arthur Nusser

J. A. Nusser, one of the most popular singing society directors in Cleveland, was born in this city on 28 April 1876 on the South Side, then called Brooklyn Village. His parents were among the German pioneers. Even as a boy Arthur showed musical talent, enjoyed a musical education, and, after he had graduated from West High School, he dedicated himself totally to music. He took piano instruction with the noted piano teacher Mr. Kösen, and under the leadership of Professor Emil Ring he studied piano counterpoint, harmony theory and directing, and under Professor Hartmann the playing of the organ. Prof. Nusser has taught music over the last 12 years. His studio is in the bank building at the corner of Pearl Street and Clark Avenue. The following musical societies are under his direction: Vorwärts Singing Section for the last ten years, with a brief interruption; Orpheus Men's Chorus for the last eight years; Newburg Germania Men's Chorus for the last eight years; Workers' Singing League for the last six years, and the Bavarian Men's Chorus for the last four years, a proof of the great love and reputation as a director he enjoys. Further, Mr. Nusser has been director for the last six years of the Church Choir of the Sacred Heart Church, South Brooklyn, and for the last three years he plays the organ at the Church of the Annunciation on the West Side.

Charles Feller

Charles Feller has passed through the troubles and pressures of the foundation period such as few of the old German pioneers of Cleveland, seeing how many of whom great things were predicted went down to ruin, while others obtained fame, honor and riches. A straight-forward man, he has always hated appearances and perceived true character through many a gleaming raiment seeking to mislead. It is a true pleasure to listen to the reminiscences of this pioneer, so rich in experiences, and it would be useful for many a young man to choose the old man as a teaching master and follow his advice. Mr. Chas. Feller was born on 5 March 1834 in Rossbach, district of Gellhausen, Hessia-Nassau, and he came to America at the age of ten, in June, 1844, along with his parents, five brothers and a sister, arriving on the 20th of that month in Cleveland. The parents were honest peasants and sought to turn at once to farming. They obtained a farm of 33 acres in Newburg Township and set to work with their children to make the earth fruitful. Newburg was larger than Cleveland in those days, consisting of what is today the 18th and part of the 17th ward, and Cleveland was a village of 5000 inhabitants. Mr. Feller has been blessed with the opportunity to see our city develop from a spot with 5000 residents to the metropolis of Ohio with 500,000 inhabitants, one of the most important cities in the country.

In 1860 Mr. Feller married Miss Sophie Zweig, daughter of a pioneer from Bavaria who settled in Baltimore, with whom she came to America as a child of nineteen. This happy marriage was blessed with 16 children, of which three unfortunately died. Mr. Frank Feller, an outstanding citizen of our city and currently superintendent of the municipal cemeteries, is the eldest of the children.

Of his siblings, only a brother by the name of August is still alive. His mother died in 1874 and his father followed his wife in 1881 at the high age of 81.

Even during the lifetime of his parents, Charles was their support, taking to farming with zeal. In addition to his father's original property of 33 acres, he obtained another 40 acres, and now he has a significant property, on which he has built a pleasant home on Harvard Street, Newburg Heights Village, where he lives with his wife. During the Civil War, Mr. Feller worked in a powder magazine, producing the material to end the rebellion and preserve the Union. He took an intense interest in public affairs, and even today the events of economic and political life interest him. Mr. Feller enjoys the best health despite his advanced age, and he expects many more years.

Albert Petzke

It was in 1866 that Albert Petzke, then barely 12, arrived with his parents and siblings in Cleveland from Woldegk, a little town in Mecklenburg-Strelitz. He continued the schooling he received before departure in the local schools here, going after the age of 14 to the printing plant of the _Wächter am Erie_ as an apprentice typesetter. After the completion of his apprenticeship he wandered to the East, hiring out in various large cities such as New York, Newark, and other places. After a couple years he returned to Cleveland, finding employment in the publishing house and printing operation of the Evangelical Community on Woodland Avenue, where he worked continually for seven years. In 1883 he gave up his typesetting profession and entered partnership with his brother Otto and their brother-in-law Stern to establish a tailor shop, called Petzke and Stern, on St. Clair Street. After the departure of Stern the firm was changed to Petzke Bros. Otto Petzke died in December, 1902, at the age of 55, and Albert Petzke continued the business under the same name, now located in the Y. M. C. A. building at 934 Prospect Avenue.

Mr. Albert Petzke had his first marriage with Miss Paulina Wendtland, contracted in 1883, which produced five children, four sons and a daughter. Mr. Petzke unfortunately lost his first wife in 1902 through death, and since then he has married the widow of his brother, born Hermine Stern. Albert Petzke has long participated in an outstanding and enthusiastic way in society life. He held the rank of colonel in the second regiment of the uniformed knights of the State of Ohio.

It is a measure of how much he is esteemed by his comrades that the encampment of the Knights in Youngstown was named after him. Further, he is the president of the Cleveland Skat Club, a proof that he is not above the convivial game, and is a master. Mr. Petzke is also a past master of the Concordia Lodge of the Freemasons, is a member of the Holyrood Commandery, Knights Templars, and he has received all the degrees through the 32nd.

Mr. Albert Petzke is in fact a man with the inborn genius and character to make many and lasting friends, giving him influence, popularity and business success.

Friedrich Wilhelm Striebinger

Friedrich Wilhelm Striebinger comes from one of the oldest German pioneer families of Cleveland. He received a very careful German education from his parents. Destined for architecture, after attending preparatory school he was educated at Columbia College, and after graduation he set off on a long study trip to Europe. He remained in Paris for four years, attending the famous École des Beaux-Arts. He also studied the most important architectural creations of great cities in Germany, Italy, England and other states of Europe, and in 1897 he returned to Cleveland with rich knowledge, fundamental experiences and the best-honed professional judgment, establishing himself in the New England Building and beginning his practice as an architect. Since then he has brought into being a significant number of buildings whose completion was entrusted to him, and which give witness to his creative and technical talent.

Incidentally, Mr. Striebinger is not only one of the most talented young local building masters, he is also an artist and connoisseur and as such well known here in educated and artistically sensitive circles. A member of the American Institute of Architects, the Cleveland Art Club, and the Water Color Society, he participates actively in everything having to do with art.

His enjoyment of good company which arises inevitably from German blood and shows itself wherever it appears, also has caused him to join the Freemasons, the Knights of Pythias, the Shriners and the Century Club. Even if he does not belong to German societies as such, one may not deny a German element in Mr. Striebinger, which expresses itself in his artistic activities in this way.

Dr. Daniel C. Dennerle

The histories and tales of descendents of German pioneers can be very interesting, such as those of the dentist Dr. Daniel C. Dennerle, told in the following sketch. Dr. Dennerle's mother was born Geib, coming from the area of Darmstadt. She was a cook from 1853 to 1857 in the then-famous Hotel America. She then married Adam Dennerle, a student and political refugee from

Landau in the Rhenish Palatinate. Our Dr. Daniel Dennerle comes from this marriage, born on 10 March 1858. After a brief marriage, the father, the former German student, participated in the Civil War and was a victim of Yellow Fever in the South. His bones lie buried in the Calvary Cemetery in Memphis, Tennessee. After the loss of her husband, the mother moved in with her elderly parents and cared for them until their deaths. The very aged mother of Dr. Dennerle still lives in the old pioneer home on the West Side, built in 1850. In those days the house still stood in a forest, quite alone, and the place was called Ohio City. The forest has long since vanished and Ohio City is part of Cleveland. As a boy Dr. Dennerle attended the parochial school at the corner of Bridge and Kentucky Streets. The school fell down in 1870, burying 75 pupils under the rubble, including him. Fortunately, the Fire Department was able to rescue them from this terror. Later he attended the public schools and finally Western University as a student of medicine. Since he had to care for his ailing mother, he turned to dentistry and established himself several years later, in 1882, in the Carlton Block, corner of Woodland Avenue and Eagle Street, above Rave's pharmacy, where his office is still located. Alongside his practice as a dentist, Dr. Dennerle pursues his passion for biology and phrenology, and the astonishing knowledge he possesses from this often appears in his dealings with friends and clients, to their benefit. Without doubt this inclination to philosophical research and scientific experiments derived from his father by inheritance. So far as societies go, in which Dr. Dennerle is always enthusiastically involved, he was for years a member of the Social Turners, and he is past chief of the Order of Knights. In 1881 he married Miss Elizabeth Wilson, and four children have come from this marriage, three boys and a girl, of which the last sadly died. Every member of the family plays a musical instrument, and in 1904 they all appeared before a large audience in the Grays' Armory. Dr. Dennerle is one of the oldest residents of Holmden Avenue, near Jennings, and there his children saw the light of the world. The names of his surviving sons are Carl Gibe, Harold Shetuck, John Wilson. Later the family moved to State View Cottage, State View Avenue, South Brooklyn, to a home built according to Dr. Dennerle's own plan, and most recently Dr. Dennerle lives at 40 Elmwood Street, Lakewood.

Joseph F. Lampert

Joseph F. Lampert was born on 31 May 1854 in Weissenburg, Alsace. His father, Michael, was a respected building contractor and manufacturer of heavy hand tools. At the tender age of 18 months the boy had the misfortune to lose his mother, whose maiden name was Barbara De Bergère, and as a result he was raised in an institution near Heidelberg until his father entered marriage with a Miss von Himmelbach six years later, moved to Karlsruhe and sent the young Joseph to the elementary school there. Then the boy attended the Volksschule in Wiesloch and finally the Catholic seminary in Freiburg im Breisgau until the outbreak of the French-German War in 1870, which led to the institution's closure. For three months the young man held a position in the administrative division of the army until a severe illness forced him to give up his position and seek recovery with an aunt. In 1872, Lampert emigrated to America, and after three months in New York he went west and settled in Galion, Ohio. Here he took a position as a traveling salesman with a tobacco company and established himself in 1876 as a wholesale cigar and tobacco dealer, which he carried out with ability despite his youth and soon made into a flourishing business. Six years later he was hired as general representative by the Anthoni Sons brewery in Delaware, Ohio, and he remained in this position for three years. Then he went into the same business in the service of the Greenway Brewing Co. in Syracuse, New York, remaining there 14 years while also managing a wholesale busines in malt beverages and wine at 20 Merwin Street, which he did with great success. Finally, three years ago he moved to 133-135 Seneca Street, and since then this has been the location of this flourishing business.

His desire to travel has taken him across the ocean three times. He is as experienced in the geography of the United States, since he has visited almost every place worth naming in the Union while a traveling representative of the companies mentioned. Mr. Lampert belongs to the Elks, the Knights of Pythias, with the position of a staff officer in the uniformed ranks, the Cleveland Singing Society and a number of other lodges and societies.

Henry Ohmenhäuser

Henry Ohmenhäuser was born on 19 August 1853 in Schönbuch, Württemberg. As a young man of 15 he came to Cleveland on 2 November 1868 and apprenticed here as a cooper. In 1878 he participated in the North Pole expedition under the leadership of Swatky of the United States Army. This expedition lasted eighteen months, which was primarily launched to recover Franklin's remains. On his return, Olmenhäuser joined the U. S. Navy as a cooper, serving three and a half years. This gave him the opportunity to get to know a beautiful part of the world, particularly the coastal regions of the Mediterranean. He visited the Holy Land, Palestine, and the places we all know from the Bible. Mr. Ohmenhäuser can tell some very interesting observations and experiences about this.

Returning to Cleveland, which Mr. Ohmenhäuser always regarded as home, he took a large role from a society point of view. He is a member of the Harugari Order and is currently Grand Bard of the state of Ohio, chairman of the Pioneer Society and for the last four years chairman of the trustees of the Vorwärts Turners, former president of the National Union and former president of the Cabinet, an association of the various councils of the National Union. He is also a member of the Western Reserve Manie, a higher degree of the Harugari. One may rightfully say that nothing of general importance is done in German circles in which Mr. Ohmenhäuser is not involved.

He married on 2 May 1888 to Miss Margaretha, née Yockel, the marriage producing four children, of which two, a boy and a girl, are still alive. Since 1884 Mr. Ohmenhäuser has been successfully involved in insurance, and he enjoys a great circle of friends in this city.

C. H. Hengst

Mr. Hengst was born on 14 January 1848 in Olbernhau, Kingdom of Saxony. He was the sixth of nine sons of his father, Karl Friedrich Hengst, who supported his large family as a farmer. As was the case with so many, he participated in the Revolution of 1848, and his sense for freedom was inherited by his son, born in that year of revolution and in that sense a Forty Eighter. After attending the Volksschule in his home town, Mr. C. H. Hengst underwent a five year apprenticeship as a rigger and metal worker, then passed through the usual time of wandering and worked in the cities of Prague, Leipzig, Chemnitz and Dresden. We find him in the last city in the years 1872-82 as the works leader in a factory for metal items and buttons. Later he entered the Royal Court Bronzewares Manufactury in Röle, and he later had the opportunity to help prepare the gala coach which the city of Dresden gave to Crown Prince Albert.

Equipped with fundamental experience in all branches, Mr. Hengst emigrated to America in 1882. He landed in Baltimore on 28 May in that year, going directly to Cleveland, which became his home. During his passage it happened that one of his children died in the old homeland where his family was temporarily staying. On his arrival in Cleveland, he worked his first two years in the Non-Explosive Lamp Works, then at W. S. Taylor's Wire Works, which produced its first brass goods under his direction, and Mr. Hengst then made himself independent by establishing his own workshop on Ontario Street, where the German-American Bank now has its office. Later he moved his office to the corner of Seneca and Long Street. There he carried on his business until 1890, when he was hit with the hard blow of losing his wife. His true life companion, born in Gehringswalde near Waldheim, had married him as Miss Anna Stoppel in 1870. She gave him ten children, seven boys and three girls, of which one son still lives, the young Hengst active in his father's business.

After his wife's death Mr. Hengst was a widower for 2 1/2 years, and he also gave up his business until he married Auguste Grundmann in 1891, also from Saxony, from Dresden. After a pleasant journey with her to Germany he resumed his business, and he moved it to Sheriff Street in September, 1898, where it remains to this day. The success of his business is shown by the fact that it employs eight men. The object of his manufacture is metal articles, and as mentioned, his son of 33 is also in the business.

Mr. Hengst is well known in wide circles because of his active participation in German society life, and he has deserved this notoriety for his efforts to support German causes. In the Vorwärts Turner Society, where he is the oldest and most respected member, he is trustee, and with the Harugari he is a member of the board of directors for the death-payment fund. He was also one of the founding and most zealous members of the German Central League. Furthe, he belongs to the Knights of Pythias, the Concordia Lodge of the Freemasons, the Harmonie and the National Union.

Despite his domestic disasters and the years he has passed, Mr. Hengst continues to be the picture of unbroken strength.

Mr. Hengst, Jr., was gone from here for some time about ten years ago, and he passed through stirring times. In 1897 he went to Nashville, Memphis and St. Louis. When the Spanish-American War broke out, he participated and entered the Artillery. He was ordered to Puerto Rico. After the war was over, he returned to St. Louis and resumed work there. The young Mr. Hengst also married in St. Louis.

Wilhelm Plotz

Mr. Wilhelm Plotz takes a leading position among the German businessmen of Cleveland. He was born on 17 April 1847 in Wildberg, district of Demmin, Prussia, grew up there and received his education. He then went to Tetzleben to learn smithery, and he remained there for four years until he understood the craft and decided to emigrate to America. In 1865 the young journeyman smith came here. He was here for two years in Cleveland, then absented himself for three years and visited various cities of the country, until he returned in 1870 to take up permanent residence in the Forest City. As a result of his energy and hard work, he soon was able to make himself independent, and from modest beginnings he rose to owner and leader of an important business, as he is known to be in Cleveland today. Along with his zeal for business, Mr. Plotz has always harbored a lively and righteous zeal for German causes, and he happily participates in German society life. He is a member of the Concordia Lodge, holding the 32nd degree of this order. He holds the office of treasurer in the Heights Men's Chorus. Further, he belongs to the Order of Foresters and the Red Men, and in all societies he holds honorary offices, a proof of his popularity and the respect he enjoys naturally. In 1869 Mr. Plotz married the first time, to Miss Marie Thessendorf from Anklam, Prussia, who had come to

America with her sister. Five children came from that marriage, of which only one daughter survives. She is now married to Mr. E. S. Hall, who is active in Mr. Plotz's business.

After the death of his first wife in 1884, Mr. Plotz married Miss Kathie Knoch, a child of Cleveland. Two sons, Georg and Oscar, came from this marriage, who are also involved in Mr. Plotz's business. Mr. Plotz has a fine home at 2500 Professor Avenue on the southwest side.

His shop is located on Champlain Street, from 401 to 411. A considerable number of mostly German workers produce the stamps, mallets and other tools and small machines for iron construction and smith work on buildings and in the open air, whose fabrication has been Mr. Plotz' work for years.

John Meinel

A thoroughly modest man in appearance who has risen to such success that he is regarded as a self-made man in the true sense of the word is Mr. John Meinel, whose place of business is in the building at 918 Payne Avenue. He was born in Rehau, a town in the Bavarian district of Upper Franconia. His father ran a tawing works, but he died while John was still a small child. His education was in the schools of his home town, where he also apprenticed as a slaughterer for 2 1/2 years.

After completing his apprenticeship, he went on the road as was still the practice there, and for the next three years he worked in various cities of his old fatherland, including Frankfurt am Main, Chemnitz, Dresden, Hof, Erlangen, etc. On 1 October Mr. Meinel was called to military service and mustered into the 10th Bavarian infantry regiment.

When the hereditary enemy of Germany disturbed world peace in 1870 and 1871 and sought to humiliate our old fatherland, Mr. Menel entered the struggle as well in the company of many others to defend his home. Wounded by a grazing in a battle, he had to spend much time in a hospital. Fortunately the wound was not dangerous, and soon he recovered and was placed in the Bavarian train battalion at Sedan as a field slaughterer.

At the start of 1872 Mr. Meinel emigrated to America, landing in New York, where he worked in his profession for 1 1/2 months before moving to Providence, R. I., where he was active for some time. His view, however, had turned west. In 1874 we find him in Cleveland, where he has been resident without interruption ever since, and where his life took a pleasant turn. Only during the first two years did he work for an employer, and then in 1876 he began his own business, and Mr. Meinel bought that shop on Payne Avenue, where his business is still located, and where he has achieved a certain prosperity. Besides his own business, he is also financially involved in other enterprises.

Mr. Meinel has always shown great interest in German causes. He is a co-founder of the Vorwärts Turners, a member of the Bavarian Support Society no. 2, of the Odd Fellows, the Cuyahoga Society, the Comrades in Arms and the Bismarck Lodge, as well as of the Pioneer Society, in which he often holds honorary offices.

In 1878 he married Miss Mina Zentner, from Mecklenburg-Schwerin, who came to the country as a young girl. This happy marriage produced four sons, of which the eldest and the youngest help in his business. John, the eldest, is 28, Georg, 25, Frank, 22, and William, 18. Georg is in New York, and Frank holds the office of delivery clerk at the Forest City Brass Works.

On 5 October 1895 the Meinel family was visited by a terrible blow of fate when death took their beloved wife and mother. Mourned by many and missed particularly by her husband, her memory is treasured. Since he is in those years when a companion is needed for life and business, particularly for the welfare of the children, Mr. Meinel decided on a second marriage with Louise Beyer, with whom he lives in a pleasant union.

Adolph Diener

Mr. Adolph Diener is well known in German circles, since in partnership with his brother he owns a sculpturing and gravestone business at 367 Woodland Avenue. One must know the story of his life and family to comprehend the strength required to wrest success from the storms which have enfolded his life. He was born on 26 March 1845 in Radolfszell on Lake Constance as the eldest son of Johann Nepomuk Diener, a sculptor. A man enthused for liberty, he joined the revolutionary movement in 1848 which had risen to great dimensions in Baden under Hecker, Franz Sigel and Brentano. After the failure of the movement, he fled to Switzerland and then to Italy, where he joined Garibaldi's bands, fighting the Austrians. In 1855 he emigrated with his family to America, and he was able to dedicate himself to his artistic activity for several years in New York, until war broke out. He was naturally one of the first to sign up for the liberation of slaves. He was recruited into the 1st Artillery Regiment, but later he joined along with the Garibaldi Guard in the 39th New York Infantry. He served in this unit for 3 1/2 years in many battles. His adventurous life carried the germ of a treacherous illness, tuberculosis, which overcame him in 1870 at the age of 52. His mother, who moved to Pittsburgh while her husband was still in the field, and then to Cleveland, was so upset by her husband's death that she followed him two years later.

Of the children left behind, Albert, Adolph, August, Heinrich, Joseph and Anna, Albert and Joseph died soon, August and Anna found homes in Indianapolis, and Adolph and Heinrich remained in Cleveland and ran the sculpture shop together they had founded. Adolph is the intellectual leader. Initiated into his father's business, it was he who was the support of the family while his father served in the war, as well as afterwards with all their troubles. Coming to Cleveland from New York with his mother, he worked in the firm of McDowell & Gibbs before he became independent in partnership with his brother. For a time he was in Canton, Ohio, and became acquainted with his wife, Miss Elisabeth Ohliger, the daughter of a respected German family. Her father was the owner of the Jackson Hotel. A brother in law, L. Ohliger, has been manager of the Canton Water Works for several years. During his residence in Canton, Mr. Diener was himself a member of the local volunteer fire department. Today he heads his well-established sculpture shop on Woodland Avenue, and Mr. Adolph Diener warmly supports German causes. He is a member of many German societies and associations. He belongs to the Concordia Lodge of the Freemasons, Cleveland Lodge no. 61 of the Knights of Pythias, is a member of the Order of the Harugari, in which he also belongs to the Western Reserve Manie, as well as the Pioneer Society, the Vorwärts Turners, the Harmonie Singing Society, the Swabian Society, an honorary member of the Baden Society, and many others. Drawn at such an early age into his father's passions, Mr. Diener has become a man of earnest and deep-looking character, and he is generally respected as such. The creations of his shop demonstrate how masterful he is in the art of sculpting.

Lorenz Leopold

Mr. Lorenz Leopold is known as the owner of a hotel including a fine restaurant and cafe at 201 Champlain Avenue, N. W., which bears the original name of Hotel Barbarossa, which the owner has given it in memory of his Swabian homeland. Mr. Leopold was born on 1 May 1858 in the district center of Tuttlingen in the Kingdom of Württemberg. His father was a respected and wealthy master slaughterer, which made possible a good education for Lorenz. He was sent to the Realschule in Spaichingen and then to the mercantile school in Ravensburg. After graduating the latter he commenced a mercantile career for which he had been prepared through being an apprentice in the writing office of the world-famous machine factory of Escher, Wyss & Co. in Zürich. His intentions were directed to America, however, and he carried out his intention to go there in 1878. On arriving in New York he found his first position with Hammacher, Schlemmer & Co. as a bookkeeper and remained there for two years, until he entered the service of L. Foreman, Fechtman & Co., where he remained for 15 years. After this long period of mercantile activity, he was in the situation to move elsewhere and become independent. He went to Cleveland and established himself in the restaurant business, which he has pursued for the last 12 years with the greatest success. Capable and jovial in dealing with all, Mr. Leopold has managed to build a great circle of friends. His restaurant and hotel are among the most proper and best-led in the heart of the city, and they receive high approval from the professional element, particularly the Germans. Various societies have found him to be a worthy member. Especially the Harmonie Singing Society gained in him an active singer. As a Swabian, Mr. Leopold also belongs the Swabian Singing League and the Schiller Lodge, and as a friend of the Swiss and a Turner he belongs to the Swiss Turner Society, and as a singer, though passive in this case, he also belongs to the Swiss Men's Chorus, and he also belongs to the Order of the Eagles and that of the Knights of Pythias, the Bayard Taylor Lodge of the Odd Fellows and the Retail Liquor League. Beyond his participation in society life, Leopold Lorenz can always be relied on in a good cause, which does him great honor and distinguishes him from many others to his benefit.

Louis Thöme

Mr. Louis Thöme was born on 9 December 1853 in Lüneburg, Hanover, as the son of Mr. Johann Thöme. His father ran a distillery and a farm, but he held a respected position among his fellow citizens and enjoyed general popularity. Young Thöme attended the outstanding schools of his home town, and after completing school he was apprenticed as a saddler. Later he traveled through the whole of Germany and trained himself thoroughly in his craft. Enthused by the drive to see other lands and find a wider field for his talents, he came to America on 6 May 1881 and settled in Cleveland, where he was pleased to make his permanent residence. His original goal had actually been Chicago, but his travel companions were so enthusiastic in their description of Cleveland that he was moved to remain here, and he has never had to regret that decision. Mr. Thöme found employment at once in his branch of work, and he later founded a saddle business of his own, which he ran for nine years with success. For the last two years, Mr. Thöme has been connected with the Standard Knitting Co., holding the office of treasurer and superintendent. Possessed by the spirit of progress, Mr. Thöme may always be found on the right side in struggles on behalf of freedom and individuality. Always taking part in German societal life, he is a member of many societies. Earlier he was a respected and active member of the Frohsinn Singing Society, and now he is a zealous member of the Harmonie Singing Society. Mr. Thöme was elected treasurer at the founding of the Central Ohio Singing District, an office he held for two terms. Further, he is one of the founders of the Hanover Society as well as a long-term member of the Independent Order of Foresters and a member of the Allemania Support Society. Through his modest and tactful presence he has gathered a wide circle of friends, and he often holds offices of honor and trust in societies and in German undertakings. On 20 April 1876 he married Miss Maria Lambe from Wittingen, Hanover, and the happy union produced two daughters, Martha (the present Mrs. O. F.

Schmidt), and Miss Lucy, who has held a position of responsibility for the last five years in the firm of Ernst Konigslöw & Bro. before going into teaching, which has always been her desire, and she is currently a capable and respected teacher.

Adam Isheim

Adam Isheim first saw the light of day on 15 September 1857 in Grüningen, Hessia-Darmstadt. He was educated in the Volksschule of his birthplace, apprenticing as a butcher in Frankfurt am Main. He practiced his profession until he entered military service. From 1877 to 1880 he served with the 116th Infantry Regiment in Giessen. It was not long after his release that he decided to emigrate to America. He arrived in Cleveland in 1881, and he was independent a mere two years later. His current place of business is 10310 St. Clair Street.

A year after his arrival in the Forest City, in 1882, Mr. Isheim married Thekla Müller, his first wife, who sadly died in 1895, leaving five children: Mary, Kathy, Emma, Karl and Willie. In order to give them a new mother, Mr. Isheim decided on a second marriage in 1896 with Pauline Reiss, producing one child, Albert.

Mr. Isheim is not only a capable businessman enjoying general trust and love, but he is also active in society life. He has been a member of the Woodward Lodge of the Freemasons for years.

Edward Schumann

Germans of Cleveland can look with happy satisfaction on the sons and descendents of German pioneers who, despite being born on the soil of free America in the middle of a mixed population, never deny their German origins but rather display it and are proud of it in trade and character. One of the best examples is Edward Schumann, the son of an old German pioneer family. Mr. Schumann's parents came to this country at the beginning of the 1840s, settling in Cleveland. The fact that Mr. Schumann can trace himself to a respected family derives from the fact that his father was born on his parents' property in Bingen on the Rhine, and that his mother, born Wilhelmine Seckler, came from the lovely Rhenish Palatinate. In Cleveland his father established a brewery although the business was then not as propitious for the undertaking, and this later went into the hands of Mr. Oppmann, and it is today well known as the Phoenix brewery. In his best years, at the age of 49, the father was carried away by death in 1876. In 1889 he also lost his mother. The marriage was blessed with five children, two daughters and three sons, of whom Edward was the second oldest, born on 8 October 1858.

While growing up, the boy attended public schools before turning to the tavernkeeper's profession, where he has remained without interruption. As the very best of hosts, Mr. Schumann today possesses one of the most beautiful and fine taverns in the city in the building at 513 Superior N. E. In 1885 Mr. Schumann married Miss Louise Schenk, the daughter of a respected German family in Buffalo. A member of a great number of societies, Mr. Schumann supports all noble German causes to the best of his ability.

Julius Firchow

In recent times our city has won a reputation for buildings not just due to their number but also their architectonic beauty. This leads us to conclude that it is not just our architects who prepare plans but also our master builders who carry out these plans who are better than those in other cities. Among these master builders an important position is taken by Mr. Julius

Firchow. He was born on 9 March 1852 in Neu-Langsew, district of Lebus, region of Frankfurt on the Oder, and he received an excellent education in the schools of his birthplace. Even as a little boy Julius built little structures of small blocks, and this interest in building continued to drive him after he left school, so that he dedicated himself to construction, becoming an apprentice in masonry. After finishing his apprenticeship, he traveled through a great portion of Germany, and then he attended the famous drafting school in Berlin. After completing his military duty for three years in the Third Posen Infantry Regiment, he went on the road again, reaching America in 1882 and coming straight to Cleveland. Here he worked for a long time as a masonry-polisher, moving in 1884 to Sioux City, Iowa, where he resided for three years, hence until 1887. Returning to Cleveland, Mr. Firchow established himself as a building contractor, and as such he has been active ever since, with brief exceptions. We shall only mention the local South School, Case School and the High School in Warren, Ohio, the High School in Collinwood, Ohio, the High School in Brooklyn, Ohio, and most of all the First Methodist Episcopal Church at the corner of Cedar and East Madison Street among the major private and public buildings. Further, Mr. Firchow has also built many so-called terraces, and he continues this activity with restless zeal.

In 1886 Mr. Firchow married Miss Mathilde Sickmann, the daughter of an old pioneer couple, and the happy marriage was blessed through the birth of two girls and two boys. Unfortunately, he lost his loving wife on 25 January 1898 after a wearing illness, and he remained single until April, 1900. He regarded it as a duty to provide his motherless children with a feminine soul to care for them, and once he came to know Mrs. Casey Cowley, an honorable widow, he married her as a second mother for his children and a lifetime companion.

Mr. Firchow lives in Euclid in a house in an idyllic setting, equipped with all modern conveniences, happy and contented and surrounded by a fine family circle.

His office and building lot is located at 1234 East Third Street. Mr. Firchow has always had an intense interest in public life and society life, and he is a member of the Royal Arcanum Order, the National Union and the order of the Knights of Pythias. A lovable personality, Mr. Firchow has deserved the happiness and satisfaction of his success, won with hard work.

Robert H. Opitz

An outstanding position among principal Germans in Cleveland is taken by Robert Opitz, who was born on 21 September 1861, in the town of Netzschkau, Saxony. He lost his father, who died when Robert was a boy of two, and he came to the comital estate of Schönberg, where he proved useful, after completing the Volksschule in his birthplace. Yet the young man did not long remain there, but rather he went out into the world and to America. To him America was the land his hard work deserved. In June, 1881, he reached Cleveland. At first he worked on a farm, but then he got a job at the Cleveland rolling mill and finally his star rose as he won a position as a porter with the Lake Shore Line. He worked up from that position until Thanksgiving 1893, when he was made chief of the tools and writing material department. He holds this interesting, but also very responsible, position to this day. He held this position with such tact that the company regards him as one of its best acquisitions. Robert Opitz is intimately befriended with innumerable persons. What created his great circle of adherents is his limitless liberality. In this there is no equal. His office is constantly full of those who have business with him and flee to him as a savior to those in need.

His joy at interaction and sociability has always caused him to take intense part in society life. It is the Vorwärts Turner Society which has in him one of its greatest promoters.

His efforts and sacrifices were the reason the Society has its Turner Hall and has become the gathering place for the best Turners. Other societies to which Mr. Opitz belongs include the German League, the Knights of Honor, the Elks, the Vorwärts Singing Section, the Forest City Lodge of the Freemasons, and various others. Since he is popular everywhere, he has many honorary offices as well. Robert Opitz is also a great and prize-winning bowler, as well as a great friend of animals and flowers. Further, Mr. Opitz is owner of a decorative garden business in the vicinity of Wade Park, which he has leased because his official position with the railroad takes all his time. He is invested in various business enterprises, so that he was a partner in the Bryan hat busines on Seneca Street. Mr. Opitz has been married since 1886. He married a Miss Gut, who was born in Zürich, Switzerland. Two boys have resulted from this marriage, of whom one recently died to the great distress of the parents. In 1904 "Bob" Opitz used his vacation for a trip to Germany. He had not visited his old homeland since emigrating, and his visit was a pleasant change from his strenuous work and activities in Cleveland. Of his relatives, he found two brothers and a sister still alive. The sister had made the visit to her brother some years before, returning to Saxony with the best memory of Cleveland. It is to be wished in the interests of Cleveland Germans that Robert Opitz long remains here, since he is a rare credit to them, and in him they have a firm hold and an irreplaceable support.

Jacob Bommhardt

One of our most respected German pioneers, who has already lived in this city for half a century, is Jacob Bommhardt. He came here in 1857, at a time when Cleveland was a relatively small place, so that Mr. Bommhardt has had full opportunity to see Cleveland grow to a large city.

Mr. Bommhardt was born on 20 April 1837 in Schierbach, Electoral Hessia, to honorable parents who gave their child a good education. After Jacob finished school, he learned the hard craft of a large-scale smith. At the age of 20 he came to America and settled in Cleveland. For eleven years, from 1857 to 1868, he worked as a craftsman before establishing himself as a grocer and a tavern-keeper, a business he still pursues and in which he has achieved some prosperity.

When the Union was in peril, he rushed to arms and joined the First Ohio Artillery Regiment, where he served for three months, participating in the battle of Shieds River in West Virginia.

Mr. Bommhardt has married twice, the first time to Miss Elisabeth Gluck on 9 December 1861, which produced three sons, John, Christian and Willy, and the second with Miss Caroline Geissinger on 11 April 1875. Four children resulted from this union, Elisabeth, Ellen, Henry and Emma.

Mr. Bommhardt is a member of the German Order of the Harugari, belonging to the "Mannie," and he is a member of the Pioneer Society. As such he enjoys the greatest respect from all those with whom he has contact.

Friedrich Axel

Friedrich Axel is a striking example of the fact that a man equipped with good health, fresh courage and decisive action can easily find his advancement in America and rise to respect and wealth.

Born on 9 July 1862 in Dielkirchen, Rhenish Hessia, he found his first employment in a quarry after leaving the *Volksschule* of his locality later going to Kreuznach, where he worked first in a dairy, then as a teamster. Then he earned his bread as a waiter until called to military service. In 1882 he was mustered into the 8th Bavarian Infantry Regiment, serving his 3 years in Metz. After the end of his term of service he took up a position as a waiter in the Mainzer Hof in Wiesbaden, where he long remained until he came to Cleveland, with his ticket paid for by the widow Schlegel, the now-deceased owner of the Schlegel's Garden on Woodland Avenue.

During his first time here he worked during the day in a tanning yard, and in the evening at both Schlegel's and Haltnorth's Gardens. Yet soon he established himself independently ran his own business on Columbus Street and later on Orange Street, where he took over the Luther Grocery with its tavern. In a few years he was able to build Mount Pleasant View House on Kinsman Road, a mile beyond the city boundary. In this building, passed by the cars of the Cleveland and Chagrin Falls line, Mr. Axel supplied a large store with groceries, iron goods, porcelain and other items needed for households, and there are also a tavern, a dance floor and a summer garden, all enjoying considerable popularity.

The respect and trust our successful compatriot won in his neighborhood may be seen by how quickly they came to like him and the extraordinary abilities he had developed, as is shown by his political career. His energy was not restricted to establishing his own business, but he soon passed to public matters. Only two years after getting the right to vote, he was named a delegate to the state convention. He has held the office of a member of the county Democratic central committee for ten terms. During this period he was also elected a school director. He declined reelection to this office after one term. Then he was elected to the city council, and for a long time he was its president. After the annexation of a part of Newburg, he became mayor of the non-annexed portion. He held the office for two terms, and then he declared the office took too much time he owed to his business. Further, Mr. Axel has been first policeman and assistant city marshall.

Later he withdrew from all public offices, since he had plenty to do with his own business. Finally, Mr. Axel has now bought a large farm in Independence.

Mr. Axel also belongs to all branches of the Harugari Order, the Concordia Lodge no. 345 of the Freemasons, the Lodge of the United German Union, the German Comrades in Arms, the Palatine Society and he is a member and president of the *Liederkranz* Singing Society.

On 14 April 1888 Mr. Axel married Magdalena Herrmann from Imbsweiler, Rhenish Palatinate, the daughter of a wealthy quarry owner and tile maker. The marriage has produced four children, of which two are still alive.

Mr. Axel lived at his place on Kinsman Road, Mount Pleasant House, until he recently leased it to move to his new farm.

Joseph Heim

Joseph Heim was born on 26 January 1857 in Hochfelden, Alsace, and attended the communal schools in his birthplace until he was 14, when he apprenticed as a barber in Strasbourg. After his apprenticeship he returned to Hochfelden, working here for a time in his business, and from 1875 to 1878 he went to Paris, where he was employed in several of the great hairdressing salons of the Seine metropolis. The two following years returned him to his birthplace. Then he decided to emigrate in 1881, coming directly to Cleveland, where he owned a barber business from 1883 to 1891 at the corner of Superior and Seneca Streets. After the death of his father-in-law, D. Kuntz, he took over the Atlantic Garden, earlier Kuntz' Garden, on Columbus Street, which maintained its popularity under his management as a summer resort for the West Side, and in 1898 he became an agent in the Schnauffer & Heim Insurance business, earlier

Seelbach & Schnauffer. Since the death of Mr. Heinrich Schnauffer, he leads his business alone, and his office is found in 1003 Rockefeller Building. In 1885 he married Miss Louise Kuntz, who gave him three children, Victor, Alma and Edwin, in the course of the years. Mr. Heim is a member of Concordia, of the Social Turners, of "Orpheus" and the Alsace-Lorraine Support Society. He is very popular in singing circles, and Mr. Heim is the local representative of the executive board of the North American Singing League.

Wm. Buse

When one proceeds along the lower portion of Prospect Avenue, N. E., the unusual façade of one building surprises, on which the inscription reads, "Hofbräu-Haus," and which is particularly intended for Germans. That house was built in 1903 and 1904 by Mr. Wm. Buse according to plans of the famous architect Mr. John Eisenmann, who has made Old German architecture his special study. The interior corresponds to the interior in every respect, and on entrance one might think himself in an old German court beer taproom of the seventeenth century, since not only the entire furnishing but even the illumination corresponds to that of old Bavaria in that time. The owner, Mr. Wm. Buse, was born on 1 September 1865 in Oldenburg, and he came to Cleveland with his parents as a child of two. Here he attended public school and grew to a young man, possessed by the drive to get to know the world. He left Cleveland and went to Chicago, where he dedicated himself to the tavern-keeper's profession and learned it in all its branches, winning so much knowledge that he later made a significant career. He was employed in Chicago for three years before returning to Cleveland. On his arrival here, he took jobs with various large locales until he took employment with Mr. John Schuster, who was then managing the German place made famous under the name of Rathskeller, located on Sheriff Street. This became the gathering place for Germans, and Mr. Buse obtained many friends here. After Mr. Schuster bought the brewery in Massillon, Ohio, Mr. Buse bought the Rathskeller and continued it with success until he sold it to Mr. Trinkner at the start of 1904, since his new place was almost ready and he wished to make a trip to Europe with his wife before it opened. Mr. and Mrs. Buse then went to New York, accompanied by several friends, and set off on their journey to the old homeland which Mr. Buse had left as a child. The traveled through Germany, France, England, Austria amd Switzerland, and then they returned here, where the grandiose opening of the Hofbräu-Haus took place on 29 March 1904. Mr. Buse is a member of the Concordia Lodge of the Freemasons as well as of the Order of Elks, and he takes an active part in public events. His amiable wife, Marie, is the daughter of the noted pioneer of Fred. Frey and his wife, and Mr. Buse has been married since 1889. The Hofbräu-Haus is at 141-143 Prospect Avenue.

Friedrich Mattmueller

In the Breisgau, in the Baden village of Tenningen near the district town of Emmendingen, Freiburg Region, Mr. Friedrich Mattmueller first saw the light of day on 30 October 1840. After confirmation he apprenticed in Malterdingen to a furniture cabinet-maker to learn the trade. He remained there until he was 17, and when his apprenticeship ended he went on the road. He worked for eight years in various places in Switzerland, France and Italy, training himself in his craft. He came to the United States in 1867 at the age of 27. His intention was to see this part of the world, to learn something, and then to return to his old homeland. A serious illness befell him here, however, and he changed his plans after recovery. Despite excellent offers received from home, he settled permanently in Cleveland. For four years he worked at the

Beilstein Furniture Factory, making himself independent in 1871. He established a furniture store and funeral parlor at 100-102 Pelton Avenue, which he still runs with great success. Two years later, in 1873, he started a furniture factory, although that burned down in 1886, bringing him no small loss. He then gave up furniture manufacture completely and concentrated on his other business.

In 1869 Mr. Mattmueller married a friend of his youth, Miss Carolina Trautmann, also born in Tenningen. This marriage produced six children, two sons and four daughters. The elder son Fritz, age 26, is associated with his father in his business. The younger son, Albert, 22, is working as a clerk in the Mattmueller shoe business. The eldest daughter Carolina is married to Mr. Georg Armbruster, bakery owner in Elyria. After his marriage, Mr. Mattmueller had his mother come to him, who died in high old age after a long life's evening on 23 January 1901.

Mr. Mattmueller has always taken an intense role in social life. He was one of the founders of the Heights Men's Chorus; he was an active member of the Baden Singing Society until recently, and he was its delegate to the League of the United Singers of Cleveland. He was a founder of the Humboldt Tribe of Red Men, and in 1880-82 he was the highest officer of the order in the state of Ohio. He was president for three terms of the West Side Baden Support Society, and he held the responsible office of treasurer of the Buckeye State Beneficiary Society, which grew out of the Equitable Aid Union. The Independent German Order of Cleveland organized itself when the previous group dissolved, and Mr. Mattmueller is today chair of the trustees.

In all of these societies in which Mr. Mattmueller held office, he stood out for his strict punctuality and conscientious fulfillment of duty.

He is known and respected in the entire city, not just in the South Side where he lives, as a fine businessman.

Joseph Tillman

A personality known and loved here, one might almost say a typical figure, is Mr. Joseph Tillman. He emigrated to America in 1852 with his parents at the age of 10 from Nehren, Prussian Rheinish Province. For years he was in the grocery business, and he applied tireless effort to it so that he could eventually retire and leave the business to his sons. As is well known, the home and business are to be found at 6302 Quincy Avenue, S. E.

Mr. Tillman is a convinced and unshaken Democrat, and he has often been elected as a delegate to conventions. Although it would be easy for him to get a lucrative office, he has never exploited this position. When it is a question of going into the lists for the Party, he is there, and still is, but the rest he leaves to others. Mr. Tillman is a respected member of the C. M. B. A. His marriage of 38 years with his wife, born Therese Melch from Kentucky, has produced six children, 4 boys and 2 girls, who have long since become important supports to their parents. Mr. Tillman wishes to make his life as comfortable as possible. He enjoys traveling, and he has taken several with pleasure, and he is always missed by his many acquaintances in Cleveland.

Friedrich Lehr

This gunmaker, well-known in many circles, Mr. F. Lehr, was born on 10 December 1845 as the son of the nail-smith Martin Lehr in Gross-Bieberau, Hessia-Darmstadt. After attending school briefly in his hometown, he emigrated to America with his parents and ten siblings in 1852, coming directly to Cleveland, where he had his remaining schooling. During the war years of

1861-1862 he was an apprentice with the _'Wächter am Erie,'_ under August Thieme. Then he went into the profession of a machinist. As such he trained himself thoroughly, later turning to gunmaking. Soon he became independent, and for the last thirty years he has owned a business in the building at 656 Lorain Street, one of the most sought-after gun-dealers in Cleveland.

Taking an active role in public life, citizens elected him in 1885 in what was then the eleventh ward to the city council, where he served tirelessly until 1887. Enthused for German causes, he has turned in his leisure hours to noble gymnastics, and he became and is still a member of the Social Turners, and he was chief Turner, first speaker, and for years Turner instructor. Mr. Lehr is also a member of the National Union, an insurance association with a large membership.

In 1873 he married Miss Anna Strebel. Unfortunately his true wife was taken away by death, leaving the sorrowing widower with three girls, Cora, Martha and Ida. Since the motherless children needed a woman's heart and a sure leading hand, Mr. Lehr decided on a second marriage after finding a related spirit in Miss Elise Möller, a lady from Hessia-Kassel. He married her, and she became his wife and the mother to his children. Mr. Lehr, wife and children form a true German family circle, and he enjoys the highest respect as a citizen and as a businessman.

Theodor Holz

Among the younger Germans in Cleveland who have managed to achieve a respected business position in a few years and to make themselves socially beloved in wider circles, there is Theodor Holz, 2911 Lorain Avenue. The named gentleman was born in 1860 in Danzig, West Prussia, and after completing the Realschule, he apprenticed as a sheet-metal worker and emigrated to America in 1889. He found here a wide field for the use of his knowledge and experience as well as for his energies. He settled in New York, moving his residence in 1896 to our Forest City. Here he quickly realized his hopes and desires. He is today the owner of a prosperous construction sheet-metal shop, 2911 Lorain Avenue, and he enjoys the trust of all people he comes into contact with in business.

Mr. Holz is an enthused disciple of Turner-father Jahn, and as such he is a zealous member of the Social Turner Society, that shrine of Turnerism on the West Side of Cleveland. It is not just that he actively participates in the physical, spiritual and musical activities of that society, no sacrifice in time and trouble is too great to advance the interests of the association and of Turnerism in general.

Wm. F. Fiedler

Mr. William Friedrich Fiedler has been Police Judge of our city for the last twelve years. He first saw the light of day on 8 October 1862. His father was born in lovely Swabia, emigrated to America in 1850, and lived here as a masonry contractor until his death in 1857. The Fiedler family was blessed with five children, of whom three died in infancy. Two sons are still alive, and one of these sons is the object of this article. Mr. Fiedler attended the public schools in his early youth, later the high school, and Adelbert College in 1883. There he completed the classical course, after which he prepared himself for law school at Cincinnati in the offices of the lawyer F. C. Friend. He began law school in 1888, graduating in 1889 with an bachelor of laws. A year later Adelbert College granted him the title of master of arts., and Mr. Fiedler began practicing as a lawyer. In 1891 Mr. Fiedler was one of four candidates for the office of police attorney on the Republican ticket. He was elected with a majority of over 1500 votes. During this term Mr. Fiedler completely justified the confidence placed in him. In recognition for his true fulfillment of duty and his great conscientiousness, in 1893 he was reelected to this position with a majority of over 3000 votes.

In 1895 Mr. Fiedler was elected as police judge, an office for which he was born and in which he has earned many warm and upright friends. Rarely has a police judge exercised his office so seriously as Mr. Fiedler, and seldom has a police judge enjoyed so much respect from his fellow citizens as he, to whom all his colleagues can give only the best reviews. So far as politics go, Mr. Fiedler has been a strict, convinced Republican, yet both tolerant and liberal. He is a member of the Knights of Pythias and the Tippecanoe Club. On 23 August 1893, he married Miss Clara C. Woldmann, who had been an esteemed teacher in the Fowler School. Mr. Fiedler now is in his best years, and the time will come when he will climb the highest ladder as a judge. He always judges properly and wisely, and he is a mild judge when that is what is called for, and a strict judge when strictness is demanded by the circumstances. His dutifulness, his gregarious nature, and his understanding for practical life, with its shadow side, won in his experience as a police judge, make him particularly suited for the office of judge.

Carl H. Nau

The current municipal treasurer, Mr. Carl Nau, is a German-American. His father, Andreas Nau, came in 1853 to Rochester, New York, where he remained until 1860. On a visit he made the same year to his home town, Marburg in Hessia, the father came to know his future wife, Miss Elise Bieber, who came in 1856 to visit her sister in Michigan, lived there for two years and then returned to her hometown of Breitenbach, near Herzberg in Hessia. Several years after the wedding, performed by the American consul in Frankfurt am Main, the young couple left Germany and settled in Berea, where a brother of Mr. Nau lived. But after the passage of a few months they moved to Cleveland to take up permanent residence. Mr. Andreas Nau built a house on Scovill Avenue, in which he pursued his work as a butcher until his death a few years ago.

Mr. Carl Nau was born on 12 April 1866. He was educated in public schools and high schools. At the age of 16 he entered the service of the Standard Oil Company, remaining there for 14 years. He gradually worked his way up from office helper to the heights, holding several responsible offices in that giant business. For years he was cashier of the naphtha department, later he was promoted to traveling auditor, where it was his duty to review and check the books of various stations. At the time of his voluntary departure from the business he held the responsible post of manager in the lubricating department.

In 1896 there was a reorganization of positions in the company, as is often the case, and Mr. Nau was offered a well-salaried, responsible position in New York. Mr. Nau declined the offer since he did not wish to leave Cleveland and had long considered making himself independent.

Mr. Nau has made it his mission for years to do all in his powers to have measures adopted by the municipal administration which benefit the citizens, and to elect such persons as officials who have the welfare of the community at heart. In 1890 he was one of the committee which introduced the federal plan. In 1892 he was candidate for the city council in the sixth district, but he was defeated by his Republican opponent. In 1895 Mr. Nau was nominated by the Democrats as candidate for the office of County Treasurer, but although he ran 9000 votes ahead of the ticket, he lost due to the political currents which ran heavily in favor of the Republicans. He was a member of the local library board during the years 1895-98, and, as mentioned, he was called to the responsible office of municipal treasurer. Mr. Nau possesses all the ability and character needed by a person in his position to administer an office bestowed by the people.

Jacob Fickel

Whoever has made the old saying, "Where there is a will there is a way" the guiding motto of his life can never fail of the success which is rightfully his. This sketch deals with just such a man. Born in the lovely, venerable city of Worms, which has held gatherings of world-historical importance within its walls, Mr. Jacob Fickel saw the light of day on 28 March 1858. After reaching the necessary age, he attended the municipal Volksschule and later the Real-Gymnasium, where he did a splendid graduation examination. Mr. Jacob Fickel apprenticed from his 16th to his 20th year with a wholesale wine dealer in his native city, learning the business of commerce and enriching his knowledge in every direction. The municipal administration recognized his eminent abilities and took him into its service, and over the next three years he was entrusted with important missions in the mayor's office. When Mr. Fickel conceived of the notion to emigrate to America, the municipal officials were reluctant to part with him. In 1881 Mr. Fickel stepped on the shores of America, going to Pittsburgh, Pennsylvania, and finding a position in a wholesale liquor business, where he stayed for four years. Cleveland drew him. Here Mr. Jacob Fickel was active as an insurance agent, first of all for Metropolitan Life Insurance Co., and later for the Western and Southern Life Insurance Co. His energy and social tact had the result that Mr. Fickel was named superintendent by the latter-named company, moved to Hamilton, Ohio, and later Cincinnati.

He resigned this position on 15 August 1898 in order to respond to the flattering call of the Gund Brewing Co. On 1 January 1900 he received the responsible position of secretary of that firm, where he could apply his knowledge to best advantage.

Alongside a native joviality and inborn goodness of heart, Mr. Fickel has a solidity of character, and the respect and success of his efforts which he sought in earlier positions will not fail him here. Mr. Fickel is a member of the Knights of Pythias and the Vorwärts Turner Society, and beyond that he possesses a circle of friends won through his friendly nature.

Georg Wilhelm Müller

Georg Wilhelm Müller was born on 8 June 1853 in Dimautstein, region of Swabia, district of Neuburg in Bavaria. His parents, who were quite respectable, provided a fine education for their son; he attended the Volksschule for four years, then the trades school in Bamberg. After an adequate preparation at school, he began his bourgeois activities under his father's eyes, in an agency and guarantee company which enjoyed the trust of the burghers in the entire region around his birthplace.

When the Franco-German war broke out, Mr. Müller volunteered as a 17-year-old and received a shot wound near Bazailles. In 1872 he came to America, remaining two years in New York before traveling to Cleveland, where he arrived on 2 February 1874 and settled permanently. During the first period of his residence he found a job as a collector in a brewery and later he opened a tavern. Mr. Müller has been active in real estate and insurance for years. His office is in the building at 1006 Clark Avenue. Through his strict sense of legality and tact he has managed to win the trust of a wide circle of local citizens. He is a member of the Concordia Lodge no. 345, F. & A. M.

He married the widow Mrs. Magdalena Bastian on 1 October 1900, who brought four well-raised children, Lena Sommers, Willie Bastian, Konrad Bastian and Louise Grabenstetter, into the marriage.

Heinrich Bach

Mr. Heinrich Bach, the noted bakery owner, was born on 2 December 1857 in Reichsdorf, Bohemia. After receiving an outstanding education, he went into apprenticeship at the age of 14 and chose baking as his profession, to which he has remained true to the present day. After completing his apprenticeship in his home town, his desire to wander drove him into the world, where he wished to get to know lands and peoples, but also to find opportunity for further training in his profession. At first he visited the lands of Croatia and Hungary before returning home to fulfill his military duty, in the 73rd Infantry Regiment quartered in Eger. After completing three years, which was the compulsory service then, he traveled to the Imperial city of Vienna, where he worked steadily for ten years. It was also here where he met and came to love his future wife. In 1884 Bach decided that the Old World did not appeal to him, so he emigrated to America. He came directly to Cleveland, working here for two years, then returned to New York for a year before returning to the Forest City on Lake Erie. It was hard for him to find work after the bakers' strike in 1892, so he made himself independent, and his charming nature won him a great circle of friends. In October, 1884, he had his bride, Miss Maria Eiselle of Iglau, Moravia, come to Cleveland. Five children, all boys, have come from this union. Mr. Bach is a member of the German Order of the Harugari and of the Lyra Singing Society, and he takes an active role in German causes.

Nicolaus Jacobs

Nicolaus Jacobs, the noted building contractor, was born on 20 July 1863 in Hillsweiler, district of Saarlouis, Rhenish Prussian Province, as the son of a respected carpenter Peter Jacobs. After Nicolaus had attended the Volksschule and spent two years in construction, emigration fever seized him on 28 March 1875, and he landed in New York on 4 May of the same year with his two brothers, Johannes and Peter. They settled at first in Rochester, New York, where Nicolaus practiced his trade. It was also here that he met his future wife, then Miss Katharina Rheinstadter, born in Wissen on the Sieg, district of Cologne. It was a strange accident that Miss Rheinstadter landed in New York on the same day as Mr. Jacobs, though with a different steamer. They were married two years after arrival. In 1895 Mr. Jacobs settled in Cleveland, and since then he has been very successful as a building contractor, a self-made-man in the true sense of the word. After his father died, Mr. Jacobs had his mother come to him, who is now 76 and still lives healthily with him. During the Cleveland administration, Mr. Jacobs held the office of U. S. Marshal, and he also functioned a number of terms as ward clerk. He has been a member of the C. M. B. A. for 22 years, and he also belongs to St. Joseph's congregation. Seven children have been born to his marriage, of which the first daughter sadly died: Maria Magdalena, born 13 May1886, died 24 February 1893; Peter, born 27 December 1887, apprenticed as a pastry baker; Johann Wilhelm, born 9 December 1889; Katharina, born 5 December 1891; Maria Magdalena, born 11 July 1894; Franciscus Xavierus, born 4 April 1897; Antonius Heinrich Joseph, born 20 December 1903.

Due to poor health, Mr. Jacobs was compelled to take a four month journey in 1904, and he visited the state of California, where he recovered completely, and where he was so enthused over the climate there that he left Cleveland to settle there.

Wm. H. Beavis

On 18 October 1859, W. H. Beavis, son of the respected Benjamin A. Beavis, saw the light of day in North Brooklyn. W. A. Beavis enjoyed an education in the local public schools. After completing West High School he entered the law division of Cincinnati College in order to dedicate himself to law, and he graduated in 1883 with the degree of bachelor of law. After leaving law school, the young gentleman associated with his father under the title of Beavis & Beavis, continuing on by himself after his father's death the next year. Mr. Beavis is a strict Republican in national and state politics, and he is independent in municipal matters, although he has never sought a public office, as his profession takes up all his time. In 1890, on 25 December, he married Miss Julia, daughter of the well-known and respected citizen Mr. H. W. Lütkemeyer, and a child has been produced by that union. Mr. Beavis is a member of the Ohio State Bar Association and the Cleveland Bar Association, secretary of the German American Savings Bank Co., as well as one of the directors of Consolidated German Newspaper Company, and is as well involved in various commercial undertakings.

Mr. Beavis is one of the most prominent younger German-American lawyers in the Forest City, earning his reputation through his basic knowledge of the law, his strict sense of duty, and his modest conduct.

Frank Sarstedt

As the descendent of an old Hanoverian family, Mr. Frank Sarstedt as a German-American combines in his character all those qualities through which the Germans have made a name in this country and by means of which they stand at the pinnacle of industry, business and social life.

The Sarstedt family is one of the oldest in Germany and belongs among the most important of the Province of Hanover, where it possessed extensive estates. The little town of Sarstedt in that province was founded by forbears of the family and is today a sign of the entrepreneurial talent and prosperity of the family.

It was in 1852 when a descendent of the builders of this little town, the mill owner Bernhard Sarstedt and his wife Sophia, née Kesselmeier, sold their properties in Hildesheim, Hanover, in order to seek their fortune in the New World. Here they first settled in Medina County, Ohio, where Mr. Sarstedt also ran a mill. In 1864 Mr. Sarstedt gave up this business and came to Cleveland to run a cooperage.

Here it was, on 27 August 1864, that Frank Sarstedt was born as the second child. On attaining school age, the little Frank attended the public schools and later West High School, from which he graduated with high honors. Possessed by the desire to become independent, he renounced further study and took a position as cashier in the noted dry-goods business of Mr. John Meckes on the West Side, where he remained for three years.

After the end of this period, in 1881, he took up service as an agent with the Cleveland, Columbus & St. Louis (Big Four) Railroad, where he did such good service that he advanced to bureau chief of the company, which he was doing when he left it in 1893 to become manager of the Barrett brewery. Three years later, in 1896, he exchanged this position for that of manager of the Columbia brewery, where he succeeded Mr. Wm. Pollner, who had resigned to concentrate on his legal practice. After leading this brewery to the satisfaction of the company, he resigned in order to accept the call to become the bureau chief of Mr. Wm. Craig, who had just been elected county auditor.

Although he had taken interest in public affairs for some years, it was in this position that Mr. Sarstedt attracted popular attention. He made the tax system his special study, and he is regarded as one of the best-informed men in the county so far as tax legislation, real estate values and other taxable properties.

Representing his views without fear, there were many conflicts between Sarstedt and certain tax reformers, from which he always emerged the victor. As a result of this situation, he was named under the new law creating a unified taxing authority for all the counties of Ohio to a five year term on the board of review by the state taxing authority on 2 June 1902, to represent Cuyahoga County.

After the end of his first term, he was renewed in view of his fearless and just procedure in fulfilling the duties of his office, which he richly deserved. Although Mr. Frank Sarstedt's time is extensively claimed by his official duties, he still finds leisure to participate in the social and society life of Cleveland. He is a member of the Cleveland Singing Society, the Order of Freemasons, where he has reached the 32nd degree, the National Union, the Cleveland Commercial Travelers' Association, and a number of political societies and groups.

Mr. Sarstedt married Miss Martha Fellmann daughter of an old settler, in 1887, and the happy marriage was blessed by the birth of a son, who is named Arthur Gordon.

R. H. Fetterman

Mr. R. H. Fetterman was born here in Cleveland on 7 January 1860. His father, Johann Fetterman, came from Hessia — he was born in Darmstadt — in 1845 to Cleveland. The mother of R. H. Fetterman was from Baden by birth, but she married her husband here in Cleveland.

Fetterman attended the public schools, then a business college, and at the age of 18 he entered service of the shoe firm Weber & Bender on Superior Street as a clerk, but he quickly earned the trust of his principals, winning the confidence of the customers, and after three years he was owner of the business. For years Mr. Fetterman owned a shoe business on Euclid Avenue, and for the last two years his business is at 1922 E. 6th Street. In 1885 Mr. Fetterman married Miss Theresia Emilie James, a Clevelander whose mother is of German origin. Three children have come from that marriage, two boys and a girl. Mr. Fetterman takes an active part in public life, particularly German life. He was earlier president of the German-American Club, he is a member of the Chamber of Commerce, the New Century Club, the Cleveland Yacht Club, and he belongs to various other societies. He is known throughout this town as a solid and helpful businessman.

Moritz M. Gleichman

Mr. Moritz M. Gleichman was born in lovely Hungary in 1866. At the age of 6 he came with his parents to Cleveland. Here he attended the public schools and later dedicated himself to the study of architecture. A number of buildings have been built according to Mr. Gleichman's designs which give eloquent testimony to his capacity as an architect. Among others, these include the designs for the Majestic Theater, Keith's Theater, as well as for theaters in Erie, Pennsylvania, and Columbus, Ohio. He is a member of the following masonic lodges: Forest City Blue Lodge, Webb Chapter, De Witt Clinton Lodge, Grand Rapids, Michigan, and he holds the 32nd degree. Further, he is a member of the H. B. S. U. In 1895 he married Miss T. R. Rothenberg and the marriage has produced four children, two boys and two girls.

Emil Bierfreund

One of our German fellow citizens of this city who managed to achieve respect was Mr. Emil Bierfreund, owner of the noted dye-works and steam-cleaning business at 6925 Colfax Road, which was incorporated in 1902 under the name of The American Dry Cleaning and Dying Co. with a capital of $50,000 with Emil Bierfreund, founder and previous sole owner, as president, a position which he retained until his sudden death on 6 May of this year.

Besides the head office located in the factory, there were five branch offices in various parts of the city and a business in Akron, Erie, Pennsylvania, and Pittsburgh, since the company's success had exceeded the borders of the city.

Mr. Emil Bierfreund first saw the light of day on 17 August 1854 in Rastenburg, East Prussia, Germany. When he reached the obligatory age, he attended the local *Volksschule*, and after completing that he apprenticed in the dyer's craft, working subsequently in various establishments in Berlin, Stettin, and other cities of Germany. After the completion of the glorious campaign of 1870-71 in the fall of 1871, Mr. Bierfreund was mustered into the 42nd Infantry Regiment [Prussian Army] and served 2 years in the garrison of Metz, the reconquered fortress. Although he had already seen much of France and Germany, he wanted to see the New World once as well. So he came to New York in 1888; went later to Scranton, Pennsylvania, where he found work; and finally settled in Cleveland. Here he quickly set up a business of his own, which has greatly expanded through and where he would also find his final resting place.

Besides being president of the American Dry Cleaning and Dying Co., Mr. Bierfreund was also president of the Euclid Building Co., where he was heavily invested, whose management and direction he had taken over, and which he managed to his death.

In this capable compatriot Cleveland lost one of the chief promoters of its prosperity and Germans lost a man whose heart always beat for its interests, for which reason his premature loss must be mourned.

In 1890 Mr. Bierfreund married to Miss Emma Messer, a German-American born in Egg Harbor, New Jersey. Two daughters, Elsa, currently 7, and Emma, one year old, came from the marriage. He made an extended visit with her to Germany a few years ago to show her the old fatherland.

The Concordia Lodge, F. & A. M., the German Scat Club, the Order of the Harugari and the Cleveland Singing Society lost in him one of their most treasured and beloved members.

Julius and Wilhelm Köbler

One of the heroes of freedom who directed their voices against the deeds and directions of a tyrannical government and who had to seek refuge in America, the land of freedom, was one of the oldest pioneers of Cleveland, Mr. Carl Köbler. He was born in lovely Baden and came to Cleveland in 1848 with his wife Anna, née Sänger, a solid woman from Hessia-Darmstadt.

Mr. Köbler established a furniture store here at the corner of Charles Street and Woodland Avenue, and he also ran an undertaking service. In the course of years the Köblers had four sons, Charles, Louis, Julius and William, of which we mention the latter two here.

Mr. Julius Köbler was born on 19 July 1860, receiving a solid education before committing himself to his father's business until his father withdrew to private life in 1883, shortly after his wife's death in September. After his father's retirement, the son Charles took over the business, and Mr. Julius Köbler and his brother William were under Charles' direction through 1897. On 22 April 1884 Julius Köbler married Miss Elisabeth Reinhart, and four daughters came from this marriage.

Mr. Julius Köbler has a leading position in both American and German social circles. He is a member of the Aurora Lodge of the German Order of the Harugari, and for a long time he was their supreme bard, and he also belongs to the Mutual Support Society, the Baden Support Society, the Independent German Order, the Cleveland Singing Society, the Freemasons, the Order of the Knights of Pythias, the Pyramid Council of the National Union, and the Order of the Knights and Ladies of Security.

Mr. William Köbler, the younger brother of the person mentioned above, was born on 7 October 1868, attended public schools and was also active in conjunction with his father and his brothers. On 7 October 1896 he married Miss Loretta Dearman, who became a true helpmate. Like his brother Julius, Mr. William Köbler also took an active part in social and societal life. He is a member of the Cuyahoga Tribe of the Red Men, the Freemasons, the Knights of Pythias, the Pyramid Council of the National Union, the Order of Elks and the Order of the Woodmen of the World.

After both brothers had been active in their father's business, and in association with their brother Charles and thoroughly learned undertaking in all its branches, they established themselves independently in a building built for the purpose at 421 Woodland Avenue under the name J. & W. Köbler as undertakers. This was in May, 1897, and they have not only earned an enviable reputation as undertakers by bringing the business to a flourishing state, but they have also established an ambulance service equal to none, and they have not only provided coaches built for the purpose with trained personnel, but they have also introduced the first invalid coaches in the United States.

The Köbler establishment is located at 2340 E. 55th Street.

Julius H. Hildebrandt

Julius Hildebrandt, well-known in business and social circles, is one of those German-Americans of Cleveland who not only rose as a result of their own strength, raising themselves from small beginnings to success through hard work and righteousness, but also one who has contributed to the prosperity of the community and deserves to be a shining example to others. Mr. Hildebrandt was born on 25 March 1868 in Tiegenhof, West Prussia, and came to Cleveland in 1887, at first associating with his brother Robert, who had a wholesale meat business, but in 1891 Julius established his own business which must be regarded as one of the most important wholesale sausage businesses. The factory is located at 148-156 Buhrer Avenue, and it is equipped with the most modern machines and most practical appointments. He manufactures all sorts of sausage, and in the course of time he has won an extensive clientele due to the quality of his wares and professional treatment,

Mr. Hildebrandt is married for the second time. His first wife was a Miss Martha Fährmann from Schöneberg, West Prussia. She died in 1895, leaving a little daughter who soon died. The second marriage took place in 1898, with Miss Rosalia Schneider from Schönau, district of Olpe, Westphalia, and four children have been born, two girls and two boys, Selma, Hermann, Leo and Amanda.

Hard tried by the loss of his first wife and his child, a self-made man in business in every sense of the word, Mr. Hildebrandt is worthy of the trust and respect he enjoys from all sides, as well as the love he is surrounded by from his second marriage.

David Barner

Mr. David Barner is without doubt one of the oldest German pioneers in the city of Cleveland, born on 10 August 1825 in Oethlingen, Württemberg. His parents, Jacob and Anna Barner, were simple but reputable and hard working rural people who had worked from their youth, but who permitted him to attend the communal school until he was 14. Barely confirmed, he decided for the crafts, and David became an apprentice to a wool weaver in Oethlingen, where he worked for four years until he was released by his master. Then followed his traveling days, which led him through many of the cities of Baden and Württemberg, bringing him both joy and suffering along the way. Such a wandering journeyman in the old fatherland had many destinies. Good and bad quarters, cheerful and uncomfortable company, good and nasty masters, money in the purse or none, and he had to accept it all according to the circumstances and be happy with it. Barner did not need to serve and wear a colorful coat, since his father had already died, and as the eldest son he was free of military service. For two years he worked in his home town, the following five years in Stuttgart in a corset-weaving shop, and this led him to the understanding that he could survive in the old homeland, but that there were no better prospects for the future. He then decided to seek his happiness abroad and joined the stream of emigration leading to the land of the Star Spangled Banner. Barner reached New York after a crossing of 46 days on the sailing ship 'Memphis,' and after a short stay in New York he went to Cleveland. At the start he earned his keep through hard work on the steamers running between Cleveland and Detroit, and he did other work, until the he received the first job in the wool-weaving shop set up by the German Society. This undertaking, which was established by prominent Germans, unfortunately did not survive. This weaving operation, the first such in Cleveland, was located in the Hurlbut Block on Ontario Street. Now Barner went to Wisconsin as the foreman of a wool weaving factory there, and he experienced the surprise that Uncle Sam wanted him as a soldier due to his being hard pressed by Southern rebels. Through the efforts of his employer, who did not want to lose his workers, Barner did not come to exchanging lead balls with the Southerners. He soon left Wisconsin and sought to become a farmer in Newburg for two years. Still, over the long run he did not like country life, so he started a tavern on Broadway which was later moved to Richland Avenue, and he ran it for twenty years, from 1873 to 1893 with good success until he entered a deserved retirement. Mr. David Barner has been a respected member of the Hermann Tribe of the Red Men as well as a member of the Swabian Entertainment Society and the Swabian Singing League. From his marriage, contracted in 1851, came two daughters, Emma and Rosa, and seven sons: Georg, who died in 1899; David; Wilhelm, a boy who died before baptism; Jacob; Heinrich; and Albert.

Mr. Albert Barner has risen to independence in business by his own efforts. Born on 4 July 1864, after leaving school he learned the oil business from the ground up, and he was active with both the Excelsior Refining Co. and the Eagle Consolidated Refining Co. in Lima. He is a partner of the Lino Painting Co., which has its factory in Collinwood. He is married since 11 January 1883 with Therese Futterer from Rastatt, Baden, who came to America with her parents as a child of four. This happy marriage has produced three children, Emma, Albert and Esther. Albert Barner is a prominent member of Cleveland Lodge no. 13 and Cleveland Encampment no. 181 of the I. O. O. F. He holds the office of major in the Cleveland Canton, Uniform Rank no. 33. He lives in a splendid home at 310 Parkgate Avenue, and he, as does his father, enjoys a wide circle of friends.

John Naumann

Mr. John Naumann was born on 1 November 1853 in Borna near Leipzig in lovely Saxony. He attended the civic school of his home town and served in the 3rd Saxon Dragoon Regiment. During his period of service he enjoyed the special favor of Cavalry Captain von Meyer, who did everything he could to keep the sharp soldier Naumann in the service. But Naumann could not be convinced, and after the conclusion of his enlistment he took his discharge and, with Captain Meyer's recommendation, he entered the service of Colonel von Walther in Borna. Here Naumann remained for eight years, holding the office of master of stables and enjoying his lordship's confidence. Mr. Naumann speaks even today of the grace he enjoyed from the Colonel during this period with enthusiasm and respect. Mr. Naumann describes these years as the most beautiful of his life. But the narrow situation of his home town did not please him. He emigrated to America in 1888 and settled in Cleveland, working in various taverns here, and in 1898 he took over the place known to all Clevelanders at 111 Ontario Street. This tavern gained a great reputation under his control. Germans with something to do in the city do not fail to come to John Naumann, since he understands how to make guests feel at home. He is also a Nimrod in the best sense of the word, an enthusiastic hunter and sure shot. His love for noble field hunting is indubitably from Colonel von Walther, for in that service he was able to dedicate himself wholly to hunting. In German societies and all German undertakings, Mr. Naumann also shows lively interest. His two sons, Richard and Albin, are partners in the business. What patience and energy combined with an intelligent exploitation of circumstances can accomplish is shown by Mr. John Naumann, the genial host though his glittering success, and when we add that he is a man of unshaken integrity, we express what his acquaintances all know.

Richard Friedrich Naumann

The eldest son of Mr. John Naumann, Richard, who is generally popular and who supports his father in his business, was born on 13 February 1878 in Borna. He attended Volksschule there and came on the day after his confirmation, utterly alone, to Cleveland. Here he worked for the first six full years with the now departed tavernkeeper Schlitz while attending night school until his father took him into his own business. Richard belongs to a great number of societies, such as the Order of Red Men, the Eagles, the German Support League, the Forest City Outing Club, the Sycamore Club and the Heights Men's Chorus. On 20 April 1898 Richard Naumann married Miss Emma Kohler, the daughter of a local pioneer family. Unfortunately, his first wife died on 26 January 1903 after bearing him three children, a boy and two girls. His second wife, married on 15 June 1904, Margaretha, is the daughter of the earliest German settler in Parma, Stumpf, and the children from the first marriage have found a good mother. This image of the perfect German housewife dedicates herself utterly and tirelessly to the leading of the household and the education of the little ones. The home of Richard Naumann is 362 Walton Avenue.

Albin Naumann

John Naumann's younger son is Albin. He was also born in Borna on 15 November 1879. He also attended the schools until he was 12, and in 1892 he came over with his mother and sister to join his father and brother, who were already there. Here he completed his schooling and entered his father's business, and he is well known to the guests in Naumann's place as a quiet man, dedicated to attentive service, an amiable and courtly young host. Since he is unmarried and dedicated to his mother, he lives with her. Albin Naumann resembles his father insofar as he is also a great lover of hunting. The noble field sport has led him to many states where there are still deer and bears to kill or trap. The fact that he captured a brood female bear is shown with living proof in the zoological collection in Wade Park. This funny example, which leads a cheerful life and does her bit to entertain, was taken from the concerns of wild nature in the state of Maine, brought here and given as a gift to the city. The Red Men, the Harugari and the Eagles number Albin Naumann as one of their most respected young members, and he is beloved and respected for his modesty and honesty.

Joseph Zell

In the Kingdom of Württemberg, in the pleasant little town of Biberach, Joseph Zell first saw the light of day on 3 February 1875. His father died when Joseph was only one year old, and when he was nine he lost his dear mother. He was passed to an aunt, who saw that he received a good education. He was able to attend the *Gymnasium*, and after his departure he became an apprentice in a bookstore. He remained in this position for fifteen months until he decided to emigrate to relatives in Cleveland. On his arrival in the Forest City, he learned baking and was active in various jobs until 1892. In that year he opened a wine and beer tavern on South Road, South Brooklyn, which he headed with good success for ten years. In 1902 he sold it to obtain a new tavern on Quincy Street at the corner of 84th Street. That has been his place ever since. Zell's place is one of the most elegant and most frequented in the entire area. Through his open, liberal nature, Mr. Zell has been able to get a wide circle of friends and acquaintances. He is also much respected in societies, and he is a member of the German Support League, the United German Union and the Swabian Singing League. Mr. Zell has not yet entered the harbor of marriage at the time of printing (22 July 1907).

Johann Kotz

"Where there is a will there is a way" would appear to be the motto of Mr. Johann Kotz; he has managed to bring himself to a position of respect in this city through hard work, persistence and energy upon which he may look with justified pride.

Born in the tiny village of Pestlin, district of Stuhm, West Prussia, on 6 September 1864, he attended elementary school in his birthplace, and after the end of his schooling he apprenticed in the hard craft of a smith. After passing the three years of apprenticeship, he followed the usage of the old fatherland and went on the road. First of all he went to the capital of Berlin, then he went to Essen, where he was employed in the famous Krupp canon factory, and later he visited the cities of Aachen, Cologne and Düsseldorf.

In 1881 Mr. Kotz decided to emigrate to America to seek his luck where so many countrymen had found prosperity, which was not as easy to do at home. And Mr. Kotz at last found what he had sought. Landing in the harbor of New York in November of that year, he went directly to the "Windy City" of Chicago, where he worked in his profession until 1889. It was also here where he found and came to love his wife, Johanna Jahnke, born in Schwetz, West Prussia, and married her in 1888. During his residence in Chicago he became aware of the vast iron industry of Cleveland and decided to move to the Forest City. Here he was fortunate enough to rise to prosperity and respect. During the last five years he holds the responsible position of a contractor in the large establishment of the Lake Erie Nut & Bolt Co., and he enjoys the respect and trust of his superiors. More than 600 persons are under his oversight.

Just as Mr. Kotz has risen rapidly in business, he has also risen in social relations. He is a Freemason of the 32nd degree, a Knight of Maccabee and a member of the German Support League.

Seven nice, hopeful children have come from his happy marriage with Miss Jahnke. The eldest daughter Anna Karolina is 17 years old and graduated the famous Central Institute on Willson Avenue. Mr. Kotz has the proper idea of giving his children a fine education. His second daughter, Margaretha Johanna, is 15, Helena Antonia, the third, is 13, Gertrude 11, the eldest boy Eddie Johann is 7, Emma 6 and the baby John Theodor is 3.

Mr. Kotz is a well-oriented and broadened man, so that it is no wonder that he has succeeded rather rapidly in his new homeland.

John Dannenfelser

John Dannenfelser was born on 22 June 1840 in Bechtheim, Hessia-Darmstadt, as the son of the farmers Heinrich and Elisabeth (née Metzger) Dannenfelser. Mr. John Dannenfelser's father was ill for 16 years and incapable of working. It is no marvel that the once considerable fortune of the Dannenfelser family melted away, and this was a major reason why the children had to emigrate and scatter in all directions. John attended the local school and then apprenticed for three years as a baker. At the age of 19 he prepared himself for emigration and came to Cleveland in 1859. During the years from 1861 to 1864 he worked at his profession in Cincinnati, but then he returned to Cleveland, where he worked as a baker for 30 years in the bakery of Gottlieb Saal. For the last ten years he has been in well-deserved retirement. Mr. Dannenfelser has been a member of the Second Reformed Church at the corner of Woodland Avenue and Putnam Street for forty years, and he holds a respected position there. He married Rose Jahrhaus, born in Leopoldhofen, Grand Duchy of Baden, on 22 June 1867. The happy marriage remains childless.

Wilhelm Johann Maier

Wilhelm Johann Maier first saw the light of day on 9 November 1859 in Ebersbach, district of Göppingen on the Fils, Württemberg. He attended the Volksschule in his birthplace until his fourteenth year and then worked for three years in a weavery. He did not care for this activity over the long run, so he moved to Stuttgart and took a position in the Royal Court Fish and Game Store. From Württemberg's capital, Mr. Maier went to Mannheim and Ludwigshafen, where he was active for a year and a half in a grocery business. He carried out his long-harbored desire to emigrate to America in 1873, and he immediately settled in Cleveland, where he has resided ever since. Mr. Maier always took an intense part in German society life. As early as 1877 he was a co-founder of the Newburg Men's Chorus, which later amalgamated with the Germania Men's Chorus and is since well known as the Newburg Germania Men's Chorus. Mr. Maier has often held positions of honor in this society, and he has been its president almost without interval and even today is an active member. Mr. Maier is also a member of the exclusively German Order of the Harugari, and for two years he was State Grand Secretary of the Order.

He married Miss Elisabeth Elsebart from Gundersheim, Rhenish Hessia, in 1875, which marriage has produced five children, five girls and a boy. Mrs. Maier is also very active in German women's organizations; she is a member of the Women's Lodge of the German Order of the Harugari and the Freedom Lodge, and like her husband she is generally beloved and respected.

Friedrich Ebert

Mr. Friedrich Ebert was born on 31 June 1833 in Klokow, Mecklenburg-Strelitz, as the son of the wagon-maker Mr. Friedrich Ebert. His mother Christina was born a Maas. The boy Friedrich attended the city school in his home town and emigrated to America in 1852. He settled at once in Cleveland, where he has resided ever since other than a brief period in the South. Mr. Ebert was a locomotive engineer for forty years on the Pennsylvania Railroad, from 1862 to 1902, and he is currently pensioned off. He took and even today takes the most intense interest in German efforts, and he is a member of the following societies: the Pioneer Society, German Union, Bismarck Lodge, Fritz Reuter Support Society, the Order of the Harugari, and for 35 years he was a member of the Locomotive Brotherhood. Although Mr. Ebert actively supported the cause of the Union during the Civil War, he was not able to take part in that war due to obligations to his family and elderly parents, who came over not long after his own immigration. Two of his brothers did serve, so that the Ebert family did its bit. In 1859 Mr. Ebert married Friederike Spattholt. Nine children came from that union, of which four have died. Five children are alive, and of those four are married and all resident in this city.

August Raber

August Raber was born on 21 April 1861 as the son of a glass-making master in Blantenloch, Baden. He had nine siblings, of which his eldest brother died. Three brothers and four sisters live in Germany, and a sister also went to America and lives in Philadelphia. When August was only six years old, his father died, so that his education fell to his mother. She fortunately lived on for another twenty years, so that all the children achieved adulthood before her death in 1885. After finishing school August went to Karlsruhe to apprentice as a baker, a profession to which he has always remained true. When he had worked for two years, he and his brother began a bakery in Blankenloch. But he did not long remain at home, since he decided in 1879 to emigrate to America, our land of freedom, before he had to do military service. He stayed in Philadelphia for half a year, then worked variously in Cleveland, Detroit, Akron and other places in the United States, finally settling here. He has run the bakery he began on Kinsman Street for thirteen years, and through liberality and the delivery of good wares he has won a large clientele. Mr. Raber participates intensely in society life in keeping with his inclination and his sense of obligation, and he is a member of the German Order of the Harugari, the Foresters, and of the Liederkranz. About 24 years ago he married Miss Henrietta Danecker, born in West Prussia, and the marriage with his fine wife has produced six children, three boys and three girls, of which one girl died.

Hard work and conscientiousness, the chief virtues of a good German, are also those of Mr. Rader, and for this reason the saying "craft has a golden floor" has proved itself with him, showing it still works.

Albert Mattmueller

Albert Mattmueller is the son of the noted undertaker and furniture-business owner Fr. Mattmueller on Tremont Street, and as such he was born here on 10 November 1874. He enjoyed an outstanding and truly German education and a basic schooling. He attended the public schools. With the knowledge obtained there, he worked for two years as the bill clerk in the Plumbing Supply House. On Saturdays and evenings he worked at his uncle's shoe business at 2519 West 11th Street, providing so much help that the business came to him in July, 1902, and he became the owner in his uncle's place.

The business which passed into Mr. Mattmueller's hands in this manner enjoys an old and reliable clientele, which is to be traced back to the business principles and methods his uncle obeyed, but which Mr. Mattmueller adheres to no less, and as a young man full of drive and knowledge of the shoe business, won the customers for himself even before he took over the business. Thus the success of this sprout from the German tree was guaranteed, as was that of his uncle.

The fact that Mr. Mattmueller makes much of his German origins is shown by the fact that he has only joined German societies. He is a member of the Heights Men's Chorus, the Stern Turner Society, and the Freemasons.

Five years ago Mr. Mattmueller, Jr., married Miss Anna Kuhl, and there is now a little son to show for it, George Emmett, who will be two years old this May.

As long as Cleveland's Germans continue to blossom in these and similar examples, the fatherland may be happy about its adoption, and this sketch may have a suitable conclusion.

Carl and Thomas Volk

The way American business life more and more drives young blood to the forefront is shown by the example of the Volk brothers, owners of the popular restaurant at 746 Prospect Avenue S.E. It was in 1883 that the father, Thomas Volk, left Sigmaringen in Hohenzollern, the origin of the German Imperial House, along with his wife and three sons, to found a new home in far America. On 23 June of that year the family landed on the shores of our free land and went to Cleveland to settle in the Forest City on Lake Erie. Mr. Volk was a furniture maker by profession, a master in his business, and he managed to find work. The family was unfortunately hit by a blow after only three months when one of the sons drowned while bathing. The two surviving sons are Carl and Thomas.

So far as the further destiny of the parents goes, their mother died at the age of 42. The father was so burdened by these blows of fate that he could no longer stay in Cleveland, and he settled in Sloan, a suburb of Buffalo, where he pursues his profession as a solid man of 59. Carl Volk, the elder son, was born on 19 November 1877. He had thus reached the compulsory age of schooling when the family emigrated. Here he attended Catholic parochial school as well as night school until he was 12, and then he took various jobs available. Possessed by the zeal to become independent, he went into the innkeeping business at the age of 15 and trained himself as a waiter, and then he and his brother took over what had once been the Schlegel Garden, remembered by older Germans, which later became the Mohawk Buffet, then the Bavarian (made famous under the control of Schüpbach and Fehl), and finally the restaurant run by the two brothers. Carl chose Miss Wilhelmine Schöne, daughter of the noted German pioneer Franz Schöne as his lifelong companion, marrying her on 21 January 1903. Mr. Carl Volk is a popular member of the Germania Turners and takes a leading role in gymnastic practice as well as with intellectual Turnerism.

Mr. Thomas Volk, the younger son named after his father, was born on 23 January 1879, attended parochial and night school, and dedicated himself to the restaurant business as a waiter. He is also as passionate a gymnast as his brother, and he has made a mark in gymnastics by defeating his opponents. He has served two terms as vice president in the Swiss

Turner Society. He is also a member of the Swabian Support Society. Thomas married a year before his brother, marrying Miss Ottilie Pfalzgraf on 29 July 1902.

The two brothers enjoy great business because of their openness and their hard work as restaurateurs, which is all the more to be praised because they also participate intensely in German activities.

Franz Knoth

Franz Knoth was born on 27 July 1868 near Nikolsburg in Moravia. He lost both his father and mother through death in his second year. His grandmother took over the orphan's education through his twelfth year, and then he was put into a bakery in Vienna, so that he never really completed Volkschule. After three years of apprenticeship, he was a journeyman at the age of 15. On the advice of his colleagues he went on the road, traveling through a part of Germany, Switzerland, Italy and all of the Austrian-Hungarian monarchy. To some extent this was the chief education of his life, since along the way he met intelligent workers who taught him in the social questions and fired him on to further studies. It was then that he won his first interest in the social movement, and the seed planted struck fruitful soil. After 2 1/2 years of wandering, he returned to Vienna, and destiny had its turn. What he had learned brought him into conflict with the government and he was as good as compelled to emigrate.

So it was that he first set foot on the shores of our free land of America as a young man barely 19. Here he had opportunity at once to express his views. Bakery workers were beginning to perceive their less than humane conditions. Entering the movement at once, the newly-immigrated man traveled almost all of the United States. Even though the government did nothing against him, he soon learned that being an agitator even for a noble cause was not easy, and he was not spared the usual disappointments. When he came to Cleveland in 1893, his situation was not to be envied. Lacking all means, his only consolation was meeting a good but equally poor girl, Agnes Kavour, who won his heart and became his wife. The happiness which grew out of this caused Franz Knoth to settle in Cleveland. After serving as foreman in various bakeries, the opportunity presented itself to become independent, a challenge he and his young, hard-working wife accepted with courage. They had the highest of gifts, which was good health, and so in the course of years they built up a lovely little business, and incidentally the stork, who does not pass a good German house by, left two cheerful boys, Franz and Erwin, to increase the life in the house and cause it to flourish.

Mr. Knoth still works together with his wife for the social cause whenever they have free time, and they are active in social and society life. He is a member of the Social Turner Society, the Turner Men's Chorus, the League of Friendship, the Woodmen of the World, the Society of Red Men, and the Workers' Singing League. Mrs. Knoth belongs to the women's section of the Turner Men's Chorus and to the West Side Women's Society.

Reconciled to some extent with destiny, the family ascribes its formation to the health which Mr. and Mrs. Knoth enjoy which makes it possible for them to forge their own happiness.

Jacob Ganss

When the names of the brave are told out, who risk their lives daily, even hourly, to protect life and private property, and who do not turn back even at the muzzle of the revolver in the hands of a criminal, the late Mr. Jacob Ganss, now deceased, deserves to be mentioned in the first ranks as one of our best citizens, doing his duty for 29 years.

Mr. Ganss was born on 19 November 1832 in Frankenthal, Rhenish Palatinate. He attended the German and French schools in his place of birth, and after completing his schooling he went into apprenticeship with a baker. In 1854 Mr. Ganss emigrated to America, living in the East for two years, alternating between New York and Philadelphia, until he settled permanently in Cleveland in 1856. Here he was active for a long time as a distiller and liquor inspector, until he was taken into the Police in 1866, where he served for 29 years, giving his best to the community. During the War of Secession he was in the commissary in Camp Chase in Columbus. Mr. Ganss was a member of the Freemasons, Odd Fellows, the Pioneer Society and the Support Society. In 1857 he married Carolina Apy, who had come as a child in 1845 with her parents to Cleveland and was one of the earliest German pioneers. Three children came from this happy marriage, Antonia, Leonora and Frank. Mr. Ganss died on 19 February 1906 after ten years of retirement, mourned by wife, children and a large circle of friends.

Friedrich Schuele

Friedrich Schüle was born in Kornthal, district of Leonberg, Württemberg, on 27 September 1857. He went throught the Volksschule in his place of birth and after confirmation apprenticed as a carpenter. In order to educate himself more thoroughly in construction, he then attended the construction school in Stuttgart. After serving three years with the 3rd Württemberg Infantry Regiment no. 121 in Schwäbisch-Gmünd, he emigrated to America in 1880. Settling at first in Detroit, he made himself independent as a carpenter and remained un Detroit until 1889. After going to Cleveland in that year, he worked in house construction until he opened a tavern in 1894 at 6922 St. Clair. Mr. Schüle is strongly supported by his capable wife, the former Miss Lena Glanz, who married him in Detroit in 1882. Three sons, William, Hubert and Karl, of whom two have grown and received a higher education, and a little daughter Ruth, have come from the marriage. Mr. Friedrich Schüle is an active member of the German Order of the Harugari, the East End Military Society and the Grand Fraternity.

Adolf R. Nunn

Adolph R. Nunn was born on 15 January 1873, the son of the old German pioneer Isidor Nunn, who emigrated to America from Königsheim near Tauberbischofsheim in Baden in 1852 and settled here. His father ran an undertaking service for years in our city until he retired in 1895 and passed the business to his sons. Adolph attended St. Stephan's School and graduated Ignatius College, which is known as an outstanding institution of education. Then he entered his father's business and trained himself to be an excellent mortician. His undertaking establishment is located at 4843 Lorain Avenue.

Mr. Adolph R. Nunn is a member of the St. Stephan's Society, the C. M. B. A., the Garfield Union 14, Knights of Columbus, the Knights of St. John, the Concordia, the Baden Support Society, and the Woodmen of the World, Harmony Camp, since society ties are useful merely from a business point of view. In 1896 he married Oliva Kramer, also born on the West Side and of German heritage. A son, Charles, came from the marriage.

Michael Urban

Michael Urban, a building contractor known throughout this city and to Germans in particular, was born on 23 August 1855, the son of a carpenter in Vilsbeburg, Lower Bavaria. After attending the elementary and preparatory school, he apprenticed at his father's trade, construction, and he was active in that business in the old homeland until 1880. He did military service for eight months as a private and two months as a non-commissioned officer, a proof of his ability in military service. In 1880 he left the old homeland, went to America, and came directly to Cleveland. He worked here for four years in his profession with the Brooks Building Co., until 1884. Then he went West to get to know the United States better, visiting several cities, in some of which he worked. Then he returned to the Forest City, resuming his work in the firm mentioned, and he remained their employee until 1893. In that year, although it was a year of panic and crisis in history, he made himself independent as a building contractor. Since then, Mr. Urban has erected a great number of buildings, and enumerating them would exceed the scope of this sketch, but the imposing St. Francis Church and School, the Greek-Catholic Church on Rawlings Avenue, the Brudnow Block n Cross Street, the Victor Block and the Rowland Block on Wade Park Avenue should be mentioned.

Mr. Urban is president of the Bavarian Support Society no. 2 and of the Knights of Columbus and the C. M. B. A. as well as the Military Society. He has stood out through his admirable and energetic initiative in the staging of German festivities over the last few years; for example, it was he who organized the parade at the dedication of the Goethe-Schiller Monument, which had an astonishing participation from German societies, doing much to give the event its impressive and popular character.

Mr. Urban was married twice, the first time with Maria Lex, born in Teggendorf, Lower Bavaria, who was torn from him by death after being the mother of seven children. On 10 August 1899 he married his second wife, born Anna Heim, whose cradle was in Marienburg, West Prussia. In her the children of the first marriage have found a second, loyal mother. Three of them are already married, three are still at home, and one has died.

Generally respected for his business ability, Michael Urban is one of the few of our fellow citizens to be designated as the primary promoter of our causes.

William Albert Nunn

William Albert Nunn, the youngest son of an old respected pioneer, Isidor Nunn, was born in this city in 1875, on the West Side. William was never to know the tender care of a loving mother, since his mother died barely six days after his birth. As was the case with all the children of Isidor Nunn, William as well received a real German upbringing, and the fact that he takes an active role in German causes is shown by the societies which have elected him as a member: the Baden Support Society; Society German Union no. 15, Independent German Order; St. Joseph's Society; Knights of Columbus. Further, he is a member of the society The Woodmen of the World, as well as of the oldest local Hungarian society, "Zerny Miklos," and many others.

Mr. Nunn married Miss Lilie Kastlow from Columbus on 28 November 1891. Three children have come from this marriage, two boys and a girl, of which the girl sadly died.

Mr. Nunn apprenticed in the upholstering business, but at the age of 18 he changed over to undertaking, entering the business of his brother John J. Nunn, making himself independent once he had learned the burial business. His splendid business and residence is located at 1553-55 Woodland Avenue. Mr. William Albert Nunn is an amiable and forthcoming businessman, and his outstanding success rests primarily on this fact.

Christian Burkhardt

Mr. Christian Burkhardt, the builder well-known in German circles, was born on 16 May 1867 in Dobels, Kingdom of Württemberg. His father ran a lumber business in the old homeland, and he emigrated together with his family to America in 1880. He settled permanently in Cleveland, and he died a few years ago. The mother is still living, active and healthy despite her age. Christian attended the Volksschule in Germany, and here the public schools. Then he learned machining, but he soon went over to building, and during the last twelve years he has dedicated himself entirely to the construction of drainage sewers. In this field he has made a name not only in this city, but far beyond the borders of the city. Among other projects, he built the largest drainage sewer in this city, the Case Avenue Main Sewer. He is also the builder of most of the sewers in Columbus, Ohio, and has done similar work in other cities.

Although his business claims much of his time and attention, Mr. Burckhardt has not neglected to participate in German societies, and he supports their noble activities in the most liberal manner. He is a member of the Concordia Lodge of the A. F. & M., the Knights of Pythias, the Swabian Support Society, etc.

Mr. Burkhardt is deeply involved in industrial and commercial undertakings. He is also one of the directors of the Rocky Rive Water Works, confirming what we have said of his wide and intense activity.

In 1891 Mr. Burkhardt married Susanna Schneider, born here of German parents who immigrated from Bavaria. Two boys and two girls have come from this happy marriage.

Early this year (1907), Mr. Burkhardt made a visit to the old homeland and Switzerland in the company of his lovely wife, and he speaks with enthusiasm of the progress he perceived there. He even harbors the desire to make a second trip to Europe.

Mr. Burkhardt is an energetic businessman and pleasant company, one of the best-loved and most-respected citizens, and wherever his name is known it has a good ring.

Ludwig Skowronski

One of the most capable German-American journalists is without a doubt Mr. Ludwig Skowronski. With an aggressiveness which is necessary for American journalism, he combines the utility of long experience and fine tact. In keeping with the motto, "Leave to everyone his right and hate nothing but what is mean," he continually attacks meanness with a sharp pen, and his articles spiced heavily with irony or biting satire are always gladly read by the people, but hated by the corrupt.

Mr. Ludwig Skowronski was born in Rosenberg, West Prussia, as the son of a Prussian official. He attended in sequence the *Gymnasien* in Bromberg, Schneidemühl, Gnesen and Nakel, but after completing the graduation examination he studied several semesters of natural science and medicine at the University of Breslau, but since the situation seemed too "narrow" there, he emigrated to America. Here he experienced several years of drifting with the stream, during which he visited all parts of the United States, getting to know the country and its people, as well as relationships. This was useful for his later profession. He began his career as a journalist in 1887 at the *'Arbeiterzeitung'* in Chicago, to whose editorial staff he belonged for many years. Then he was on the editorial staff of the *'Illinois Staatszeitung'* in Chicago for many years, and when that paper was amalgamated with the *'Chicagoer Freie Presse,'* he came to Cleveland in 1890. Here he belonged to the editorial staff of the *'Wächter und Anzeiger'* for several years. When the Cleveland *'Herold'* appeared as a daily, he entered that paper's editorial staff, where he is still a valuable force.

Carl Lorenz

Carl Lorenz, editor of the Sunday edition of the *'Wächter und Anzeiger,'* was born in 1858 in Stuttgart, Württemberg, the son of a master builder. He enjoyed a good education, attended the Killius private institute and studied architecture and painting under Prof. Kurtz at the *Polytechnic* in his native city. His preference for languages later led him to Geneva, where he entered a boarding house and heard lectures on literature at the university. From Geneva he went to Paris, then London. In the latter city he worked as a teacher and pursued a degree at the University of London. Business ties to a brother then living in New York, now deceased, brought him to the United States in 1880. Here he again took up his activities as a teacher, but he put this aside after a few years to dedicate himself to journalism, which corresponded to his literary tendencies and to which he has remained true.

Mr. Lorenz has been a member and secretary of the Library Board of the Public Library for the last three years.

John Reich

Mr. John Reich, editor in chief and president of the Herold Publishing Co., first saw the light of day in the sunny Rhenish Palatinate, in the village of Hessheim, on 27 December 1858, attended the Latin School in Frankenthal and the seminary in Kaiserslautern. From 1877 to 1885 he was a teacher, and then he emigrated to the United States. He went directly to Cleveland, where he at first gave musical instruction, and then became collector and agent for the *'Wächter am Erie.'* In 1888 he became a reporter in this paper, but in 1891 he went to Louisville, to the *'Anzeiger'* there, but he returned to Cleveland two years later, where he spent a year with the *'Neue Presse'* as local editor. From 1894 to 1900 he was a reporter at the 'Wächter und Anzeiger,' then he founded the *'Clevelander Herold,'* which appeared as a weekly until a year ago, when it passed into the ownership of the Herold Publishing Co. stock company and has since been published as a daily.

Mr. Reich was elected to the 76th Ohio state legislature by the Republican Party. He always acts on behalf of progressive and freethinking ideas.

Anton Bechler

Mr. Anton Bechler was born in 1865 in Schöneberg on the Vistula, Province of West Prussia. He received his education in the local elementary school and then in a well-known private school, where he gained extensive knowledge. This proved particularly useful in his apprenticeship in manufacturing goods, which was done in Danzig. Tired of the narrow conditions of Germany, he turned his glance to the Land of Freedom. He came to Cleveland in 1885 and was active in various businesses. Soon, however, the opportunity presented itself to take over the tavern known as Schlegel's Garden on Woodland Avenue, which was for years the gathering place for the Germans of the neighborhood. After running this tavern for several years with success, he changed and moved his location to the corner of Ocean and Woodland Avenue. After the expiration of his lease for this place he took over the tavern made famous by Mr. Krause at the corner of Sawtell and Woodland Avenue, where he has flourished ever since. Mr. Bechler's place is also a pleasant little place, and everyone feels at home there due to the accomodating nature of the tavernkeeper and his friendly wife. The value of the latter, the former Elisabeth Fischer, a Hessian woman from Hirschfeld, became obvious to him as soon as he met her, and he married her in 1889, and she has tirelessly helped at his side ever since. This truly German marriage was blessed by the birth of a son. Mr. Bechler fulfills all the civic duties placed upon him, and although he dedicates himself largely to his business and his family, he also has a lively interest in German societies. A member of the Harugari Order, he has been for years a member of its Aurora Lodge.

Julius W. Triptow

Who does not know the story of the old fortress Kolberg in Rear Pomerania, made famous by Schill's volunteers? And everyone knows that its occupants were true German patriots, showing it through their great sacrifice of goods and blood. They cherish Fritz Reuter's language and writings, and his memory is esteemed. The fact that many of these "Plattdütschen" have immigrated here and include some of our finest citizens is also adequately known. Working, saving, loving the law and peace, these qualities bring most of them to significant wealth and influential positions in public life. One of these is the noted Mr. Julius W. Triptow. He was born on 14 July 1855 as the eldest son of the furniture maker and master builder Julius Triptow and his wife Henrietta, née Sibel, in Kolberg in Pomerania. He attended the schools there and chose baking as his profession. His father was one of the most famous master builders of his time, building the military infirmary in Kolberg and other structures. But his family would not long be preserved. In 1866 cholera, which was prevalent in those days, killed him at the age of 39, and his wife followed him two years later, at the age of 42. This left his children — three sons and two girls — alone as orphans, and the little Julius had hard times ahead of him.

After completing his apprenticeship, he traveled through Germany, working in the large bakeries in Berlin, Leipzig, Bremen, etc., and then emigrated with his siblings to America in 1874. Here he first settled in Chicago, coming later to Cleveland and getting work in a bakery. Later he worked in the factory of the Eberhardt Manufacturing Co., and then he set up a carriage works, which he ran with success, and he was employed for 15 years in the factory of the Malleable Iron Works Co., and then he ran a grocery and tavern for eight years at 8305 Kinsman Road. He then built a beautiful building at the corner of Kinsman Road and 81st Street, where he currently runs an ice cream parlor and restaurant, and his son-in-law A. Rothärmel runs a tavern in the same building.

In January, 1882, he married Franzisca Grimm, born in Sitzenhausen, Baden, a relative of the noted local pioneer Grimm family, and in the course of the years she gave him seven children, two boys and five girls. One boy and two girls died, as children. Of the surviving children, the son Arthur continues the business begun by his father, and the youngest daughter Franziska helps her parents, but the two older daughters, Rosa and Anna, are married.

A brother of Mr. Triptow by the name of Ludwig runs a carpentry business in Chicago, and the sisters, Maria and Anna, are married to noted Germans there, the first to the caterer Ehrenwerth and the second to the restaurateur Manz. The second brother, who learned sheet-metal work, died several years ago in a railroad accident in Atlantic City, New Jersey.

In 1904 Mr. and Mrs. Triptow and a daughter made a three-month visit to Europe. Not only Mr. Triptow's birthplace, but also that of his wife, were visited, and longer times were spent in Berlin, Baden-Baden, Heidelberg and other towns. Mr. Triptow is a member of the Order of Independent Foresters, Court Kinsman, and has long been secretary. He also has belonged for years to the Freedom Union no. 13, United German Union. Beloved to all, the Triptow family is the image of a genuinely German family life.

Franz Richard Barth

Mr. Franz Richard Barth was born on 26 September 1849 in Reichenbach I. V., Kingdom of Saxony, to honorable bourgeois parents. He attended the Volksschule in his home town until he was 14, then he learned the craft of house painting, and after completing an apprenticeship of four years he visited several of the large cities of Germany. Hard working in his profession, he decided to emigrate in 1873, landing in New York, where he was active in his profession for several months, then moving to Cleveland. Here he found employment and worked in various companyies until 1883. In that year he established his own business in 531-533 Central Avenue, which he still runs. Through strict honesty and solid service he won a large circle of customers. Mr. Barth is a member of the Pioneer Society, the Harugari, the Cuyahoga Support Society, the Germania Turner Society and so on. In 1875 he married Miss Agnes Kuchs, and the happy marriage produced four children, three boys and a girl, Karl, Albert, Arthur and Diana.

Charles Latsch

The Fouilloux Passoire Co. is one of the newest blossoms on the great tree of Cleveland industry.

Mr. Charles Latsch, already known in German circles here, is the inventor of the apparatus produced and operated by this company. The president, Mr. Fouilloux, who gave the company its name, enjoyed a high reputation in the world of cooks, earned as chef in the Hollenden Hotel as well as in other outstanding hotels both in America and in Europe, as does Mr. Latsch. Both Latsch and Fouilloux saw and experienced much of the world before settling here in Cleveland and going to work as entrepreneurs. Mr. Latsch's invention consists of a strainer achieved after years of effort to strain purées, creams, soups, gelatines, honey and similar juices and mixtures. His apparatus is very light and can be operated with little force, and its chief advantage is that it loses nothing in the process, which is an economic advantage not found in earlier methods. Secondly, the apparatus accomplishes its work in a minute which once took an hour, so that the apparatus can strain in three minutes 25 gallons of cooked bean purée, espagnole, allemande, cream of tomato or any mixture of the sort. Thirdly, these mixtures are made finer and more tasty than previously had been possible with the use of straining cloths. Fourthly, as a result of its simple construction, the strainer cleans itself during use, which is an accomplishment from a hygenic point of view. Fifthly, it pays for itself within three months since it saves so much on labor.

It may be imagined what this newly-invented apparatus means for the kitchen and the culinary art and their productivity, particularly in hotels, hospitals, steamships, in institutions, schools, wherever it may be applied in large scale, more than in private kitchens. It has even now begun to be received everywhere. The establishment run by the company to manufacture the device is located in Central Avenue. Besides this device, Mr. Latsch is now far enough along with several further inventions that he can have them patented.

Mr. Latsch was born on 16 February 1869, in Lancaster, Pennsylvania, the son of a prominent German, the owner of a restaurant and tavern. His father made so much of German identity and education that he sent Charles to Germany as soon as he was six to be educated and attend school. Over the next eight years he received his education at German elementary school and *Realschulen*, and he can really be called a German despite not being born in Germany. After completing school, he apprenticed as a cook, and this led him to lovely Milan in Italy and other cities of Italy and the South. As a ship's cook, he made the entire journey around the world. It was only five years ago that he returned to America, and he came as a stranger. His invention is the best proof of his spiritual kinship, as well as how he created ways and means to make and distribute it.

Mr. Latsch is married, and his wife is the daughter of a deacon, Dr. Schröder, who has a high reputation in Germany and was decorated with the Order of the Eagle, 2nd class. He met Miss Schröder in her homeland, and the marriage took place there. Three children have been born to the marriage. They shall also receive a genuinely German education.

Martin Bauer

Mr. Martin Bauer, the inventor of a ladder and owner of the Bauer Safety Elevator Ladder Co., was born on 7 May 1864 in Dackenheim near Dürkheim on the Haardt, the Rhenish Palatinate. At the age of 17 he came to America and learned interior carpentry, since he had not learned a trade in Germany but had helped his father, who was a farmer. For years he worked in his profession until an accident led to his invention which was destined to create a new branch of industry. His invention, the safety ladder, is intended for house painters and others in the building crafts, and it has the advantage over previously-used ladders that they can be set automatically, so that workers are saved climbing up and down and are hence less tired.

As with all or most inventions, the safety ladder owes its existence to the effort of people to save time and hence also money. Several years ago Mr. Bauer decided to paint his house. He thought, as an amateur with little practical experience at house-painting, that it would be easy. Soon he saw that the work of a house painter was not as easy to begin as he had thought. He saw particularly that the raising and lowering of a ladder when the position was changed was tiring and wasted time. He considered how to avoid this situation as much as possible, and the invention of his safety ladder was the result of his thinking. This security ladder saves time, work and money, so that it cannot help but be generally used. A special advantage of Mr. Bauer's invention is that his ladder works together with a tackle system, called the "elevator," which is so balanced that the weight does not rest on the steps but on the long sides of the ladder, which are obviously able to bear much more weight. The factory of the Bauer Safety Elevator Ladder Company is located at 4209 Clark Avenue.

Mr. Bauer will soon obtain some patents which are destined to be epoch-making. He is continually making improvements to his ladder, of which some are already in use. Hundreds of testimonials from people using them show the advantage of this invention, and he is considering calling a stock-company into being to exploit the invention further.

Charles Haverdill

Among the local singing society directors, Mr. Charles Haverdill holds an outstanding place. He was born in Holland, but he came to America and Cleveland with his parents and siblings as a four-year-old boy in 1869. He had a splendid voice from his earliest youth, and he attracted attention when he sang in the church choir. On growing into a youth, he entered German men's choruses, and he was particularly treasured in the "Frohsinn." His love of song determined to dedicate himself wholly to the art of singing, and teachers such as Prof. Möller, Bonfie, Dr. W. Henninges, took over his training here, and it was continued in New York under Prof. Mors and perfected in Berlin, Germany, by Prof. Blum.

On returning to Cleveland, in 1900 Mr. Haverdill founded his own singing school, and outstanding pedagogy has led him to train many beautiful voices and fine pupils, male and female. His lovable wife assists him, born a Hart. Mrs. Haverdill was born in Erie,

Pennsylvania, and she has developed into a good teacher and accompanist at her husband's side.

He has had the leadership of the Harmonie Singing Society for years. When he took it over, the society had only ten singers, but under his excellent leadership it quickly flourished into one of the best societies. Under haverdill's leadership it has celebrated many a triumph.

Heinrich F. Ahrens

Heinrich F. Ahrens was born in this city on 27 July 1868, the son of a respected German pioneer family. He enjoyed a genuine German education, and he has inherited a German character from his parents, developing in all its contours despite an American context. At first working in upholstery, which he learned from H. Junge after completing school and in whose business he remained for 14 years, Mr. Ahrens is today in the beer business.

Mr. Ahrens is so widely known in German circles because of his participation in society life. He was an active member for 16 years of the West Side Turner Society, which shows that he took the right path to venerate the Germans and their ideals, embodied in Turnerism. Further, Mr. Ahrens is a singer, particularly well known in this capacity to his brethren in song. He is in the posession of a fine baritone, and he was trained by Prof. Chas. Haverdill. He is a member of the Orpheus Singing Society as well as of the Harmonie. He has belonged to the Harmonie for six years, and he is the chair of the music and entertainment committee. At concerts and similar activities where German song has its role to play, his treasured strength has always played its role in success, and as a result he has become beloved and respected.

Mr. Ahrens is married. His wife comes from the Seelbach family. Two boys have been born to the marriage.

Jacob Carl Lichti

Jacob Carl Lichti was born on 26 September 1882 in Zweibrücken, Rhenish Palatinate. At the age of four he came to Heidelberg, where his parents moved, and it was in the splendid student city, without equal on the Neckar or the Rhine, that he grew up. He attended Realschule, and after graduating he apprenticed in combination lock-making. His father, who had come over years before, lived in Columbus under the pseudonym of Otto Engerson, which he took for political reasons, and he was a teacher of music and song until 1893, when he died. Jacob Carl Lichti's mother still lives in Heidelberg. He himself came directly to Cleveland, and since his arrival he is active as a locksmith, which is sought after here. He is in possession of a fine tenor voice and enthused with true joy for song, so that as soon as Lichti set foot in the Forest City he joined the Harmonie and placed himself under the control of Professor Haverdill, who promoted his training as a tenor, and who had incidentally known and been a friend of Lichti's father.

Jacob Carl Lichti will doubtless play a significant role in local singing life, since he has already begun to be well known in German circles.

Frank Kohler

Frank Kohler was born was born on 21 June 1859 in Appenweiler, near Offenburg, Baden. His father was city clerk there, and he had taken part in the 1848 Revolution as a sergeant major. Frank attended the Volksschule, and afterwards he apprenticed as a beer brewer by working at a brewery in Kehl near Strasbourg for two years. He came to America in 1882 and first settled in Utica, New York. He worked there in his profession, as he also did in Philadelphia and Elk Harbor City, New Jersey. After going to Atlantic City, New Jersey, in 1890, and working in his profession a total of ten years, he gave it up and started interior carpentry in Atlantic City. In 1893 he came to Cleveland, finding employment in E. Bierfreund's well-known dye works. He remained there for five years, learning that business completely. Then he established his own dye works on Lexington Avenue, which he continued for seven years, after which he finally opened the tavern "zur Badischen Heimat" ["at the sign of the Baden Homeland"] on Buckeye Road, which he has run as an up-to-date host with the greatest success to the present day. He is actively supported in this by his wife. He met her on the passage to America. She was born Miss Elisabeth Roth, from Lagelshurst, Baden, and they married in Utica. The marriage has produced five children, two girls and three boys.

Mr. Kohler is president of the Baden Support Society, a clear proof that he is respected by his particular countrymen. Further, he is a member of the Cuyahoga Support Society. Every German cause has in him a warm friend and helpful supporter.

Karl Ferdinand Hackert

Mr. Karl Ferdinand Hackert was born on 19 May 1842 in Bärden near Hildesburghausen, Saxony-Meiningen, to respected parents. He attended the Volksschule in his birthplace and dedicated himself to botany, promoted by the local pastor, Prange, who affectionately supported the boy. He preserves an interest in botany to the present day. Later Mr. Hackert worked for 16 years in a toy and furniture factory, where he rose to be an artist in his area. After being briefly with his uncle in Bremen, who ran a chair factory, he decided in 1870 to emigrate to America, landing on 18 May 1870 in the harbor of New York. Mr. Hackert remained two years in New York, working as an interior carpenter during this time. He settled in Cleveland on 5 July 1872. He worked for a while as an interior carpenter here as well, but then he established himself independently and remained that way for five years. During the last ten years, Mr. Hackert has worked at the Cleveland Store Fixture Co., where he enjoys the respect of his superiors and colleagues. Mr. Hackert sent a splendidly worked table of his creation to the Columbian Exposition in 1888. The table top is set with 5442 pieces of nine various types of wood. In 1872 in this town, Mr. Hackert married Theresia Brehm, born in Wolfsdorf near Erfurt, Coburg-Gotha, whose acquaintance he had already made in New York. The marriage may be described as extremely happy. Mrs. Hackert is an amiable companion and is as interested as her husband in everything beautiful and fine, particularly for German causes.

Frank Ortkowski

Frank Ortkowski, the paving contractor well known and respected in this city, was born on 15 September 1851 as the son of the mason Jacob Ortkowski in Kosmin, West Prussia. His parents later moved to Pawlaw, and from there to Wischin, where Frank also was educated. He emigrated to America in 1873 and landed on its shores on 14 March. His first residence was Erie, Pennsylvania, where he was active for two years. Then he came to Cleveland in 1875, remaining here for three years before going to Detroit, working there and in other places until returning to the Forest City and making it his permanent residence. First of all he was superintendent in Sandusky with Collins the paving contractor, but he has been continually resident in Cleveland since 1880.

Mr. Ortkowsky soon made himself independent, and through hard work, energy and persistence he has risen to prosperity. Besides the qualities cited, he also had M. A. Hanna and other magnates to thank, since they recognized his capability and gave him paving jobs. Mr. Ortkowski speaks of this with a sense of gratitude, particularly concerning ex-Senator Hanna.

Frank Büttner, who was well known in German circles and now deceased, was manager under Mr. Ortkowski for six years. Alongside his paving business, he also runs a liquor wholesale business, presided over by his nephew, Bernard Ortkowski.

Mr. Ortkowski enjoys great respect as a ready helper in need among his particular compatriots. He has dried many tears with his strongly-marked sense of welfare. He is also active in Polish societies, such as the Polish National Alliance, with its headquarters in Chicago, as well as in the Ohio Alliance. Further, he is a member of the Sacred Heart Support Society and the St. Vincent Society.

In 1882 Mr. Ortkowski was married in St. Peter's Church with Miss Mary Wägner, born near Zempelburg, district of Marienwerder, West Prussia. Ten children have come from this blessed union, of which five, Apollonia, Julia, Leo, August and Hedwig are still alive.

The family lives in a splendid residence at the corner of Chambers and Tod Street, opposite Mr. Ortkowski's place of business. It enjoys great respect in all circles, without concern for nationality, and Mr. Ortkowski is a welcome guest wherever he appears.

Friedrich Reich

Fritz Reich, superintendent of the municipal paving operation, was born on 15 January 1861 in Hetzheim, Rhenish Palatinate. His father of the same name was a respected farmer. Friedrich attended the Volksschule and Latin school and later apprenticed as a cooper. At the age of 20 years, on 1 May 1881, he came to America and settled first in Brooklyn, New York, where he worked at his profession for a year. In November, 1882, he came to Cleveland. After spending several years here in his profession, he founded his own cooperage, running it for several years until he entered municipal service. At first he was paving inspector, but for the last seven years he has held the responsible post of superintendent of paving, and due to his years of experience he is one of the most capable officials of the city engineer department.

Mr. Reich married Miss Magdalena Maler from Dürkheim, Palatinate, in 1881. She has given life to eight children, Paulina, Wilhelmina, Johanna, Friedrich J., Adolph G., Henrietta, Henry R. and Irma, giving positive guarantee that the Palatines shall not die out.

He is a respected member of the United German Union, the Sycamore Club, the Forest City Outing Club and the Improved Order of the Redmen of America. Mr. Friedrich Reich also pursues German activities with lively interest. His brother is the journalist John Reich, active here for years, who created the notable local German paper, the *'Herold.'*

Arnold Wilhelm

Arnold Wilhelm, owner of the West Side Printing House, came to America in 1866 with his parents and siblings. His father was one of the most accomplished and respected German teachers, Lorenz F. Wilhelm, who was hired as German teacher as soon as German instruction became obligatory in the public schools in 1871. Previously he had taught in the Independent German School Congregation, as well as in the Church School at the corner of Greenwood and Scovill Avenue. After many years of activity, he died at the high old age of 87 on 20 May of this year (1907), and his death was mourned by all who knew him.

Arnold Wilhelm, his son and the object of this sketch, was born on 4 January 1866 in Schiers, Grisons Canton, Switzerland. After coming to Cleveland as a child, after his schooling he learned book printing and established himself in partnership with Mr. Hindermeister as a job printer on the West Side in 1886, and in 1886 he bought out his partner and continues the business to the present day as the West Side Printing House at 1903 25th Street on his own.

Mr. Wilhelm is a member of the Swiss Society and one of the founders of the Swiss Men's Chorus, as well as a member of the Social Turner Society, the Freedom Court, I. O. F., the Humboldt Union of the United German Union, the Lake Shore Lodge of the Knights of Pythias, the Heights Men's Chorus and other societies.

He is happily married with Elizabeth Kurz, a local lady born of German parents. Four children, two boys and two girls, have come from that marriage.

Mathias Steinen

Mr. Mathias Steinen was born on 13 March 1876 in Eller on the Moselle as the third son of the vineyard owner Joseph Steinen. He attended the Volksschule and later the Kaiser Wilhelm Gymnasium in the district capital of Montebauer, and after his graduation he trained as a cook. After doing his military duty he made himself independent, establishing a restaurant in Mayen near Koblenz, which he ran for 4 1/2 years. He was not fortunate, however, so that he had to sell the business and try to make a living as a traveling salesman for several years.

In 1904 Mr. Steinen came to America and settled in Cleveland. For nine months he held the position as chef at the old Savarin on Ontario Street, and he later made himself independent by taking over an established beer and wine tavern in the old bank at the corner of St. Clair and Willson Avenue, but he soon gave this business up and took over the position of administrator at the Vorwärts Turner Hall. After doing his duties for a full year, he bought a lot at 6915 Lexington Avenue on which he built a tavern combined with a restaurant, together with a delicatessen. His rooms are done in Old German style and are tastefully furnished, making a friendly impression. His establishment is frequented by the best elements of the neighborhood.

In Münster-Maifeld on 25 November 1898, Mr. Steinen married Miss Margarethe Marx, from which came his two children, Katie and Fritz.

Mr. Steinen naturally takes an enthusiastic and prominent part in society life. He is a member of the Aurora Lodge of the German Order of the Harugari as well as a Knight of the Golden Eagle, and he was their high priest. Other societies to which Mr. Steinen belongs are the East Side Military Society, the Society of German Comrades in Arms, and the Rhinelanders' Society.

Jacob Gund

One may see from the career of Mr. Jacob Gund what a man can accomplish when he harmoniously combines honorable striving with restless hard work and an energy which knows no barrier. He was born on 29 February 1844 in a leap year, so that the object of this sketch only has the occasion to celebrate a birthday every four years, and as a result of the advent of the twentieth century he has to wait eight years. His place of birth is Hockenheim in the Grand Duchy of Baden, where his father was a long-established and respected citizen and died last year (1906) at the high old age of 88. After Jacob completed school, he chose the profession of a painter, which was successful, so that he made himself independent in the course of time. Unfortunately he later lost his considerable fortune through the blows of destiny. Yet Mr. Gund is not one of those characters who give up easily. He gathered fresh courage and emigrated to America in 1876, settling here in Cleveland. After his arrival he worked at first at his profession, but later, in 1886, he bought a nice piece of land in Collinwood, where he ran a truck farm and a vineyard for several years. When the Lake Shore Line placed its shops in Collinwood, however, he gave up gardening, divided his property into building lots, and dedicated himself to real estate. Mr. Gund's lots, located on St. Clair, Crosby, Dunham and Gund Avenues in Collinwood, have water and gas, and paved streets lead to the lots, which are accessible on the St. Clair steetcar. It was in 1867 that he married Miss Marie Schwesinger, born in Altlussheim, Baden. Mrs. Gund is very expert in the area of German literature, and she is interested in all intellectual activities. Two sons, both of whom have taken respected positions in the Cleveland business world, have come from this happy marriage.

Mr. Gund visited the old homeland in 1905 to be able to press hands with his old father in life. Two brothers, who enjoy great respect among their fellow citizens, still live there.

Mr. Jacob Gund is an honorary member of the Baden Support Society, and he enjoys general respect not only in Collinwood but in this entire city.

Fritz Kummer

Born on 25 July 1855 in Limpach, Bern Canton, as the son of the married couple of Nikolaus and Elisabeth Kummer, Friedrich attended the schools in his home town until he was 16, when he went to the agricultural school in Bern. Then he took various positions until entering the military. On being declared free from the service, he established a mercantile business in Limpach and married Elisa Hofer in 1876, a marriage which produced two daughters, Frieda and Emma. But his wife was torn from him by death in 1879. As a result of this blow of fate, Mr. Kummer gave up his business and moved to French Switzerland, where he held various jobs. In 1886 he followed his frequently-expressed resolution to emigrate to the land of the Star Spangled Banner, and he went via Le Havre and New York to Uhrichsville, Ohio, where his brother Jacob was already resident. Here his own thorough knowledge of cheese making proved useful, making him a good living. In 1891 Mr. Kummer moved to New Philadelphia and opened a tavern in that booming town which soon became one of the most popular places in the locality. Mr. Kummer came to Cleveland three years later and took over the tavern "At the Sign of the Three Sworn Brothers" at the corner of Bank and Lake Streets, which became a gathering place for Swiss. In 1899 he sold this business and opened the restaurant known by the name of the "Swiss Casino" at 199 St. Clair Street. Located in the business district of the city, it enjoys a good reputation.

On 4 August 1901 he took over the noted tavern "At the Sign of the Wilhelmshöhe" on Denison Avenue, one of the most beloved and used picnic places for German societies.

Mr. Kummer has lived in marital happiness since 1888 with Walburga Bechtold, who has given him two girls, Dora and Bertha. Mr. Kummer belongs to the Swiss Society and its branches, to the Swiss Men's Chorus and the Mutual German Support Society, and he is a beloved member of the Freedom Court of the Foresters.

Charles Noll

Hard work, persistence, character, all combined with the command of a craft, these are the primary characteristics which mark so many of our compatriots to make it possible for them to rise to the heights, to solidify their existence and to bring themselves to respect and reputation. Among them is Mr. Noll, who was thrown on his own resources and laid the foundation for a business with no help from others. Holding to his principle of always doing his best with his full strength, he has built himself from step to step, so that he may look proudly on his success as a capable businessman.

Mr. Noll was born on 11 December 1861 in Mahlert, district of Schlichtern, Electoral Hessia. He attended the Volksschule in his place of birth, and after graduation he went to Frankfurt am Main to learn building, to which he had been inclined since youth. After six years of working in his profession in the old Imperial city, he decided to emigrate. He came to America in 1880 and settled in Cleveland, where he has lived without interruption since then, pursuing his work. Three years after his arrival Mr. Charles Noll made himself independent as a building contractor, and over this long series of years he has built many imposing buildings, not only in this city but also outside it.

Mr. Noll married Katharina Josepha Odenwald, born in Ober-Bimmbach, district of Fulda, in 1882. Eight children have been born to this couple, of which one girl sadly died at a tender age.

Mr. Noll is an outstanding member of the C. M. B. A. as well as of the John the Baptist Support Society no. 1, and he is respected by those who known him for his honorable German character. The Noll family lives at 2550 E. 67th Street.

Frank Schoene

Frank Schoene was born on 11 February 1855 in Zerbst, Duchy of Anhalt. His father ran a tawing business, but he came with his family to America in 1871, directly to Cleveland.

Mr. Schoene attended school in Germany and after the arrival of the family here he learned furniture finishing. For a long time he was employed by the once-noted furniture business of Vincent & Sturm. In 1886 Mr. Schoene took over a wine and beer tavern on Central Avenue, which he ran for 15 years. This business no longer pleased him, so that he sold the tavern he had so long run. He has been a municipal employee for the last several years, and he has done great service through punctually fulfilling the duties of his office.

Even in his earliest years Mr. Schoene, who is an outstanding singer, joined the Harmonie Singing Society, and later he was one of the founders of the old "Frohsinn." He was also an active member of the Harugari Men's Chorus. He is still a member of the Germania Turner Society, the Pioneer Society and the Aurora Lodge of the Order of the Harugari.

In 1876 Mr. Thomas Schoene married Miss Maria Endress. Six chilren, three sons and three daughters, have come from the marriage. The daughters are all happily married. His wife sadly died in April, 1906.

Mr. Schoene has his heart in the right place. Always a true devotee of Germans, he has always joined in whenever something needed to be promoted or when a demonstration in its honor was called for.

Christian Friedrich Pfeiffer

The "Land flowing with milk and honey" is praised as the promised land. The horde of silver stars passing through the night sky in a bright path is called the Milky Way. Milk is the first nourishment we receive, and without it we would not grow. These are proofs how important that liquid is and what importance has always been assigned to it. Mr. Christian Pfeiffer is a compatriot who travels the Milky Way and provides housewives with this irreplaceable food.

Chr. F. Pfeiffer was born in Gross-Sachsenheim in lovely Swabia on 28 March 1872. His father, Gottfried Pfeiffer, pursued the honorable craft of a shoemaker. He died in 1879, and in November of the same year the mother emigrated together with the children to America, where they settled in the state of Michigan with relatives. There Christian grew up on the farm, and through his seventeenth year he worked on the land, so that he came to know every aspect of farming from the bottom up.

He came to Cleveland in 1889 and learned the craft of a molder, but once he had assembled sufficient means, he established a milk store which is still operating. As a result of his hard work, the business has achieved a significant scale, and a large number of wagons belonging to him travel the city.

Mr. Pfeiffer has always has a lively interest in German societies, particularly the Harmonie counts him as one of its most enthusiastic members. He long held the first position in the arrangements committee, accomplishing great things for the society. More recently his business claims too much of his time, so that he had to pass the position of financial secretary, which he also held, into other hands. Mr. Pfeiffer is also a member of the South German League, the Woodmen of the World and the Vorwärts Turner Society. Mrs. Pfeiffer also has the warmest interest in German society life. She is a member of the Harmonie Women's Society and is its financial secretary. The Harmonie has passed many pleasant hours at the Pfeiffer home.

Mr. Pfeiffer's wife is an amiable compatriot of his, born in Aalen and formerly Miss Anna Rittelmann. Three children, two boys, Karl and Walther, and the girl Nana have come from this most happy of unions, making lively the home on Norwood Avenue, where the place of business is also located

Lorenz Dippel

Mr. Dippel was born on 28 December 1866 in Olberode, canton of Ziegenhain, district of Kassel, in Hessia-Nassau. His father, Heinrich Dippel, had been mayor of the place for many years. He still leads the destiny of Olberode in healthy old age, looking back on a service of 32 years. Mr. Dippel's mother, Margarethe née Battenberg, died in August, 1895. He himself came to America at the start of the 1880s, when he was still a young man of 16. He had gone through the Volksschule over there, and he had also done two years of musical instruction under Heinrich Schissler in the Superior School of Music. It was then his intention to become a musician. After his move to America, however, the struggle for survival became more important. He came directly to Cleveland, arriving here on 8 May 1883. The first position he had was a job in the Doan Gasoline Factory, and he remained there for two years, then he worked for a further nine years as a wire worker. After this intense and trying period as a worker he was in the possession of savings which made it possible for him to think of independence and a business of his own. During the crisis years of 1892-94 he tried to run a grocery, and although he survived, he changed over to being a tavernkeeper, where he has remained.

Dippel's Hall, or Liederkranz Hall, which he has run for 11 years now, is generally known, just as Mr. Dippel himself is known as a hard-working host and as an honorable, jovial, but also strict character, who only wants decent customers, which makes his place popular.

Mr. Dippel married Miss Auguste Krumrei on 20 September 1888. This marriage has produced seven children, Lillie M., Walter William, Herbert J., Lorenz C., Edward H., Flora E., and Georg Friedrich Dippel, of which only the last little boy died.

What should be stressed is the intense involvement of Dippel in German causes. He naturally is deeply involved in German society life, since the Swabian Men's Chorus, to which he belongs as a fine singer, has its location in his business. Further, he belongs to the Knights of Pythias, the German Order of the Harugari and the United German Union, and he also does what he can to support any undertaking derived from a German origin or a German ideal, which origins and ideals he upholds in his own life, and which have a true and respected home in his home and his tavern.

Bernhard Schatzinger

The first settlers and oldest residents of the city are called "pioneers," and we have given many examples of these in this work who are worthy of the designation. But this does not exhaust the number of pioneers. Hardly anyone deserves this designation more than Bernhardt Schatzinger, who only came here in relatively recent years, but who accomplished more as a building pioneer than anyone before him or perhaps after him, so that he should be mentioned as one of the first here.

Mr. Bernhardt Schatzinger was born on 21 January 1860, in Wesel on the Lower Rhine, a fortress in the Rhine province, and after finishing elementary school he apprenticed as a construction cabinetmaker. His apprenticeship took three years, and after he had completed it he toured almost all of Germany as well as the over the Rhine to Belgium to improve his profession.

He had heard and read a great deal about the "land of the free" during his years of wandering. The desire to see it first hand moved him to emigrate to the United States in 1881, so that he arrived in the Forest City in September of that year. He knew no one here, and he was a stranger in a strange land. It was, however, not hard to get a job in his profession. For six months he worked for a boss, and, having learned English, established himself as a building contractor. The many new streets Mr. Schatzinger opened during this period, particularly on the East Side of our city, and the marvelous cottages he built there, the modern houses and other structures that he raised here, show most clearly that his enterprise was crowned with the greatest success. Mr. Schatzinger was former manager of the real estate firm of Schatzinger and Tremaine, and he is even today invested in the firm. He is also a major stock holder and vice president of the Cleveland Gas and Electric Fixture Co., which has its office in the Masonic Temple and its factory, where about 75 workers are employed, in Seneca Street. Mr. Schatzinger is director of the Euclid Beach Park Co., and he is involved in various other enterprises. In his construction firm there are employed an average of 50 to 60 men.

Mr. Schatzinger has been living for a short time in a splendid home on Superior Street, east of the Boulevard. As the goddess of good fortune has always smiled on him, so she has also bountifully graced him in his new home. Mr. Schatzinger discovered a producing gas well sufficient to heat and light his lovely new home. But he does not owe his business prosperity to luck alone, but to his honorable German character and solid nature. Many have been put in a position by Mr. Schatzinger to have a home of their own, and it is no wonder that he enjoys the love and respect of his fellow men to a high degree.

In 1883 Mr. Schatzinger married Miss Sabina Kröckel, who was born in Westheim near Kissingen, Bavaria, and who came to Cleveland in 1881 with her parents. The marriage produced two sons and three daughters.

Dr. Arthur Winter

Among the well-known physicians of the younger generation, the name of Dr. Arthur Winter is one of the best-known. His cradle was located in lovely Hungary. He was born on 17 March 1867 in Miskolz, Hungary, and came to the United States in 1890 to join his parents, who had immigrated a few years earlier. In 1896 he graduated as a physician from Cleveland Medical

College and settled in Youngstown to practice, where he worked for nine years, enjoying great popularity. After nine years of intense medical practice, the literarily gifted young physician was tired of small-town life and came back to Cleveland, where he recovered his many friends, who esteemed his intellectual as well as his medical capabilities. Dr. Winter soon began to play a major role among his compatriots. He wrote essays and popular medical articles, gave lectures and was chosen as the physician of many societies and associations, which now claim much of his time.

William J. Geier

As the name already betrays, W. J. Geier, the local police attorney, is of German origins. He was born here on 21 October 1875. His father, Sebastian Geier, settled in Cleveland after immigrating and lived in this city without interruption until his death in April of this year (1907), in high old age. He was always respected and honored for his integrity by those who knew him.

His parents provided him with an outstanding education. After attending elementary schools, he continued on at St. Ignatius College and later studied law, graduating Baldwin University in 1901 and [was] received by the Bar. In autumn of the same year he took up practice as a lawyer and formed the law firm of Geier, Farrell & Edwards, with its offices at 631 Williamson Building.

W. G. Geier holds a prominent place in the guild of lawyers, and he is regarded as one of the sharpest and most adept defenders of the law. His intensity and ability won him public attention, and in 1902 Geier was named assistant city sollicitor. The next summer he received the office of police attorney, and since then he has rendered unequalled service to the community since he is eminently qualified, as his electors foresaw. It should not be forgotten that this position is one of the stormiest and confronted with all the tricks of those allied with the criminal element. It demands great insight, superior decisiveness and an understanding which does not go awry. We have recently had occasion to see that the young police attorney is equipped with these qualities, and knows well what punishments should be given to the guilty who have been arrested and convicted.

Police attorney Geier has been married since 1903 to Miss Agnes Horn from Fremont, Ohio. A son, John Newton, has been born to the union.

Adolph J. Haas

Adolph J. Haas, secretary of the district election board, a man popular in political circles but also thoroughly capable, is a German Hungarian. He first saw the light of day in Busita on 30 March 1858. His father ran a grocery in the old homeland, which he also did after moving to Cleveland. He was successful in this business for years, and he died at the age of almost 80 in the July of this year (1907). Adolph Haas came to Cleveland on 13 January 1877 as a young man of 19, when his father had already been established, and after various jobs he ran a cigar store. He as well was successful in business. But from the very moment he arrived, he was interested in the political institutions of this free country, which he still admires. It was natural that this interest should lead him to politics, and he joined the Republican Party, going through many a hard battle in the ranks. In 1899 he was elected secretary of the Republican Central Committee, which he held until 1904, when he moved to his present position as secretary to the election board, which had just been created by law. The election could not have fallen on a better person, since it is known that Adolph J. Haas excercises his office with strict conscientiousness and non-partisanship.

Adolph J. Haas also takes an intense part in social and society life. He is a member and president of the H. B. S. U., grand master of the Order of the Sons of Abraham, as well as a member of the Western Reserve and Tippecanoe Club.

He married Rosa Newman on 17 October 1882. Two sons and a daughter came from this union.

Adolph J. Haas demonstrates that it makes no difference whether a person is born here or overseas, and that every position is open to that person regardless.

Alexander Sandory

What German in Cleveland has not met the fluent, amiable, genial director of the former German Theater in Cleveland, now manager and partner of the fashionable Wohl Restaurant at 1280 West 3rd Street, Mr. Alex. Sandory? Mr. Sandory can rightly be be numbered as one of the divinely blessed artists who always bring excitement and profit to those fortunates with whom they deal. It is too bad that his beautiful talent is no longer in the service of Thalia, so often applauded by the theater-going public of Cleveland, but — one may hope for the future! Mr. Sandory is still young, and it entirely possible that conditions might so change that he will once more be able to dedicate his full efforts to the artistic mission which has enthused him from youth.

Alexander Sandory was born in Kaschau in Hungary in 1865, and he attended the Premonstratensian *Gymnasium* there. His inclination to the stage was so intense in his youth that as a boy of 16 he abandoned both his parents' house and the *Gymnasium* in order to join a Hungarian acting troupe. His father, however, was not in agreement; he desired that Alexander should at least get a good education before following his artistic inclinations. He had the fugitive brought back by the police, and Alexander was compelled to complete his studies. Today he blesses his father's superior experience, who compelled him to gather the fund of knowledge without which even an artistic career is never successful. After graduation, Mr. Alex. Sandory dedicated himself completely to the stage without any further contradiction from his father.

The fiery, handsome young man, a gifted performer, was soon a favorite of the public in roles as a young lover. His first important engagements were in Hamburg and Frankfurt am Main. Soon he turned to more important roles. He had triumph after triumph playing bonvivants and officers in engagements in Metz, Carlsbad, Wildungen, Marienbad, Norderney, Kohlberg, etc., attracting so much attention from theatrical leaders that Alexander Sandory soon became a director, then superior director, and finally, at a relatively young age, theater manager. He was only 25 when Prince Georg II made him theatrical manager of his court theater in Rudolfstadt, a position which he held until the death of his princely patron. For one year, Mr. Sandory also led the summer theater in Erfurt, in conjunction with the Metropole Theater Weimar and the Park Theater in Gotha. He has particularly fond memories of two tours he arranged. One started from Marienbad and became a triumphal procession across Bohemia, Upper Austria, Lower Austria, Tyrol and Styria. The second, which was no less successful, started in Lindau and passed through all the communities around Lake Constance and Switzerland, ending in Geneva. In 1902 Mr. Sandory was invited by the Cleveland German Theater Society to take over the management of the Cleveland German Theater. He led it for two seasons with great success, as everyone may recall. The companies assembled by him were very accomplished, and the repertoire was a model. But what good was art or ability? As one may recall, the local German enterprise could not be maintained as a paying enterprise. The passivity of most of the Germans here caused it to bleed out, so that in the end it also lost the inspiring force of Sandory himself.

There is no more popular person in Cleveland than Sandory. He has the true soul of an artist, a warm heart, a naïve, childish character. Whoever comes to know him has to love him, and once won as a friend he is totally dependable. Sandory made his reputation as leader of the local German Theater. Under his two years of leadership, we received classically perfect, genuinely artistic performances, and when he gave up the leadership and bade his artistic goodby, he won our universal respect by sacrificing himself for his parents and siblings and taking over the management of the restaurant. By staging international music evenings he raised the establishment to a national reputation which is certainly unique in the United States, a gathering place for the elite of the citizenry.

Sandory has often performed small labors of love for our Germans. As often as one turns to him to help at larger festivities and presentations, he was always glad to give the best of his taste and his ideas.

Georg J. Sommer

Georg J. Sommer, the manager of the Gehring brewery, was born here in 1864 as the son of the grocer and old pioneer John J. H. Sommer. He attended the public schools and the West Side High School. In 1881, at the age of 17, he entered the service of C. E. Gehring, and he has worked there a full 25 years. He has proved to be not only one of the most loyal, but also one of the most capable officers, and he was elected one of the directors at the founding of the Gehring stock company, and named manager of the business. He has had control over the entire business for some time.

Mr. Sommer is a member of the Knights of Pythias, the Elks, the Shriners and the Freemasons, in the last of which he has reached the 32nd degree. The fact that Mr. Sommer cleaves to the Germans despite being born here is shown by what has been said. He is also married with German blood, and his wife is the former Miss Dietz, daughter of an equally old and well-known Cleveland German pioneer. Four children, three girls and a boy, have come from the marriage.

In Geo. J. Sommer the Gehring establishment has an outstanding chief officer, since he possesses the tact needed in his position, which brings him into contact with persons of all levels every day, which is how his business wins so many customers, which may be ascribed to the general popularity and respect which he personally enjoys. Mr. Sommer recently took over a leading position with the Isaac Leisy Brewing Co.

Louis G. Seibel

Mr. Louis G. Seibel is a child of Cleveland. He first saw the light of day in this city on 2 February 1857. His parents came to America at the beginning of the 1850s and settled permanently in Cleveland. His father was from Hamm, Hessia-Darmstadt, and the mother, born a Haman, was born in Malberg, Grand Duchy of Baden. The marriage was blessed with five children, of which Louis, the object of this sketch, is the eldest. As a boy he attended public school, as well as a German private school for two years, and he graduated from the East High School. He at first chose the machining business as his trade, but then he entered the service of Western Union Telegraph Company, where he remained for 20 years. For years he held there the position of a telegraph engineer, and over the last seven years of his service he led the operations division. Health compelled him to withdraw from the trying conditions of the company, and he accepted a more comfortable position in the management of the Leisy Brewing Co., where he has been working the last few years.

Mr. L. Seibel married Miss Lina Fix, daughter of the late, popular German pioneer Georg Fix, in 1880. Four children, including three sons (William, Randolph, Emil) and a daughter, Mamie, have come from the marriage. The eldest son, William, is currently an assistant to the superintendent of the East Cleveland Water Works.

Mr. Seibel is an outstanding member of the Ellsworth Lodge and Hillman Chapter of the Freemasons, is a Past Master and held the position of secretary for 16 years. He is also a member of several telegraph societies, etc.

He distinguishes himself in all his positions through his conscientiousness and loyalty to duty, and Mr. Seibel is loved and treasured by all who know him well.

Ernst Heyse

One of the most beloved among younger German businessmen, who has managed to build a good business in a short period of time through hard work and persistence, is without a doubt the noted pastry chef, Mr. Ernst Heyse. He was born in Kolmar in Posen on 17 April 1865 as the son of the merchant Heinrich Heyse. After he attended the *Gymnasium* in Kolmar through his fourteenth year, he apprenticed as a pastry maker. At the age of 17 he emigrated to America and settled first in New York, where he was employed for three years in the famous Sherry Pastry Bakery. Then he held a prominent position for four seasons in the Grand Union Hotel in Sarasota Springs.

In 1890 we find him in Cleveland as the manager of the firm of Heyse & Weissgerber, a position he held until he established his own business in 1893. Mr. Heyse has been able to build a great circle of customers among German as well as American families, and now his business holds a prominent position among companies of its sort. His shop is at 6212 Superior Avenue.

Mr. Heyse has been a member of the German Freemasons' Lodge, Concordia, for many years. He belongs to the Oriental Commandery and the Al Koran Temple. As a member of the Cleveland Singing Society, the Harmonie Singing Society, the Germania Turner Society and the National Union no. 36, Cleveland Council, Mr. Heyse is a beloved personality in society circles.

Edward S. Meyer

General Edward S. Meyer, retired officer in the regular United States Army, a veteran of the War of the Rebellion and one of the most noted jurists in the state of Ohio, was born on 20 August 1843 in Canton, Ohio, to German parents. His father was the late Judge Seraphim Meyer, and his mother was born Eleanora Schuchardt. Both of these families, the Meyers and the Schuchardts, were among the most esteemed in their home towns of Mannheim and Heidelberg, respectively.

In 1827, his grandfather Jacob Meyer, who had moved a few years earlier from Mannheim to Belfort on the Swiss-German border, decided to emigrate to the America, and he settled in Canton, Ohio.

General Meyer took his schooling in the public schools of Canton and later attended St. Vincent's College. At the outbreak of the Civil War in April 1861 he gave up his studies and enlisted, although only 17, in the 4th Ohio Volunteers, and served through the entire war. He also served in the 19th and 107th Ohio, as well as in the 5th United States Volunteer Regiments.

Hence he participated in the 1861 campaign in West Virginia under the command of General McClellan. In 1862 he participated in the battles of the Armies of the Ohio and the Cumberland. In the next year we find him in the ranks of the warriors of the Army of the Potomac. In the siege of Charleston, S.C., he took an active part with his men, and he participated in all the actions of the Army of the Potomac in 1864 to 1865 under the command of General Hancock.

After only 6 months in service, when he was only 18, he was named a lieutenant. In the course of only a few years he held all the ranks, and on 13 March 1865, at the age of 21, he was named a brigadier general for his bravery and ability. As a reward for his services in the Battle of Shiloh, he was advanced to the rank of major, and after the Battle of Chancellorsville, from which he took severe wounds, he was granted the rank of lieutenant colonel. He was struck by an enemy bullet that passed through his back, neck and right lung, seriously wounding him, and he fell into the hands of the Confederates.

After the end of the war he was named a captain in the regular army and stood out here as he had in volunteer service through his military judgment even in very difficult situations. Entrusted with the command of cavalry against Indians in Texas and the far West, he participated in campaigns against the Lapan, Kickapoo, Apache, and other tribes.

In 1875 the consequences of the wounds suffered in the Civil War became palpable, he commenced internal bleeding, forcing him to apply for discharge from active service if he were not to put his life in jeapardy. His release was granted with the remarks, "Released at his own request due to incapacity arising from wounds received in service and while carrying out his duties."

In 1870, as commander of the occupation forces in Baton Rouge, La., he was granted the title of brigadier general by the State Legislature and voted thanks for service to the state. He had suppressed a bloody uprising against which the local and state authorities were powerless.

Called to the Texas border to command troops at Fort McIntosh, he managed in 1872 to encircle the insurgents under General Pedro A. Valdes and force them to surrender, using cavalry troops under his command. The insurgents had been trying to invade Mexico from the American side of the Rio Grande. General Valdes put up intense resistance, and he could only be moved to surrender after he himself was seriously wounded. For his heroism during the campaign and its rapid conclusion, General Meyer was officially thanked by the War Department and the State Department.

During his free hours that he was granted in the course of his military career, he revived with great zeal the legal studies interrupted by the war. Six years before he left the military, he passed the bar examination and received a license as a lawyer in the courts of Ohio, and later the right to practice before the United States Supreme Court and federal circuit courts.

Through intense rest and various successful surgical operations, his weakened state of health was bostered, if only in part. For that reason he was able to accept the position of assistant United States attorney for the northern district of Ohio, to which he was named. At the time he took this office, he established himself as a legal counsel in Cleveland. Named United States attorney by President Garfield, General Meyer held this important position until 1883.

On the introduction of the Federal Plan in April, 1891, which led to a complete transformation of municipal administration, he was named corporation attorney of the city of Cleveland. As such it was his obligation to draft new laws or to modify the existing ones in such a way as to benefit the municipality or eliminate abuses. The fact that he brought clarity to the operations of many city departments, accomplishing much good, cannot be doubted by anyone. It is due to his truly heroic intervention that guarantees for the sum, $279,413, embezzled by the absconded city treasurer Thom. Axworthy, were called in.

General Meyer also managed to force the gas monopoly to lower its prices significantly, despite massive opposition, and to pay the city 6 1/2 percent of its annual gross income for the privileges granted. His comments at the time that enough money would come from this to build a new city hall in a few years were at first scorned by many and even attacked in the English press. How wrong his detractors were is shown by the contributions that flow into the municipal treasury from this source every year, amounting to over $600,000 after 10 years. The savings to the gas consumers amounts to almost $ 2 million annually, which once went straight into the pockets of money-hungry monopolists. Through this alone, General Meyer deserves the lasting recognition of local residents.

It is entirely natural that his activities in office made him a politically popular man. It was particularly the Workers' Party that praised his conduct as municipal attorney, and it offered to run him as candidate for the office of mayor in 1893. Despite his decided refusal, he was still nominated as a candidate by the independents and Workers, and he would surely have been elected if he had shown the slightest interest in the election. After the end of his term as municipal attorney, he resumed his old practice as a lawyer, which won high reputation under the name of Meyer & Mooney.

At the outbreak of the war with Spain in 1898, General Meyer offered his services to the president and would have received a command if the Spaniards had not been forced to sue for peace after the rapid succession of American victories.

When the German Day celebrations was being staged by the German-Americans in 1890, General Meyer commanded the German-American Division of the parade. He takes an intense interest in public matters as a member of the chamber of commerce.

In August 1865 General Meyer married Miss Jennie Hauser, daughter of the late respected citizen of Canton, Mr. Johann Hauser. This truly happy marriage, unmarred by any disharmony, produced seven children, of which five are still living. His sole daughter was torn from him by death at the age of 12, and his eldest son also was taken a few months later.

Two of the sons, Oren B. and Ralph E., are officers of the United States Army. Oren B. is first lieutenant in the 3rd Cavalry Regiment, and he was seriously wounded in the taking of Santiago, Cuba, on 1 July 1898. Ralph E. is serving as a second lieutenant in the 12th Infantry Regiment. Oren B. graduated from the United States Military Academy at West Point. The third son, Edward S., studied at the Western Reserve University, and after his graduation he took another course at the University of Heidelberg, Germany, receiving the degree of doctor of philosophy, and he currently holds the position as Professor of the German Language at Western Reserve University.

Mrs. Meyer was always a true companion to her husband, sharing his perils and troubles. At the age of 19, she accompanied him on horseback across the seemingly endless prairie and mountains to all of the various military posts, seemingly isolated from all civilization, on the border of New Mexico and Texas. During the seven years she went through this, she bore 3 of her sons, one of them — who was wounded in the attack on Santiago — in Fort Bliss, which was then more than 1000 miles from the nearest railroad or telegraph.

Although Mr. Meyer was born and raised here and his profession as a soldier and as a lawyer put him almost exclusively in contact with Americans, he has still remained true to his mother tongue, which he speaks whenever the occasion offers itself. He has also given his sons an education in both English and German. Further, the large number of German authors in his private library gives the best proof that he values German literature.

Louis Ritter

On 3 February 1902 the Germans of Cleveland lost one of its oldest pioneers, Louis Ritter, who died on that day at the age of 76. Not only did Cleveland lose one of its oldest pioneers, but the Germans of the entire country were poorer by one of its best sons, who had always struggled in the first rank for more than a half century when it was a matter of humanity and liberty, which is why a monument is still set for him on this page.

Louis Ritter was born on 29 January 1826 in Kirchheimbolanden (Rhenish Palatinate), where his father was postmaster. His mother was born a Kölsch. After graduating from the Gymnasium in Speyer, the son attended the universities of Würzburg and Heidelberg. In the latter institution, where he studied law, he was hit by the revolution of 1848, in which he actively participated with musket like thousands of other students. After the suppression of the uprising in the Palatinate and Baden, he went to Switzerland in 1849, from whence he emigrated to America. Here as well he studied law, with the earlier U. S. Senator Henry B. Payne and Hiram V. Wilson. In 1854 he was admitted to the Bar, and he was assocated with the firm of Ritter, Beavis and Mueller. No sooner did he enter practice than agitation began against Negro slavery, in which he involved himself more than served his personal interests. As a result of his and former-governor Müller's efforts, the _'Wächter am Erie'_ was founded in 1852, and August Thieme, who was then in Buffalo, was called to Cleveland as editor. Ritter was also enthusiastically involved in the newspaper as assistant editor. In 1861 he was named assistant tax collector, a position he gave up in March, 1862. He took this position again years later, but only briefly. At this time he entered the 37th Ohio Infantry Regiment as a volunteer, participating as a member of Company H in Sherman's campaign in Georgia, the taking of Atlanta and Savannah, as well as in the march through South Carolina and North Carolina, and he was mustered out at the end of the war in Louisville as a lieutenant. He composed an account of his experiences on campaign entitled "The 37th Ohio Regiment" in the history work published by Whitelaw Reid. He was named a commissioner by Governor Tod to lead the care of the sick and wounded.

After the war, Ritter was one of the founders of the Hemlock Coal Co. in Perry County, Ohio. Further, for years he was active in real estate and insurance, from which he abstained only in his last years, when he withdrew from everything. He was also one of the co-founders of the Cleveland Singing Society. Other than the aforementioned work on the war, he also wrote useful press articles on the gold and silver question when that matter agitated the public. These articles attracted wide attention, showing him to be as ever a fighter who put his full strength behind his convictions.

When Louis Ritter died, he was mourned not only by German but also by English writers who recognized the efforts of this Forty-Eighter hero of freedom, who brought the fire of enthusiasm with him from Germany and never ceased to cause it to burn for his holiest and best goals even in his adopted fatherland and to dedicate himself continually to those goals. Like so many others who were his comrades and companions of destiny, who were brought into the country in hordes, it can be said that he did impress himself on the consciousness of the country. Those still remaining are contually fewer. Louis Ritter was one of the most important.

In 1854 Louis Ritter married Miss Harriet Lambert, on the same day when Ohio City was amalgamated with Cleveland. Mrs. Ritter was born in 1836 in Saarbrücken, coming to the United States in 1848 and settling permanently here with her parents. She died on 21 June 1907, and she was an educated lady who was widely known for dealing deeply with German literature. The marriage produced seven children, five sons and two daughters. The eldest son, Homer P. Ritter, is United States Engineer and commissioner for the Mississippi River, Louis E.

Ritter is a construction and civil engineer, Thomas J. Ritter has been here in the drug firm of Benton, Meyers & Co. for years. The youngest son, Horace G.

Ritter, whose twin lived only a few days, was unfortunately taken by death in the blossom of his years. Of the two daughters, Miss Jessie L. Ritter has been an assistant at the public library for over 20 years, and she oversees the German division, where she has accomplished great things. The second daughter, Hattie, is the wife of Mr. Chas. Carren, Deputy Auditor, and before her marriage she was active as a German teacher in the local public schools and prized by her superiors. She has often charmed her friends and listeners as an outstanding violinist.

The memory of this departed fighter for freedom will be treasured by descendents as well as all who know of his accomplishments.

Louis E. Lambert

Louis E. Lambert was born in Saarbrücken in 1842 and came with his parents to Cleveland as a boy in 1848. Here he passed his youth and ran a men's haberdashery in the city for years. He moved to St. Mary's, Ohio, where he is one of the most prominent and respected residents, and where he held the office of mayor with honor. At the outbreak of the Civil War he joined the 37th Ohio Infantry Regiment, the third German regiment, at the time of its organization in Cleveland, participated in all its marches, battles and problems the regiment endured over four years, and after its end he returned to Cleveland, from whence those few returning (189 of 1133) departed for their homes.

Capt. Lambert entered the regiment as a private, being promoted in recognition of his service to corporal, sergeant, orderly sergeant, second lieutenant, first lieutenant, regimental adjutant, and finally as captain of Company G of the 37th Regiment, and he commanded this company until the end of the war and brought it back home victorious. During the war he was wounded four times, once quite severely, so that he briefly fell into the hands of the enemy. Mr. Lambert was loved by both his superiors and those placed under him.

A Clevelander from childhood, he belongs to the G. A. R., and he was earlier a member of the Cleveland Singing Society and the Germania Turner Society. Many local citizens will recall this gentleman, always friendly.

Mr. Lambert is married to a lady born in St. Mary's, and the family is decorated with two children, Karl and Flora.

Currently Mr. Lambert is active in the insurance business in St. Mary's.

E. H. Klaustermeyer

Our respected fellow citizen E. H. Klaustermeyer is certainly one of the pioneers of the city, resident in the city for over a half century. He was born in Osnabrück, Hanover, parish of Buer, on 22 August 1830, the son of Mr. John Friedrich and his wife Eliza, née Heucher. His father, born in 1800, died in 1839, was the owner of a grocery business. The parents — his mother died in 1853 at the age of 50 — gave their children a careful education. E. H. Klaustermeyer, the eldest of five children, supported his parents in the store after leaving school and being confirmed in the Lutheran Church at the age of 14, and he continued to work in the store until he was 21. Then he emigrated with his brother Martin in 1851, and both came directly to Cleveland at the special invitation of Mr. Hempy, a friend of the Klaustermeyer brothers' youth, who had settled there a few months before. His brother Martin died in 1854.

In late 1858, Mr. Klaustermeyer set himself up in business in partnership with Mr. J. H. Melcher at 386-388 Prospect Street under the name of J. H. Melcher & Co., which was run with profit until 1884. In that year, Mr. Klausermeyer bought the share of Mr. Melcher and took his sons Martin, Edwin and Carl into the business. At the same time he established an ironwares business at 474 Woodland Avenue which was run by his son Henry. Besides these two businesses, Mr. Klaustermeyer also opened a second grocery in a new building at 2729 Euclid Avenue.

In 1858 Mr. Klausermeyer married Miss Mary Stegkemper from East Cleveland, and that happy marriage has produced eight children: Emma, Maria, Henry, Friedrich, Martin, Edwin, Dora, Nowa (now the wife of Mr. Ed. Fürst), and Carl. Mr. Ed. H. Klaustermeyer's wife died in 1889 at the age of 50, mourned by a large circle of family and friends.

Albert Urban

The vice president and manager of the *'Cleveland Herold,'* Mr. Albert Urban, was born on 16 January 1846 in Berlin. His father, Carl Urban, was a master builder there. After Urban graduated the Royal *Real-Gymnasium*, he chose a mercantile career. He pursued this career until he emigrated to America in 1896. In that year he came directly to Cleveland and settled here permanently. At first he worked for the Werner Publishing Co. (Akron), then he was collector for the German Theater Society in 1901-2. Then he went to work for the *'Cleveland Herold,'* and it is largely his doing that the *'Herold'* became a stock company and a daily.

Mr. Urban is a member of Concordia Lodge no. 345, F. & A. M., as well as of the Social Turner Society. He is naturally closely identified with German interests as a result of his business, and in him Germans have a column of strength and a vanguard.

Mr. Urban married Louise née Eckardt in 1873, and in a second marriage Antonie née Anders in 1895. The son Hans Urban and the daughter Kath. Urban are currently 31 and 21 years old respectively.

Jacob E. Mueller

Jacob E. Mueller, the publisher of this work, was born in Gundersheim, Rhenish Hessia. His father was the owner of the famous Prairie Mill. After attending school and taking private instruction, he was committed to the mercantile career and was put with relatives for an apprenticeship. He survived a severe winter with this business, during which he got a severe cold, so that he had to take to a sickbed. After his recovery he wanted nothing to do with mercantile life, and he entered the Ackermann Book Printers in Alzey, where he learned book printing, the profession he now pursues.

In 1869 the object of our sketch came to Cleveland. He found employment in the publishing house of the Evangelical Community, remaining there until 1872 before passing, after a brief time in New York, to the *'Wächter am Erie,'* where he passed 15 years as foreman and two years as manager. In 1889 he established the first German penny-paper, the *'Deutsche Presse,'* with which he had an unheard-of success. After the controlling shares of the *'Deutsche Presse'* passed into the hands of Wm. Kaufmann and it was amalgamated as a result into the *'Anzeiger,'* Jacob Mueller published the *'Neue Presse,'* which prospered originally as a weekly, but later, when it was transformed into a Republican daily, it needed so much money as a result of the crisis of 1893 that he finally sold it, after which he created the *'Deutsches Magazin'* as well as the German-American Historical-Biographical Company. He hung the first on the "nail" in 1904. The investor, Mr. Nagel ["Nail"], changed the name of the *'Deutsches Magazin'* to *'Nagel's Magazin,'* and within six months it was "nailed." Mr. Mueller, who came to dedicate himself exclusively to the editing and publishing of historical and biographical works,

178

then had good success in various cities, including Cleveland. As was the case with the *'Deutsche Presse,'* he was creating something new, and there can be no doubt as to the service performed for Germans and the enumeration of their accomplishments. Besides the newspapers mentioned above and the *'Deutsches Magazin,'* Jacob Mueller founded in 1888, while he was at the *'Wächter am Erie,'* the *'Hessische Blätter,'* which is currently published in New York.

In his earlier years Mr. Mueller took an active part in German societies. Right after his arrival, in March, 1869, he entered the old Cleveland Turner Society. In 1870 he was a cofounder of the Social Reading Society, a literary association of young men, mostly immigrant Germans. He helped call the Frohsinn Singing Society into existence, and he was long an active member. At the singing festival of the North American Singing League in 1893, he held the office of corresponding secretary.

After the completion of the second edition of his work *Cleveland and Its Germans*, Mr. Mueller will edit a historical work on the state of Ohio and the participation of Germans in its development, as well as a biographical lexicon of the outstanding Germans of the state, of which preparations are already being made and good collaborators obtained. This, his next undertaking, is already assured of success.

Edward Meyer

Secretary and treasurer of the Cleveland Herold Publishing Co., born in Cleveland, he attended the public schools here and received a careful mercantile education at the Ohio Business University. His father ran a furniture business, and the young man inclined to that branch. He worked at the National Furniture Co. for four years and distinguished himself as a capable businessman, achieving a respected position in the area of commercial life.

In May, 1907, he began a relation with the German-language daily and was elected into the board of directors of the Clevelander Herold Publishing Co., and he was elected its secretary and treasurer.

Mr. Meyer knows how to make friends in the course of dealing with his fellows, particularly those who value a straight-forward man. He is happily married to Emma Teufel, who comes from a respected German bourgeois family.

John Koch

Mr. John Koch was born on 11 December 1835, in Osthofen, district of Worms. His father was a farmer who also owned a wagon factory. The boy attended the *Volksschule* until he was 14, then attended the *Bürgerschule* until he was 17. John Koch entered the postal service at the age of 17, but he did not want to pursue this permanently, and like many others from his area he sought to cross the ocean to find a more promising field of action. In 1857 he emigrated to New York, and after beginning difficulties, through hard work and strict fulfilling of duties, he made it to collector and assistant bookkeeper of a brewery. For a time he was active as a salesman in a wholesale cloth business. In September 1862 Mr. Koch married in Hoboken, N. J., to Miss Maria Krämer, a young lady from Ober-Flörsheim, Alzey district. The couple have had two daughters survive, of which one is married and in Georgia, while the other still lives in her parents' house.

It was in May 1863 that Mr. Koch gave up his residence in New York and went to Cleveland, where he has remained. He once more entered a clothing business, soon becoming a partner in the large enterprise of the firm Thomas, Goodville & Co. He was active there until 1880.

In the meantime a new movement began in his life and activity. Cleveland developed rapidly, and the time of streetcars had come. The project to build a horse railway along Superior Street emerged in 1874, and Mr. Koch was one of the warmest supporters and promoters. With his wonted energy he went into carrying out the plan and helped call meetings, to call the stock company into existence. The first meeting took place in his own house. He was deeply involved in winning a charter from the city council. The final order came in March 1874, and the organizing meeting of the shareholders took place in May of the same year, with Mr. Charles Hathaway elected president and Mr. Koch director and vice president of the new company. They worked away, and the line was already in operation in October, 1874. The line stretched from Public Square to Giddings Avenue. Mr. Koch was the true promoter of the enterprise and remained its manager, and in July 1883 Mr. Koch's efforts added the Payne Avenue line as a branch of the Superior Street line. Until 1889 he remained in his position as director and vice president, until the horse railway had been rebuilt into a cable system.

In the meantime Mr. Koch had completely severed his ties with the cloth business in 1884, and he dedicated his full attention to running the street railway. When the cable line was consolidated with the St. Clair-Street Railway and the West Side lines (the Little Consolidated), he entered the new firm as its solicitor and adjuster of claims, a responsible position that he held until 1904.

Mr. Koch belongs to various organizations, since 1882 to the Cleveland City Lodge No. 15 and the Webb Chapter No. 14, R. A. M. He was one of the founders of the German Support Society, and after Thieme's death he was one of the stockholders and codirectors of the *Wächter am Erie* Co., which passed the paper into the hands of Mr. Hotze. He has always taken an intense interest in German efforts and undertakings.

While the Superior Street Railway was under construction, Mr. Koch became ill and on the advice of Dr. Weber he accompanied the doctor for seven months to Germany, France, and England. His brother lives in England.

In politics, in which Mr. Koch has always been intensely involved, he has been a solid Democrat since 1871. He has never sought an office nor held one, but he takes great interest in political developments inside and outside his party. On the electoral ticket for 1888, Mr. Koch was elector for the 21st Ohio district. He was member and official (cashier) of the German Independent Club, which existed from 1876 to 1884 and stood in the first row in all struggles for personal liberty against intolerance in Ohio. Mr. Koch's interests in public events continues today unabated.

August Zwierlein

Mr. August Zwierlein first saw the light of day near the world-famous watering place of Kissingen, in the town of Holstadt in the Bavarian district of Lower Franconia. The boy grew up in simple rural circumstances, and when he had completed the village school at the age of 13, he was apprenticed to a master shoemaker of his home town. The determining factor for his choice of profession was the result of a local custom which prevailed in many parts of Germany. In keeping with this custom father Zwierlein took into the house for a few weeks every year a shoemaker, who took care of the shoe needs of the family and did the repairs needed. August was able to watch the craftsman at work for hours, and the fact that he profited from it is shown by the fact that when he was barely 12 he made a pair of shoes for his sister, five years younger, of which he had even correctly cut the lasts. After completing his three years' apprenticeship the young journeyman took up his wandering staff, not so much to look around the world but to perfect his craft, to which he had committed himself heart and soul. He worked in the various large cities of South Germany, including Stuttgart. Even today Mr. Zwierlein recalls an incident from his period of residence in the capital city of Swabia with great fondness, which strengthened him in his resolve to improve himself. One evening he had come by chance to the Court Theater; a new world opened to him. For the first time he had the genuinely noble enjoyment only a truly good theater could afford, which he had previously done without because he had not known it.

As with so many of our compatriots, a longing awoke in August Zwierlein for the land of liberty, and so it came about that around Christmas, 1872 he shook the dust of Germany from his feet and left for America, which he reached in January, 1873. After working for a year in various eastern cities, he came to Cleveland in 1874, where he settled down. For three years he was a shoemaker for various local companies, but in 1877 he established his own shop on Pearl Street, which he was able through hard work and talent to bring to such a level as to win it the reputation of one of the best in Cleveland. In keeping with modern demands, the shop, remodeled last summer, presented the products of the famous shoe factories of the country in rows on the shelves, and there is a good market. Still, the part of the business to which Mr. Zwierlein dedicated special effort was individual creation of outstanding shoes, particularly for those whom nature has more or less disadvantaged, as well as crippled feet. Through long, penetrating study and as a result of the rare interest he applied to his profession, Mr. Zwierlein has advanced himself to be an artist in his business. The products of his shop are known far beyond the limits of Cleveland or the borders of Ohio.

In 1880 Mr. Zwierlein married Miss Louisa Heil, daughter of the old German pioneer Mr. Henry Heil, who arrived in Cleveland in 1846. She has given him five children, of whom the eldest son, Arthur, is active in his father's business.

Mr. Zwierlein has obtained a treasure of knowledge through zealous self-directed study, through good reasoning and a carefully cultivated discussion with men of higher education, making it possible for him to participate in any conversation, of whatever level. He enjoys a great circle of friends, within which he is held in high regard because of his splendid character. For more than 30 years he has belonged to the Orpheus Singing Society, and he is a member of the Social Turner Society and the German-American Club.

Joseph Reuss

The noted local building contractor Mr. Joseph Reuss was born on 17 April 1870 in Grossenlüder, district of Fulda, Hessia-Nassau. After leaving school he commenced the same craft his father operated in his birthplace, which was that of a mason, and he learned the business in all of its branches. In 1888 he came to this country as a young man of 18 and settled at once in the Forest City. For ten years he worked for various building contractors, then he made himself independent, and since then he has built many handsome buildings, and he has done his bit to erect homes.

In earlier years Mr. Reuss belonged to various societies, but now he dedicates his free time to his dear family. He is still a member of the Protective Home Circle, and he has insured himself with the Home Life Insurance Company in order to protect his family against unforeseen events.

In June, 1894, Mr. Reuss married Miss Elisabeth Schön, who was born in St. Johann, Rheinish Palatinate, and came as a child to Cleveland with her parents. This happy marriage produced six fine children, two boys and four girls.

In 1903 Mr. Reuss visited his parents, who were still alive in Germany, and on this occasion he also traveled through a great deal of the rest of the fatherland.

The home of the Reuss family here is the lovely house at 896 East 99th Street.

Christ. Geiger

Christ. Geiger was born on 3 November 1859, in Eichelbronn in Baden. After schooling he learned cabinetry like his father and forefathers. As a journeyman he perambulated Switzerland, Austria, and all of Central Europe until 1879, obtaining a basic knowledge of people and places. Then he had to enter the Third Baden Infantry No. 111, serving his three years and receiving his discharge with the rank of a sergeant. His desire to know the New World drove him across the ocean, and so he came directly to Cleveland, where he opened an inn, combined with a bar and a restaurant on Sheriff Street, which enjoyed a good clientele due to his own amiability. About ten years ago Mr. Geiger sold this business and took over the well-known and idyllic summer place, "Idle Wild" on the Rocky River, where the best people gather in the summer months. There are few who show so much love for German lodges and societies to promote German sociability as Mr. Geiger. He has been a Harugari since 1884, belongs to the Order of the I. O. F. and the Odd Fellows since 1893, and he belongs to the Knights of Honor and the Red Men. He is also a member of the Society of German Warriors and the East Side Baden Support Society, and he belongs to the German League. In 1892 he was first made treasurer of the Baden Central League of North America, and he still holds that office now. He was president of the East Side Baden Support Society from 1889 to 1895, and since 1890 he has been dictator in the Knights of Honor. He has held offices of honor in all the lodges.

Mr. Geiger is one of those open characters with their hearts in the right place. Wherever the interests of Germans are involved, Mr. Geiger is certain to be there.

John Wilhelm Ohlsen

John W. Ohlsen was born on 20 November 1851 in the Free Imperial City of Bremen. His father was a cigar maker, for which reason John apprenticed as a cigar maker after completing his schooling. He trained himself thoroughly, and he then traveled through the greater part of Germany before emigrating to America, arriving on 13 November 1880, and settling in Cleveland. Here he worked for eight years in his profession before establishing the Ohlsen Cigar Factory on Lorain Street, which he led for eight years before he took over the old Kurz Hall on York Street, a place with a bit of history behind it. It had been built when the West Side was still called Ohio City, but under Ohlsen's regime it was renovated and is generally known as "Ohlsen's Hall." Mr. Ohlsen led that business for twelve years, and then he led the well-known amusement place, "Scenic Park." For a while Mr. Ohlsen has been leading his café, "The Ohlsen," corner of West Sixth Stret and Frankfurt Avenue, which enjoys a significant clientele.

Mr. Ohlsen has always been an upright and zealous promoter of the cause of workers in this town, and he is so today. In the earlier Trades Assembly he represented the cigar-makers' union, and it was through his initiative that the current Central Labor Union arose, of which he is first speaker. As an employer the constitution of the cigar-makers' union forbids him to represent it in the central bodies, but he is still a member of the association.

He is also active in societies. He was one of the founders of the Workers' Singing League and the only one still belonging to the Singing League. In the same way he is the founder of the Workers' Singing League of the Central Northern States of America, an association of workers' singing societies of various cities. The first singing festival this league held, in 1897, was held here in Cleveland, and Mr. Ohlsen was the festival president. Further, he belongs to a number of societies as a member, including Central Union no. 7, United German Union, the Baden Singing Section, etc.

Mr. Ohlsen married in 1872 to Miss Anna Wilkens, also born in Bremen and a former schoolmate. Four sons have come from this happy marriage, John W., Arnold, Hermann and Willie.

Otto C. Berchtold

Mr. Otto C. Berchtold was born in New York on 27 January 1859. His father, Andreas Berchtold, emigrated from Bavaria and ran a successful meat business in the city on the Hudson. When young Berchtold reached school age, the family moved to Cleveland. Here Otto attended the private school on Mechanic Street so prized by the Germans then, which did wonders under the direction of Mr. Roeder and later under Cobelli. It should be added that this institution became the Turner School. Then Otto attended public school, and after graduating from there he attended the Spencerian Business College and then the Calvin Institute. Then the young man was hired by the noted firm of W. P. Southworth as shipping clerk, then he passed in a similar capacity to the John Weidemann business , and then he took a position in the Hayes Bros. haberdashery on Water Street. Here the young Berchtold had his first great business success. He invented a very practical safety device for the elevator there which he later patented and sold with good success. Mr. Berchtold made himself independent at the age of 25 and established a butcher shop on Clark Avenue, which soon was a great success. On 4 August 1890 Mr, Berchtold founded a sausage factory with his brother Paul on Mill Street. This is regarded by specialists as one of the best-equipped in the country. In 1883 Mr. Berchtold married Miss Amalie Leopold from Cleveland, who gave him four children, two boys and two girls. Mr. Berchtold was elected mayor of Lakewood in 1899 with a great majority. He has a splendid home in Lakewood. He did this despite the fact that his opponents said that Lakewood had never had a German mayor. Nothing more is heard about this any more. The progressive, energetic administration which Mr. Berchtold introduced has made many of his opponents into enthusiastic supporters who cannot love their German mayor enough. Mr. Berchtold is a very well-known personality among the Knights of Pythias. He is one of the Big Five, those Pythias pioneers who are wont to march in parade in advance of the order of "preux chevaliers," always attracting comment because of their great size. As president of the Cleveland Gun Club, Mr. Berchtold has done much for German shooting.

H. J. Mühlhäusler

H. J. Mühlhäusler is a child of Cleveland. He was born on 22 August 1873 as the son of the noted restaurateur August Mühlhäusler, who emigrated at the start of
the 1860s from Friesenheim, Baden, and settled permanently in Cleveland. Mr. H. J. Mühlhäusler's mother came from the Rhenish Palatinate. His father died on 16 March 1887 after running a popular tavern on Michigan Street certainly recalled by older Germans. The

young Mühlhäusler had an excellent education in his youth. After he completed the public schools, he attended a business college and prepared himself for the positions he received after completing the course. He was first of all an assistant bookkeeper at the Baptist Publications Company, and he later held a similar position with the Lake Shore Railroad.

During the last ten years Mr. Mühlhäusler has dedicated himself to the tavern business. His place of business, located at the corner of Willson Avenue and St. Clair Street, is the most elegantly equipped tavern in the East End and enjoys great popularity. Mr. Mühlhäusler knows how to serve his guests in the most accommodating way, and that explains his great success.

Mr. Mühlhäusler is a member of the Woodward Lodge of the Freemasons as well as of the Order of the Eagles. In 1895 he married Miss Frieda Köhler, born in Saxony. Three children, a boy and two girls, have sprung from this happy marriage.

Although born here, Mr. Mühlhäusler is proud of his German origins and takes great interest in German causes.

Paul Meinke

Paul Meinke first saw the light of day on 16 September 1859 in Gross-Glogau, Lower Silesia. His father was an honest master shoemaker, representing the citizenry of his hometown in the city council. The Meinke family consisted of five boys and three girls. Three of the sons, Julius, Paul and Emil, as well as one sister, Auguste, emigrated to America and settled in Cleveland, where one of the brothers, Julius, sadly died. Auguste, the sister, has since married and lives as Mrs. Nieske on Fairfield Street, South Side. Paul, the subject of our account, attended the Volksschule as a boy as well as the Realschule, and then he went into apprenticeship with a jeweler to learn that profession. When he had completed the apprenticeship, which lasted four years, he went to Berlin, attending the university for two semesters, where his uncle, Professor Elker, worked, and he heard lectures in philosophy and law. He got the money to do that from the work of his hands. He worked at the court jeweler, Schaper, Potsdamer Strasse 3. He also did a course in drafting in a Berlin academy. In 1880 he fulfilled his military duties with the 43rd Infantry Regiment in Lötzen, East Prussia. The next year Paul Meinke emigrated to America and came directly and permanently to Cleveland. As a talented jeweler and engraver it was not hard for him to find a post at once, and his first position was with Lehmann Bros. on Bank Street. He then went to Brunner Bros., where he remained for two years. In 1885 he became independent, and he has been such ever since. His current place of business is 6910 St. Clair Avenue. As a draftsman and engraver Mr. Meinke has won considerable renown. Many designs for society banners and insignia come from him, including the souvenir for Goethe and Schiller. He plays an important role in society circles. He is former grand president of the United German Union, and member of the German Support League, the Woodmen of the World, the Vorwärts Turner Society, the Orpheus Singing Society, and Lyra, in the last one active; he is also in the Swabian Singing League, the German Comrades in Arms, and finally the German-American Central League.

Mr. Meinke married in 1844 to Miss Christina Schaabm who was born in Bürgenau, Hessia-Darmstadt. Six children, two boys and four girls, who have come from the marriage, are still alive. The eldest daughter, Ida, is married to the engineer Paul Weiss. The eldest son, Hermann, who has followed his father's profession, was hired by the renowned jewelry firm of Cowl and Hubbard, and the second son is a clerk with Sherwin and Williams.

Hugo Karman

Hugo Karman was born in Budapest, Hungary, as the son of Dr. Philipp Klein. His father is one of the most outstanding figures in medical science. There are certainly few men with such an outstanding reputation, or who enjoy such popularity among the better bourgeoisie as this doctor, still hale and dedicated to his extensive practice. He is one of the servants of Askulapius [Asclepius] of the old school, one who takes his profession seriously, doing good for a suffering mankind as a true benefactor. Dr. Klein also possesses high virtues in dealing with his fellow man, and those who know him, including almost the whole of grand, intelligent Budapest, know how to treasure him.

His son Hugo was born on 9 May 1877 in Budapest, Hungary. He attended the Lutheran Volksschule there, and the outstanding Gymnasium there for four years. Then he went to Zürich, Switzerland, to the famous Concordia mercantile academy of Dr. Phil. Bertsch, where he learned foreign languages (French, English, Italian and Spanish), which he did with the best success. During a school vacation he traveled all over Switzerland, and he experienced the most wonderful days in that splendid country. After completing the commerce school, he returned to Karlsruhe and did his military service as a one-year volunteer. He then worked in the transport and travel company of Schenker & Co., with the cable manufacturing stock company in Pressburg [Bratislava], the electricity factory in Berlin as a corresponding agent. After he worked in the same capacity in Italy, he came to America in 1902. Here he was active in newspaper advertising, and he also sold land in Texas for colonization and has been in Texas about 24 times. He has also helped many German families to a secure existence.

In recent times, Mr. Karman was a collaborator in the work, *Cleveland and Its Germans*.

He has been married to Miss Marie Pucher since October, 1902, and Mr. Karman lives with her in a happy marriage.

Robert Lenz

There is no doubt that Robert Lenz is among the journalists of the city who have understood how to make a name in the country. Certainly others before him have written in the Pennsylvania Dutch dialect, but none has done it in such a humorous way, and his Philipp Sauerampfer has become a permanent figure in German-American newspaper literature. There are thousands of readers who look first for the "Open Complaint of Philipp Sauerampfer" and thousands who enjoy the eternally bubbly source of humor that Philipp Sauerampfer brings to the surface.

Robert Lenz was born in October, 1858, in Wiesbaden. A merchant by profession, he came over to a journalistic career in 1887 after immigrating to the United States. In April 1887, he entered the editorial offices of the *Wächter am Erie*, was later local editor of the *Deutsche Presse*, then coworker of the *Cleveland Anzeiger*, and after the joining of the two papers, which is reported in this book, he entered the editorial offices of the *Wächter und Anzeiger*. In July 1898 he was named cashier of the company, which position he now holds. His Sauerampfer letters, which he issues weekly, began appearing about three years ago to great applause, so that they are now reprinted by more than 200 newspapers in the country. Mr. Lenz is a very amiable person in character. He is married and the father of three children.

Arthur Doebel

Arthur Doebel was born on 4 January 1877 in Wendisheim near Leisnig. His father, Carl Gottlieb Doebel, owned an estate there. He lost his mother when he was only six years old.

After attending school, Mr. Doebel learned gardening. He came to America in 1893 during the Chicago World Exposition, staying for one year in Chicago, then working in his profession in various cities of the country until he came to Cleveland six years ago and settled here. Here Mr. Doebel has dedicated himself to landscape gardening, and he is much in demand by the prosperous classes because of his expertise in the tasteful laying out and beautifying of private gardens. He also does a trade in trees and bushes which he grows himself.

Mr. Doebel, who no longer considers returning to Germany or leaving our Forest City, is a member of the Red Men and the Knights and Ladies of Security.

He very happily married to a Springfield lady born a Hermann, and four boys have been born to the marriage.

Mr. Doebel's residence and place of business are located at 10710 Morrison Avenue N. E.

Leo Kraus

Leo Kraus was born on 19 August 1861 in Klein-Chiska, Bohemia. After leaving school, he went into the grocery business and worked in that profession until departing for America. This happened in 1879, when he came here with his family to Cleveland and settled here. His first employment was in a wholesale haberdashery business. In 1875 he made himself independent and opened a tavern on Quincy Street, which he later moved to Woodland Avenue, and when this district began to go dry, he moved again, to 8602 Buckeye Road. There he serves his many friends and acquaintances.

He was one of the founders of the Freedom Lodge no. 13 of the United German Union, and for the last thirteen years he has been president. The Union has 286 members, and it has a fund of $4000. Through his tireless efforts and agitation he has brought this society to its blossoming. He is also a respresentative at the Grand Lodge for the last nine years and the Assistant Grand President of the same. Further, he is president of the Columbia Union of the same order. Other societies of which he is a member are the Foresters, F. F. of A., Sons of Benjamin; he was also one of the founders of the Bohemian Turner Society, and he is president of the Bolton Social Club.

In 1883, in the old fatherland, he married Miss Rosa Steiner. Eight children, four sons and four daughters, are the result of that marriage. The oldest daughter, Clara, is a teacher in the public schools, and the two eldest sons are active as bookkeepers, the eldest (Alfred) with Landesman, Hirschheimer & Co., and Rudolph with the Cleveland Gas Co.

Christian Friedrich Kubach

He was born on 21 April 1862 as the eldest son of the tinsmith Christian Kubach in Liedolsheim near Karlsruhe, Grand Duchy of Baden. He attended the Volksschule in his birthplace and came with his parents in 1880 to America, directly to Cleveland.

Mr. Kubach did not always have it as nice and independent as he does now. After coming to Cleveland he threw himself into the labor which our industry offers, and he worked for twelve long years as a form-maker. At the end of this period he became independent for the first time by opening a wine and beer business at the corner of East Madison and Kinsman Street. Mr. Kubach knew how to make it a good financial success. In 1901 he obtained an inn in Warrensville, at the corner of Chagrin and Kinsman Road, combined with a property of 7 1/2 acres. Here as well, his combined inn and tavern prospered, but the drying out of the township where he was located and lived by temperance fanatics forced Mr. Kubach to give up his tavern and change it into a grocery, which flourishes on the place, known as East View, and is run by him.

Mr. Kubach is a member of the Baden Support Society.

In 1887, Mr. Kubach married Miss Emilie Schuler, also born in Liedolsheim and come to Cleveland as a little girl, where a sister and a brother already lived. It may be said of Mrs. Kubach that she is a strong support in the business.

The marriage has produced two daughters: Louise Auguste, the elder, is already 13, and the second, Prisca Emilie, is 10.

In the course of the years, Kubach has accumulated a fine fortune as a result of his prudence and persistence. Due to his open and straight nature, he is respected by all who know him.